ENCOURAGING THE DEVELOPMENT OF EXCEPTIONAL SKILLS AND TALENTS

Edited by

Michael J.A. Howe

BPS
BOOKS

Published by
The British Psychological Society

First published in 1990 by The British Psychological Society, St Andrews
House, 48 Princess Road East, Leicester, LE1 7DR, UK.

Distributed by The Distribution Centre, Blackhorse Road, Letchworth,
Herts SG6 1HN, UK.

British Library Cataloguing in Publication Data

Encouraging the development of exceptional skills
    and talents.
    1. Gifted children. Development
    I. Howe, Michael J.A. (Michael John Anthony) 1940–
155.455

ISBN 1-85433-038-1

Printed and bound in Great Britain by BPCC Wheatons Ltd., Exeter.
Whilst every effort has been made to ensure the accuracy of the contents
of this publication, the publishers and authors expressly disclaim
responsibility in law for negligence or any other cause of action
whatsoever.

CONTENTS

INTRODUCTION
Michael J.A. Howe

Natural resources are the life-blood of human existence. We recognize this by trying to preserve forests, by looking for more effective ways to utilize sources of energy, by helping farmers to be more efficient. Efforts are made to protect, nourish and extend those resources that are most necessary. To help achieve those aims advanced societies make efforts to gain a fuller understanding of their resources. In agriculture, for instance, scientists conduct research aimed at discovering more about the circumstances in which crops and livestock thrive. A nation which depended on wheat production but made no efforts to discover the causes of variations in that plant's quality would be seen as foolishly short-sighted.

But the most valuable of all our natural resources receive precisely that kind of neglect. Human abilities, particularly exceptional ones, are vital resources for the well-being of all cultures. Few goals can be more desirable, or more valuable, for the human race than understanding the origins of exceptional abilities and knowing how to nurture and increase them. Yet both the language and the logic of debates on the causes of outstanding achievements – even by 'experts' in education and psychology – are often primitive and inadequate. The kinds of illumination that scientific rigour and empirical research can provide have been glaringly absent. Vital as the issues are, the ways in which they are discussed continue to be tied to the thinking of a pre-scientific era.

For better or worse, accepted viewpoints about the causes of high abilities largely determine the kinds of policies which educational systems adopt towards them. As Colin Berry points out in Chapter 3 of this volume, current policies towards the promotion and encouragement of outstanding abilities owe more to ill-informed folk beliefs than to real knowledge of the circumstances which actually give rise to exceptional human accomplishments. This results in tragic wastefulness.

A TRADITIONAL VIEWPOINT

According to a view that is still widely accepted, extraordinary human accomplishments largely depend upon individuals inheriting certain talents or gifts. The implication is that only a person who possesses such a gift for, say, mathematics will be able to become an outstanding achiever. For someone who lacks that gift, the most exceptional mathematical accomplishments will simply not be possible. And if we wish to encourage gifts and talents to flourish, the best we can do is to 'identify' them as early as possible, and to help provide conditions that will nurture them. Essentially, all that society can achieve is to wait for gifts and talents to appear, and then take supportive measures. As to the question of what precisely an innate gift is, or that of how it exerts its effects, or why one person but not another receives such a gift, these are all matters of deep mystery. Gifts and talents are presumably transmitted via a person's genes, but the mechanisms and the processes by which they make their presence known are just as inscrutable as are their forms and structures.

On many of these issues ignorance has seemed to reign unchallenged. How are we supposed to know when an innate gift or talent is present? That is easy, or so it appears: if a person has an extraordinary ability, they must have a talent for it. And if, like Mozart, someone produces achievements which are so extraordinary that most people cannot even imagine themselves becoming capable of them then, according to this view, there is indisputable evidence that a special talent is present.

It does not take long to discover that there are serious flaws in the logic of viewing unusual abilities and their causes in this manner. As Anders Ericsson, Clements Tesch-Römer and Ralf Krampe point out in Chapter 6, in terms of its explanatory power this view is not unlike the belief that the earth's various species and geological formations were separately created by divine powers. One obvious problem is that on the one hand innate gifts are seen as being the cause of special accomplishments, whilst on the other hand the existence of special accomplishments is the very reason for claiming that innate gifts actually exist. Thinking here has turned full circle: a gift is supposed to be the cause of something that provides the sole evidence for that gift's existence. It is as if I were to attribute some unexplained footprints to the presence of Martians and, when asked how I know that the Martians are here, reply, 'It's obvious: I've seen their footprints!' And the very word 'gift' begs the question of its origins by implying that the quality it refers to has been donated to the individual concerned, rather than gained by the person's own efforts.

That it is based on circular thinking is by no means the only thing that is wrong about the kind of thought processes in which exceptional human abilities are attributed to the workings of inherent gifts and talents. This way of reasoning also involves the error of 'reifying'. To reify is to assume that the sheer fact that a word exists is sufficient basis for assuming that there is a corresponding concrete thing. Take the word 'talent', for instance. It is reasonable to introduce the term 'talented' simply to describe a person. We find this term very useful: it performs a function that is not quite achieved by other broadly synonymous terms such as 'clever', 'competent', 'able' or 'capable'. But when writers pass from the adjective 'talented' to the noun 'talent', they find it all too easy to forget that a word is not necessarily more than a word. The error is an easy one to make, because in most cases where a noun exists – ball, engine, book, for instance – there also exists something concrete to which that noun refers. But the fact that this is often the case should not deceive us into believing that this is always the case. And in the case of a concept like 'talent' or 'gift' or 'natural aptitude', there is no justification at all for assuming that the existence of the noun provides sufficient grounds for believing in the existence of a corresponding concrete entity.

There are more flaws in the kind of thinking which sees innate gifts and talents as the causes of exceptional abilities. One problem is that such terms are simultaneously used to describe and to explain the same phenomena. It is as if I were to decide on a term (say 'productive') to describe a factory which is particularly successful at producing gifts, and then assert that the *reason why* the factory is so successful is because it is productive. Similarly, with a term such as 'talented', there is no harm in using it to describe a child who is unusually good at playing the piano. But if we then answer the question 'Why does she play so well?' by saying that she is talented, we may be illegitimately using what is in fact simply a *descriptive* term as if it were also an *explanatory* one.

THE REAL CAUSES OF OUTSTANDING ABILITIES

Nevertheless, the idea that the origins of exceptional abilities lie in innate gifts and talents does contain a substantial degree of truth. Even if the notions of gifts and talents as customarily defined are ill-conceived, it is still possible that an explanation based on them is not far off the mark. It may be true that to be able to acquire exceptional abilities a person needs to have inherited the potential for some special quality or mental mechanism: some kind of special genetic blueprint might be necessary. And if that were the case, the practical implications would be broadly the same as those implied by the view that extraordinary capabilities reflect the workings of gifts and talents. Namely, the role of society in the production of special abilities is a limited and largely passive one, and all we can usefully do is identify exceptional capacities when they appear, and help nurture them.

Is there any truth in this view? If there is, then the implications are gloomy. But if it is substantially wrong, the exciting prospect opens up that the size of our potential resources of exceptional abilities – indicated by the number of individuals who are capable of mastering exceptional abilities – may be vastly larger than it has been thought to be. In that case, if we are seriously interested in increasing the number of people capable of mastering the most difficult skills and creating the most impressive human achievements, it makes sense to work far more actively at cultivating exceptional abilities than we do now.

The way to answer questions about the real circumstances in which extraordinary abilities are formed is to obtain hard evidence on the matter. Some of this evidence can be obtained from historical records (Howe, 1982). Sometimes it is essential to conduct empirical research. A substantial amount of evidence is reported in this book, the causes and origins of exceptional capabilities being primary concerns of a number of the chapters. Other chapters place more stress on directly practical issues, such as the effectiveness of specific procedures that have been designed to help young people to master difficult skills.

Evidence from recent research presented here and elsewhere shows that the widely accepted belief that extraordinary abilities can only be gained by a comparatively small number of individuals who happen to have been born with particular gifts or talents is mistaken. The facts show that the majority of children are born capable of acquiring impressive levels of expertise in most spheres of competence, if the circumstances of their lives make this possible. The contents of the book's chapters demonstrate that the case for this view is overwhelming. And readers who are convinced by the evidence that abilities are indeed largely forged by the conditions of a person's life will find it hard to resist concluding that since exceptional abilities are an undeniably valuable resource, the passiveness of current policies towards the promotion and encouragement of them cannot be justified.

Of course, because humans are complicated organisms, the cultivation of superior capabilities is by no means a straightforward matter. It is far from being a simple manufacturing process. Each person is a unique individual, whose development is controlled as much from within as from without, and whose progress is by no means entirely predictable or controllable. Dimensions of variability such as temperament and personality affect the interests and development of abilities in a person in ways that are just as powerful and just as complicated as are the strictly cognitive determinants of learning. To complicate things even further, although the notion that people's lives are determined by inborn gifts and talents may be largely fictional, it is equally wrong to believe that everyone is born identical. At birth, babies are very different from one another, and the dimensions on which they differ can influence future development in a number of important ways. For instance, newborns differ in their cuddliness, in the ease with which they are soothed, and in their sensitivity to different modes of perception. All of these can influence learning and development.

So there is no denying that characteristics in which babies already differ by a very early stage of their lives – and which may originate in genetic sources of variability – can influence a child's later development in ways that may increase or decrease the likelihood of the individual eventually becoming exceptionally accomplished in certain areas of ability (Howe, 1990). Moreover, genetic differences can undoubtedly have outcomes that will affect an adult's performance in an intelligence test, although in many of the investigations that have been undertaken in order to examine this matter it is likely that assessments of the potency of genetic effects have been inflated by the confounding influences of other factors and by the absence of substantial and adequately measured systematic differences in the quality of the learning environments experienced by different individuals (Howe, 1989).

But for practical purposes, acknowledging that babies are not identical is very different from believing that some of them are born with specific gifts or talents. Whereas gifts and talents are seen as having outcomes that are direct and irreversible, the actual effects of those kinds of early variability that are known to exist have none of these characteristics. Far from affecting a baby's future capabilities directly, the eventual outcomes of initial differences between babies in temperament and other dimensions of variability are uncertain, probably modifiable in most instances, very indirect – operating at one point in a long chain of causes and effects – and largely unpredictable. Our understanding of the precise ways in which genetic variability affects the likelihood of different individuals gaining exceptional abilities is extremely limited. Concerning the long-term effects on learning of innately-caused differences between babies there is much speculation but little hard evidence. The one thing that is clear, however, is that the ways in which early differences do influence people's later capabilities are not at all like the scenario implicit in the notion that exceptional abilities reflect the workings of innate gifts and inborn talents.

It has been said that the fluttering of a butterfly's wings can have effects that eventually affect the course of a typhoon in a distant ocean. That is correct, but it is equally true that the wing movement is just one event among thousands or millions that need to occur in a particular sequence: to say that the butterfly causes a typhoon is only true in a rather trivial sense. The statement that early individual differences cause later abilities is not entirely dissimilar. Such differences may have implications that have further outcomes, eventually linking-up with variability in people's skills: but the number of other factors involved at each of a large number of stages is so great that it would be misleading to identify one particular early difference as *the* cause of eventual differences in ability.

Within the chapters of this book there is a substantial amount of reported evidence which demonstrates that the causes of exceptional human abilities in children and young people largely reside in those events in a child's world that determine how the individual's life is experienced. Essentially, what a person becomes depends on what happens in that individual's life. Taken one at a time, those influences that are especially important are typically neither complicated nor mysterious, although the manner in which they work together and interact in the course of a person's life may be complicated in the extreme, to the extent that for all practical purposes they cannot be fully disentangled.

To some extent the most obvious candidates for the roles of causes of high abilities turn out to be the most crucial ones. First, for example, the presence of appropriate opportunities to learn is absolutely vital. You will never be a great violinist if you had no opportunity to play the violin in the early years of your life. Sheer lack of opportunity is the major factor ruling out young people from becoming experts at many kinds of accomplishments.

Also, the amount of time a person spends practising a skill is extremely important. That is not to say that practice alone is sufficient to ensure the highest levels of competence. However, the finding that in a number of separate areas of expertise there are very substantial correlations between amount of practice and level of performance (Ericsson, Tesch-Römer and Krampe, in Chapter 6 of this volume) firmly contradicts the notion that 'mere practice' is relatively unimportant: it is vital. And the empirical evidence also disproves the common view that certain especially talented individuals can achieve the highest levels of ability at difficult skills without having to undergo years of intensive practice preparation. That simply never happens.

People do not spend long hours practising a difficult skill unless they are highly motivated. For that and other reasons, motivation is the third essential ingredient of outstanding capabilities. And since practising is not, by and large, an intrinsically motivating activity, there need to be additional sources of support and encouragement, especially in the case of young people, to help sustain a person's efforts. Hence the support and encouragement of other people, typically parents, is another important ingredient of success in acquiring exceptional abilities. Moreover, the kinds of activities that the parents support and encourage largely depend on the parents' own interests and values, and on their broader cultural background.

So even though the ways in which the circumstances of a person's life combine to produce, say, a Newton or an Einstein may be complex in the extreme and are clearly unique to each individual case, the essential broad ingredients of outstanding success are not too hard to designate. Specifically cognitive ingredients in the form of skills and knowledge are clearly vital, but it is at least equally important for the individual to have other attributes that depend upon temperament, character, and personality. To be capable of the sustained hard effort on which outstanding success typically depends, a person needs to be attentive, determined, persevering and independent, and to have developed a sense of purpose and of direction, and perhaps single-mindedness. It is not unknown for the experiences of an intense childhood, in which great pains have been taken to equip a child with knowledge and intellectual skills, to leave an individual ill-equipped in terms of the non-intellectual resources that also need to be drawn upon if a person is to be outstandingly successful. Such an individual will not be at all prepared to follow the long and arduous route towards the highest levels of human achievements.

OVERVIEW OF THE CHAPTERS

Each of the first four chapters looks at a range of the background factors that contribute to the lives of people who gain exceptional abilities. In Chapter 1, *The timing of talent: the facilitation of early prodigious achievement*, Lynn Goldsmith enquires into the circumstances in which a small number of children become outstandingly accomplished at an early age. She suggests that one way of regarding prodigies is as examples of 'development gone right'. In these young people there has been an unusually good matching or 'co-incidence' of a number of critical factors that converge to produce exceptional abilities. She suggests that by examining how the different factors interact in an optimal way to create prodigious accomplishments we will not only understand prodigies better but also gain an increased understanding of some of the forces that result in other children's progress being less impressive.

Goldsmith also points out that the combination of felicitous circumstances that work together to produce a child prodigy may be temporary. There is no guarantee that a child who is exceptionally able will become an outstandingly successful adult. If only because the qualities that lead to a child being labelled a prodigy are not always identical to the ones that are acclaimed in the mature genius, those who eventually make the most significant contributions to a field of achievement are by no means invariably those who made the most spectacular progress as children.

Chapter 2, by John Radford, is on *The problem of the prodigy*. Those outstanding young people who have been labelled prodigies differ enormously from one another in many ways, but there are interesting points of similarity between them. For example, in virtually all cases it is clear that the parents of a prodigy have helped to make early opportunities available and have done much to encourage the child and provide facilities for practising and extending abilities. But prolonged efforts do not invariably result in outstanding accomplishments: Radford points out that too much pressure on a child, or extreme 'hothousing', may jeopardize the chances of good long-term results. The chapter also draws attention to the role of cultural factors in deciding which abilities are regarded as being outstanding. Radford remarks that Europeans would regard some of the skills frequently displayed by young people and children in an African tribe – tracking skills, for instance – as being quite phenomenal. Such skills might even appear to provide evidence of inherently extraordinary ability. But those African people would consider some of the abilities that are commonplace in European children to be equally extraordinary.

Colin Berry, the author of Chapter 3, *On the origins of exceptional intellectual and cultural achievement*, describes the findings of a major study on the cultural backgrounds of those exceptional scientists who have won a Nobel prize. The fact that family and cultural backgrounds are important comes as no great surprise, but some readers will be taken aback by the sheer magnitude of this source of influence. For example, in the vast majority of countries which have produced Nobel prize-winners in the sciences the proportion of individuals from Jewish backgrounds who have won prizes is much higher (in some instances fifty times higher) than that of Gentiles. Also, Protestant countries produce far more Nobel prize-winners in the sciences than Catholic countries. But prize-winners' backgrounds in the more productive of the Catholic countries are different from those of Nobel prize-winners in Protestant countries. In the latter, winners tend to be distributed fairly evenly between the different parts of each nation, but in the Catholic countries a very substantial proportion of the laureates are drawn from a few large metropolitan areas. The majority of Nobel prize-winners in the sciences have come from professional backgrounds.

In many people who have made outstanding achievements the individual's parents have had a dominant influence on educational experiences in childhood. That is not always the case, however, and in some instances brothers or sisters have played a vitally important role. In Chapter 4, *Sibling relationships in creative lives*, Doris Wallace mentions the crucial support given by siblings in the lives of Van Gogh, Darwin, the Brontës, and William and Henry James. The chapter by Wallace concentrates on a study of the collaboration of one famous brother and sister pair, William and Dorothy Wordsworth. Their working relationship was intense and prolonged, lasting from 1794 – after a lengthy period of separation which, Wallace observes, seems to have cemented the close relationship they had previously established – until William's death in 1850. Wallace draws attention to a number of ways in which each guided and depended upon the other and drew upon the other's responses to shared experiences.

The fifth chapter, Joan Freeman's *The intellectually gifted adolescent*, examines high abilities and their implications through the eyes of the young people who possess them. For the individual concerned, outstanding abilities are not always an unmixed blessing: they can bring problems and frustrations as well as benefits. At worst, Freeman tells us, the young child who is wise beyond his or her years and is fondly regarded by adults as a 'young professor' may too easily become a lonely and isolated adolescent, with all the troubles of that stage of life but with no real friends to share problems with, and inadequate social skills. Not surprisingly, fear of success can be as powerful as fear of failing.

Freeman reports the findings of a large-scale study financed by the Gulbenkian Foundation, in which she interviewed unusually able children, as well as children of average ability who formed a control group. As expected, the brighter children were generally more sensitive and more responsive to variations in educational facilities. For instance, in the abler children poor educational environments led to a larger decrease in intelligence-test scores, compared with children of average ability. But a number of the findings contradicted expectations. For example, whereas it is often believed that unusually able young people prefer to work independently, amongst Freeman's respondents more of the highly able than the less able said they preferred to work with a teacher. The brighter individuals saw themselves as good at remembering facts they regarded as interesting or important, and they estimated their ability to concentrate for lengthy periods more favourably than the less able children did. They also put more emphasis on the importance of high achievement. Interestingly, they were more likely than children of average ability to regard themselves as being lazy.

The next two chapters concentrate on two important determinants of high abilities, practice and motivation. Chapter 6, by Anders Ericsson, Clemens Tesch-Römer and Ralf Krampe, is on *The role of practice and motivation in the acquisition of expert-level performance in real life*. The authors note that expertise in many areas of achievement largely depends on a person having the ability to rapidly access relevant knowledge that is stored in memory. Typically, the sheer amount of knowledge necessary for expert-level performance is vast, and acquiring such knowledge involves lengthy periods of preparation and practice. Amount of practice is a very important determinant of performance level. At least ten years of intense practice and preparation are essential in order for an individual to reach international levels of performance at any of a variety of activities ranging from chess, mathematics and the arts and sciences to music and sports.

The authors of Chapter 6 go on to point out that since long and intensive practice is essential for high levels of success, an understanding of the causes of exceptional expertise must include an account of the ways in which practice is initiated and of the reasons why it is maintained at the necessary high levels. The chapter provides an important theoretical framework which describes and accounts for the circumstances in which certain individuals are able to initiate and maintain a way of life which accommodates the heavy demands and the sacrifices that are necessary if training, practice and preparation are to be as prolonged and intensive as they need to be for an individual to reach the highest levels of achievement. The circumstances in which individuals regularly practise a skill are explored. Maintenance of high levels of practice depends on a number of motivating conditions being present. These differ according to the age and stage of progress of the person concerned, but always depend to a marked extent on the resources, support and encouragement that are made available by other people, especially the parents.

Ericsson, Tesch-Römer and Krampe demonstrate how in each of three domains of expertise, chess, sports and music, individuals are exposed to the domain, then actively participate in it, and finally become engaged in systematic practice and training. In each domain the average starting age is young, with many eventual high-level practitioners becoming involved in the activity before the age of ten. An early start brings definite advantages: as the authors point out, if two individuals of the same age differ dramatically in their accumulated practice time, and both maintain the same weekly schedule, the less trained individual simply cannot catch up with the more experienced one. So it is not surprising that the starting age of chess players correlates with the age of first achievement of international-level performance, that starting ages for the best sports performers are younger than for less successful performers, and that the best musicians tend to start younger than less highly accomplished musicians.

The importance of motivational factors in one particular kind of ability is explored in Chapter 7, *Exceptional memory performers: the motivational background* by Ian Hunter. His approach is that of a field naturalist, and he examines a number of case studies each of which shows how a particular background and cultural milieu helped to shape an individual's values and interests in ways which encouraged the person to acquire extraordinary memory skills. Hunter shows that memory achievements which may strike a naïve observer as being so phenomenal that they resist any kind of explanation except by reference to rare inherent gifts or supernatural causes are in fact not at all difficult to understand once one knows the circumstances of the individual's life. It then becomes apparent that the cultural background of the individual and the values and interests that the person acquires provide a motivational background that lead to he or she directing a large amount of time and energy towards the kinds of practice and other mental activities on which memory skills are built.

Someone with an exceptional ability to remember certain kinds of information strikes us as being an 'exceptional person'. That is so, but the chances are that if a different individual was to share the same interests, values and experiences, and was equally strongly motivated to devote time and energy to activities centred on the same domain of knowledge, the second person's memory achievements would equal those of the first individual. A person may be exceptionally able at remembering certain kinds of information without being unusually competent at other mental skills. Even some *idiots savants*, who are mentally handicapped, are extraordinarily good at recalling information that is related to the things they are interested in. Memory skills are highly specific, and most people who perform remarkable feats of memory are not good at remembering in general. They are only unusual in their ability to remember information that is related to things they are knowledgeable about.

Lauren Sosniak, the author of Chapter 8, *The tortoise, the hare, and the development of talent*, looks at the implications of the fact that the events that lead to individuals becoming exceptionally accomplished musical performers occur over very lengthy periods in people's lives. Acquiring impressive skills demands sustained efforts over extended periods of time, and understanding the development of exceptional abilities is partly a matter of explaining how a person is able to maintain the motivation to keep working intensively, year after year, at a particular kind of activity, in the face of all the other attractions and distractions that fill most young people's lives. Even for the best performers, it takes a long time to progress from the point at which formal instruction in a discipline begins until the individual finally reaches the stage at which international recognition is gained. Sosniak, in an important contribution to a series of Chicago based studies of exceptional young individuals that were initiated by Benjamin Bloom (1985) and are also mentioned in Chapters 2 and 6 of the present volume, found that the concert pianists she studied took an average of 17 years to arrive at this stage. Scientists, mathematicians and sculptors all required similarly long periods of preparation. Even in swimming, an area of sporting expertise in which young competitors are unusually prominent, the average time between starting to swim and being selected for Olympic teams was no less than 15 years.

To some extent it was sheer doggedness that marked out the most highly successful performers from those individuals who never became quite so outstandingly good. Surprisingly perhaps, most of the former were not individuals who displayed exceptional signs of promise at a very early stage in their careers. (Anecdotes about individuals who dazzled everybody by their expertise at the age of two are not reliable sources of evidence.) Even after as much as seven years of preparation neither the pianists nor the swimmers who were eventually most outstanding were any more successful than scores of other young people. They were certainly doing well, and competing in local events, but by no means always successfully. Gradually however, perhaps by dint of stronger motivation, more effective combinations of encouragement and sensitivity on the part of families, and a few lucky breaks and fortunate opportunities, a few performers gradually moved ahead. But it is clear that those few did not start off any better than the others, or any more inherently talented. The most successful individuals outshone the majority as a result of combinations of fortunate circumstances that occurred over lengthy periods of time.

Chapters 9 and 10 are each concerned with the causes of variability in particular forms of abilities. In Chapter 9, *Musical excellence – how does it develop?*, John Sloboda takes a cool look at some cherished beliefs – ones which, he points out, are deeply embedded in our cultural consciousness and which are influential because they are believed – about the reasons for some individuals becoming outstanding musicians. Sloboda finds that a number of such beliefs are contradicted by the evidence. It is not true that excellence is an exact quality that can be clearly defined, nor is it a stable characteristic of the individual person. In music it is hard to find universal criteria for making comparisons.

Like Sosniak in Chapter 8, Sloboda notes that many people believe that to be an excellent musician a child has to be outstandingly capable from a very early age: contrary to the myth, however, many exceptional adult musicians did not show exceptional early promise as children. Conversely, it is also untrue that sheer diligence will produce outstanding success: diligence is a necessary but not sufficient cause of outstanding musical ability. It is not even true that teaching is an essential component of musical excellence: Sloboda points out that a number of distinguished jazz musicians were self-taught. Nor do outstanding musicians have to be intelligent. However, the individual does need to be highly motivated, and it is clear from Sloboda's own research that motivation has to be at least partly internal in origin. That is, listening to the music itself must have some positive significance for the individual. Sloboda suggests that formal musical education at school may have negative effects if it produces anxiety, especially if that leads to disruption of a child's ability to respond emotionally to music.

In Chapter 10, *Early stimulation and the development of verbal talents*, William Fowler demonstrates the importance of children's early circumstances for the acquisition of language and related skills. It is often thought that because almost all children succeed in acquiring language, the quality of a child's early experiences of language are relatively unimportant. That is totally untrue: the kinds of language stimulation that parents and others provide, the opportunities they make available and the encouragement they give have immense effects upon language development. And since language has a central place in thinking and all the skills that depend upon it, accelerating or extending a child's language development can have enormous beneficial effects.

Fowler reports findings which illustrate a number of procedures that can produce large improvements in young children's language skills. Programmes of practical intervention that have been based on such procedures, which typically involve the parent being shown how to involve a child in particularly beneficial forms of language interaction, reliably produce substantial and long-lasting practical gains. As Fowler demonstrates, the most effective procedures are generally simple and not at all difficult for parents to master. The child's home can be a superb learning environment and, if only more parents were to realize just how much children's language skills can be improved by talking to a child and by parents engaging in language-based play activities, it is conceivable that numerous children's levels of competence in the use of language would rise appreciably. Here is one human ability resource for which it is clear that relatively modest efforts to improve the quality of everyday husbandry could yield major benefits.

Chapters 11 and 12 describe programmes that have been specially designed to promote high levels of ability in various domains. Chapter 11, *Finding and helping young people who reason extremely well mathematically*, by Julian Stanley, describes some of the outcomes of his highly influential Johns Hopkins Study of Mathematically Precocious Youth. This programme, which began in the United States in 1971 and has now spread to a number of countries, provides numerous kinds of practical opportunities and facilities for helping young people who show unusual competence in mathematics. A large number of young people who have participated have done extremely well, and it is clear that in many instances individuals have benefited considerably from the opportunities that the programme has made available.

Chapter 12, *The emergence and nurturance of multiple intelligences: The Project Spectrum approach*, by Mara Krechevsky and Howard Gardner, describes an innovative approach that is designed to assess the abilities and working styles of young children and to provide parents and teachers with information about a child's strengths and weaknesses before the child's abilities have become set in a rigid profile and when schools can still be highly flexible in adapting to individual needs. The design of Project Spectrum has been strongly influenced by Gardner's pluralistic view of human intelligence. This asserts that different abilities are largely separate and autonomous, and are not constrained by any unitary factor of general ability. The Spectrum approach is concerned with abilities that are not assessed by standard intelligence tests, and it deliberately blurs the line between teaching and assessment. Krechevsky and Gardner argue that psychologists should spend more time trying to help students and less time trying to rank them. One advantage of the approach adopted in Project Spectrum is that the tasks on which children's strengths and weaknesses are assessed are ones that they find meaningful and interesting, a fact which ensures that the testing process has an ecological validity that is lacking with conventional psychometric approaches. The authors report the results of a fascinating study aimed at discriminating between specific and more general areas of strength and weakness in young children's abilities and examining how patterns of abilities can facilitate or hinder various accomplishments.

CONCLUSION

'We must make better provision for the needs of the gifted.' It is hard to disagree with that often expressed sentiment, but the statement gravely over-simplifies the problems which it addresses. As I remarked earlier, the very presence of the label 'gifted' is often taken to imply that young people can be divided into two separate groups, the gifted and, by exclusion, the non-gifted. For many people, the label 'gifted' also implies that being gifted is rather like being in a state of grace, and having a status that is somehow bestowed upon certain individuals who are the fortunate recipients of gifts. Such an account fails to allow for the fact that a person's capabilities are not givens, and that they are largely the outcomes of experiences, opportunities and various forms of enrichment that are unequally handed out in that they tend to favour the children of those parents who are relatively well-educated, affluent and successful. In place of the word

'gifted' in the statement which began this paragraph it would not be unreasonable to substitute the word 'fortunate'. And if we are confronted with the sentiment that we should make better provision for the needs of the fortunate, we would be inclined to respond that, whilst we have nothing against the idea of encouraging those young people who have already been lucky in their experiences of the world, it might be wiser as well as more just to direct our energies to increasing the number of individuals who are fortunate enough to belong to that category.

If we put aside the term 'gifted', with all the dubiously legitimate implications and connotations it seems to have, and substitute the more neutral term 'able' in its place, it is immediately clear that making better provision for the already able is but one of a number of important priorities. For instance, it is at least equally necessary to add to the number of young people who become highly able at various areas of competence, and it is as desirable to help more children to become more able as it is to support those who are already able. All these goals can only be achieved by responding to each child as an individual and by accepting the implications of the conviction that every child is a unique person who has unique educational needs, but who also has an equal right to all opportunities, support and encouragement that only the most highly favoured receive at present.

This is asking a lot, of course: it demands a transformation in the attitudes and the expectations of many families and numerous schools. But an important step in that direction will be made by abandoning the current practice of attaching simplistic labels to children – gifted, average, backward and so on – and pretending to ourselves that the labels indicate 'types' of young people who can be treated as members of homogenous groups. As Scott Fitzgerald observed, if you begin with a type you will find you have created nothing. Everybody is a unique person, and we must recognize this if we are seriously interested in taking the steps that would undoubtedly add to the numbers of people who master the most difficult human skills.

Our world urgently needs more individuals capable of helping to solve the horrifyingly difficult problems that it now faces. We have it within our means to bring up people who possess the intellectual resources that are needed. Doing so is not going to be easy or cheap, but the costs seem paltry if we bear in mind that the benefits could include, quite literally, the survival of our own species.

REFERENCES

BLOOM, B.S. (1985) *Developing Talent in Young People*. New York: Ballantine Books.

HOWE, M.J.A. (1982) Biographical evidence and the development of outstanding individuals. *American Psychologist, 37*, 1071–1081.

HOWE, M.J.A. (1988) Intelligence as an explanation. *British Journal of Psychology, 79*, 349–360.

HOWE, M.J.A. (1990) *The Origins of Exceptional Abilities*. Oxford: Blackwell.

THE TIMING OF TALENT: THE FACILITATION OF EARLY PRODIGIOUS ACHIEVEMENT

Lynn T. Goldsmith

The child prodigy provides a natural experiment in human ability which offers the opportunity to explore those dimensions involved in the expression of talent. Such natural experiments are relatively rare, yielding glimpses of experiences and accomplishments that most of us will never know directly. The phenomenon of early prodigious achievement highlights the factors involved in the development of ability by providing the opportunity to examine cases where individuals with unusual talent succeed in achieving high levels of expression. Not only does the study of prodigies yield a fuller picture of extraordinary expression of talent, it may direct our attention towards factors involved in the process of development of ability in all individuals.

It may be useful to think of the prodigy as an example of development gone right, at least with respect to the process of mastering a particular field or body of knowledge. Psychologists and educators have long maintained that much can be learned about normal development by studying cases of pathology or disability, since investigations of development gone awry can help identify factors that are necessary or sufficient for a developmental trajectory to stay on target (for example, Gardner, 1975; Miller, 1989; Sacks, 1987). An examination of ability at the other extreme of the range can also shed light on the centre by seeking to articulate factors which are optimal (rather than necessary) for development.

Child prodigies provide examples of such optimal development: they embody an uncanny match between individual talent and a given domain of expertise. Under the right 'enabling environments' this match can lead to extraordinarily rapid mastery of a domain by an unusually young child. What constitutes 'extraordinarily rapid mastery' and 'an unusually young child' has typically been left to an informal and intuitive sense. For earlier research purposes (and for the purpose of this paper), early prodigious development has been defined as a child's attainment before the age of ten of a level of performance in a cognitively demanding field that is characteristic of an adult professional (Feldman, 1980; Feldman with Goldsmith, 1986).

Within a psychometric framework the prodigy has been characterized as a child possessing a general intellectual power (i.e., high IQ) which was then directed towards some specific area of ability. This view has neglected a critical distinction between the *potential* for future high level performance (based on the predictive value of IQ scores) and the *proven* maturity of actual achievement characteristic of the prodigy. While thousands of children are identified as 'gifted' in the psychometric sense, very few actually demonstrate performance mastery that is significantly beyond their years. The child prodigy is a far more rare individual, one whose talent is tangible and observable, rather than simply inferred from predictive test scores.

By assuming that the child prodigy could be characterized in terms of IQ, at least three critical issues about the phenomenon of early prodigious achievement have been obscured:

1. early prodigious achievement represents a very *specific* match between a talented individual and a particular domain, rather than a general intelligence that happens to become focused at one of several possible areas of interest;

2. child prodigies do not necessarily display overall intellectual strength in the psychometric sense;

3. the expression and development of prodigious ability is a surprisingly delicate and sensitive process which requires extraordinary environmental support.

There are sound reasons for directing attention away from predictions about future achievement and towards actual mastery of a particular field: the factors critical to facilitating mastery, and the process by which prodigious talent develops.

'Co-incidence' and Environmental Enablers

What makes a prodigy? Historically the tendency has been to assume either that prodigies are just like everyone else only more so (the psychometric approach to prodigies as extra-high IQ individuals), or that they are blessed with a mysterious and powerful biological gift which asserts itself effortlessly and in mature form at the first possible opportunity. Not surprisingly, neither approach is correct. Based on a ten year longitudinal study of six young boys, Feldman and Goldsmith concluded that the child with the potential for expressing a prodigious talent will only develop that gift if a number of critical factors converge (Feldman with Goldsmith, 1986; Feldman and Gold-smith, 1989). A similar view regarding the conditions facilitating the development of talent more generally has been advanced by other investigators as well (Albert, 1978; Albert and Runco, 1985; Horowitz, 1987; Horowitz and O'Brien, 1985). It is the 'co-incidence' of extra-ordinary individual talent with a range of powerful personal and cultural supports which yields early prodigious achievement.

It may be useful to think of these co-incidence forces as three layers of an onion skin. At the innermost layer, representing the core of the process, is the individual child who possesses a particular ability and other supporting (or interfering) talents, interests, and strategies for dealing with the world. The second layer is composed of other individuals who monitor, guide, and facilitate the child's develop-ment – generally parents, teachers, patrons, and mentors. Encom-passing and enabling the process at the third and outermost layer are those socio-cultural forces which set the tone and opportunity for the development of unusual talent. These three layers interact one with another, and a critical factor missing from any of the three can throw the 'prodigy equation' into disequilibrium and can alter the original developmental path.

The individual child. At the innermost level we must consider the role of individual ability. This is obviously central, for without the poten-tial for exceptional achievement the phenomenon of the prodigy would not exist: the difference between Bobby Fischer and the mem-bers of the chess club at the local high school is, to a significant extent, simply one of ability. This talent can reasonably be considered to have some biological basis, although we know little or nothing about the specific biology of the acquisition and transmission of talent.

The tendency of some families to produce several generations of gifted practitioners (for example, the Calders, Peales, van Ruysdaels, and Wyeths in the artworld; the Galton and Darwin family in science and medicine; the musical Bachs; and the Bernoullis in mathematics) would suggest some genetic component. It is, of course, difficult to estimate the effect of environmental support and expectation on the development of talent in such families. It has been proposed else-where that families which value and encourage the mastery of certain areas of expertise confer a non-biological, yet familial tendency to concentrate on particular domains of knowledge. This 'transgener-ational' transmission occurs through both explicit and implicit teach-ing of family values, disciplines, and ways of viewing and knowing the world (Albert, 1978; Feldman with Goldsmith, 1986; Runco and Albert, 1986; see also Cavalli-Sforza and Feldman, 1981, for a techni-cal discussion of the cultural transmission of characteristics). At this point, however, it is not possible to do more than assert that a significant factor in the development of a prodigy is the child's own potential for the expression of extreme talent.

In addition to individual talent, certain motivational characteristics seem to be present in all prodigies which may serve to support and sustain the specific talent itself. Prodigies seem to possess a dedication to their craft and a determination to master it which engages and fuels the process of realizing their enormous talents. It seems possible (and even likely) that there exist other children with equally strong talents, but who lack the drive and passion to extend these abilities into actual prodigious achievements. Prodigies characteristically demonstrate intense, focused, and dedicated study of their chosen field. Parents of 'average' children often find that their efforts to provide enriching experiences must be accompanied by exhortations to study or practise these activities. But in the case of the child prodigy, parents often find themselves begging their children to *stop* studying or practising and to go and play outside with their friends.

In addition to the intensity of attraction between child and field, one often finds in child prodigies an unusual confidence and sense of inner security about their special abilities. As children, prodigies are rarely beset with misgivings or uncertainties about the extent of their abilities or the correctness of their commitment to intense study of a particular domain of knowledge. As prodigies approach adolescence, some of this certainty may become more elusive for two basic reasons: others' expectations for mature performance increase; underlying cognitive changes often require children who have just arrived at the Piagetian stage of formal operations to transform their old ways of knowing the field into a more abstract, intellectualized understanding. This may lead to a crisis of confidence (and performance) which Bamberger (1982) has termed the 'mid-life crisis.'

Other individuals as enablers. At the second layer of the onion skin are the individuals who serve as environmental enablers. These people assume much of the responsibility for the identification, facilitation, education, and guidance of the prodigy.

Parents play a critical role in the initial recognition and response to early indications of prodigious talent. The early products and performances of even the most supremely talented child are immature, and impressive only in relation to some range of normative behaviour for age-mates. If parents are unaware, insensitive, uninterested, or otherwise unable to respond to indications that their child is doing something quite unusual for his or her age, then the fledgling talent may remain neglected and relatively undeveloped.

Once parents do recognize a child's unusual talent and decide to foster it, they must be willing to make significant commitments, and often sacrifices, to facilitate and monitor their child's development. At the very least, this means arranging for teachers, providing transportation to provide lessons and performance, and keeping a careful eye on their child's schooling as well as his or her 'professional' and personal development. This can represent a significant burden in financial, emotional, and professional terms.

Assisting in the education of a prodigy can become a full-time job which may require reassessment of a parent's own commitment to the pursuit of satisfying work. Yehudi Menuhin's father left his post as Superintendent of Hebrew Education in San Francisco to manage his son's education and early career; the young Chinese painter Wang Yani's father has given up his own career as a painter to do the same for his daughter. Of a sample of six longitudinal cases of prodigies and their families, five were essentially single income families in which one of the parents assumed a primary responsibility for being responsive and available to the demands of educating a prodigy (Feldman with Goldsmith, 1986).

Parents of prodigies are faced with the major task of finding appropriate teachers for their children. Mythology would have it that the prodigy demonstrates uncannily mature abilities from the outset, and requires little or no tutelage. While child prodigies do make unusually rapid progress which yields astoundingly mature achievements, such progress is rarely unschooled. Teachers play a critical role in helping a prodigy to master a domain, whether the student is an extraordinary teenager or adult (Bloom, 1985) or an exceptional child (Bamberger, in press; Feldman with Goldsmith, 1986).

In the case of the prodigy, it is important to find teachers who are not only fine instructors and practitioners, but who are also able to relate to children. Despite the fact that prodigies demonstrate an unusually mature grasp of a particular area of expertise, they are nonetheless still children, emotionally and cognitively, in areas outside their domain of giftedness. Teachers must be able to tailor their instruction to deal with this extreme form of decalage between the prodigies' special areas of talent and their more age-typical overall functioning (Baumgarten, 1930; Feldman with Goldsmith, 1986; Feldman and Goldsmith, 1989). Some particularly gifted teachers become known for their work with exceptional children (for example, violinist Dorothy DeLay and chess coach John Collins; Collins, 1974); other teachers rise to the challenge of altering their teaching to accommodate the particular demands of the prodigy. Because a poor, or even uneasy, match between teacher and student can strongly influence the quality (and even the direction) of a prodigy's development, the choice of teacher is a crucial one for the process of realizing prodigious potential. (See Feldman with Goldsmith, 1986, for a discussion of how a significant career change for a musical prodigy involved a change in the dynamic between pupil and teacher.)

Institutional enablers. At the third and outermost layer of the onion skin we must consider those extra-individual factors that are central to the expression of prodigious ability. These involve characteristics of the specific domain of knowledge and the nature and extent of broader cultural support for the expression of unusual ability.

Only certain domains seem to be conducive to the close fit between individual abilities and the cognitive demands and structuring that yields prodigious accomplishments (Feldman with Goldsmith, 1986; Feldman and Goldsmith, 1989; Goldsmith, 1987). Prodigies are frequently found in fields such as chess and music (both composition and performance), and occasionally in writing, painting, mathematics (if the criteria are relaxed somewhat) and, it seems, computer programming. Significant mastery of other fields, such as bridge, medicine, economics or philosophy do not seem to occur even among the most talented of youngsters. It is not entirely clear why some domains support early prodigious achievement while others do not, although a number of possible reasons have been suggested (Feldman with Goldsmith, 1986; Feldman and Goldsmith, 1989). Prodigies are found in domains which engage primarily a single 'mode' of mentation (Gardner, 1983), are highly structured, and include well-organized pedagogies for instructing aspiring students. The more clearly structured and articulated the domain, the greater the possibility that it can be comprehended – especially by a child. Similarly, the more established the available instructional techniques, the more likely that these well-tried approaches will be useful, or relatively easily adapted, to the education of the prodigy. Finally, there is an experiential factor: domains which require the ability to reflect on rich life experiences are less likely to be mastered by children.

There may also be factors related to the structure or content of particular domains that hold particular appeal for children. Music, for example, seems to be a 'privileged' domain for everyone, occupying a central role in the experiences of both children and adults worldwide. Levi-Strauss (1969) has written about music as containing the key to the secret of humanity. It may be that this special place in the realm of human experience makes music an especially compelling area for children who are also fortunate enough to be gifted with unusual musical sensibilities.

In any case, the rhythmic and tonal building blocks of musical experience may hold a special fascination for talented young children. In a similar vein, the writings of literary prodigies are best characterized as strong in formal properties and relatively weak in substance. At age seven or eight, for example, Randy McDaniel was able to recreate the style and texture of Victorian prose, although his stories lacked significant plot or character development (Feldman with Goldsmith, 1986). There may be something particularly compelling and comprehensible to young children about disciplines that rely on an underlying spatial or temporal logic which is structured through metre and cadence.

Finally, the third layer of onion also includes the impact of the social and cultural environment in which the prodigy lives and learns. To a significant extent, cultural values and priorities support or discourage the pursuit of particular areas of study. Without some form of support at this level, the child prodigy will fight an uphill battle for the simple privilege of studying. In a very general but nonetheless profound way societal values and pressures provide or deny the opportunity for individuals to develop their interests and talents. While American children with a penchant for chess are generally only mildly encouraged to study and improve their game, children in Iceland (where chess is a national pastime) are heartily welcomed into an extensive and well-supported network of lessons, clubs, and tournaments. American children demonstrating strong interest and aptitude for mathematics and science, on the other hand, will have far less difficulty finding teachers and mentors to encourage, supervise, and even finance advanced study. The cultural milieu also facilitates or denies access to its valued domains, and gifted children who are members of minority groups may be denied the opportunity to pursue their interests (Baldwin, 1985; Eccles, 1985; Goldsmith, 1987; Mistry and Rogoff, 1985). Thus, the role of culture in the expression of talent can be profound; its effects may be quite subtle or relatively blatant.

All three of these layers of the onion – individual child, individual enablers, and institutional enablers – must be coordinated and then interact productively over time if prodigious talent is to develop. If one of these factors is missing, or even mistimed, it becomes far less likely that a prodigy's talent will continue to flourish. It is in this sense that a child prodigy can be considered a cultural creation. A child with even the most striking gifts cannot realize that talent without considerable support: early prodigious achievement requires the concerted efforts of family, friends, teachers, and mentors, as well as the child's good fortune to be born in a place and time which respects and values the particular ability, and which provides opportunities for pursuit of excellence in that given field.

Typical Development

Studying the extremes of ability yields a good deal of information about unusual gifts and unusual deficits. But what can it tell us about patterns of typical development? The case of the child prodigy highlights a number of issues which should hold for the development of normal, as well as exceptional, abilities.

Prodigies provide strong evidence for theories of intelligence which emphasize relatively independent, modular ways of knowing rather than a global and generalized intellectual power (Gardner, 1982; Gardner, 1983; Gardner and Krechevsky, Chapter 12, this volume). Although child prodigies demonstrate extraordinarily mature development in their special fields, they are not necessarily unusually talented across the board. In fact, the prodigy's talent is best characterized by an unusually mature specific ability. Feldman (1979) has reported, for example, that four prodigies exhibited significant decalage between performance in their fields of prodigious mastery and classic Piagetian tests of formal operational reasoning: while the children demonstrated adult level performance in their particular domains, their performance on the Piagetian tasks was age-appropriate and characteristic of concrete operational thought.

Though a child may demonstrate a phenomenal grasp of mathematics, he or she may not be particularly talented in terms of expressive language, nor particularly gifted in terms of mechanical or spatial abilities. A prodigious writer may have no special capacity for musical or kinaesthetic expression. Prodigies' 'profiles' of interests and abilities are often atypical in their irregularity by virtue of their exceptional gifts, but in many ways this irregularity is similar in kind (if not in degree) to those of less exceptional children (Gardner and Hatch, in press).

The rate at which prodigies connect with and begin to master their special domains is unusually rapid but the process by which they do so appears not to be. They can therefore provide some information about the ways in which successful learning occurs for any individual aspiring to master the domain. Because of this, prodigies may provide information about the optimal conditions for the mastery of specific domains.

The prodigy's command of his or her special field often appears to an outsider to be effortless and nearly instantaneous. Such mastery does not, in reality, occur of a piece, but is wrought from years of study and practice. Despite the apparent speed and ease with which it occurs, the prodigy begins at the beginning and progresses through the levels of mastery much as anyone else seeking to learn the content and techniques of a field. Early prodigious development seems to correspond to more typical development in that both forms of mastery follow the same sequence and demonstrate the same general cognitive structuring.

This suggests that prodigies are not privy to unique processes. It is, however, important to note that we know virtually nothing about the specifics of prodigies' mastery of their fields, as there have been no longitudinal, fine-grained analyses of prodigies' knowledge systems, nor of how these systems change over time. Bamberger's work (in press) with talented young musicians represents the only effort I know of to systematically explore in detail children's understanding of a domain. One direction for future investigations is to undertake a more detailed and thorough analysis of prodigies' specific knowledge and understanding of their fields, how they come to their understanding, and how this changes with instruction, experience, and maturation.

Finally, prodigies have been described as the serendipitous result of the co-incidence of a number of important factors which yield the expression of exceptional talent. These co-incidence factors are not unique to unusually talented children, but operate in the expression of all ability, whether it is Promethean or quite modest. By observing how these factors interact in an optimal way to allow the expression of prodigious talent, it is possible to understand better some of the forces that facilitate or impede the realization of potential in the ordinary case. Some of these factors are difficult to control: we cannot much alter our individual abilities, nor change the cultural *Zeitgeist* in which we live. Other factors such as parental sensitivity and responsiveness to indications of interest or ability, availability of appropriate adult models and efforts to expose children to a range of potentially engaging activities, can (and probably should) be kept in mind as we seek to identify and facilitate the expression of interest and ability in ourselves, our children, and our pupils. By making an effort to maximize the coordination and interplay of these factors, we will increase the probability of approximating optimal expression of our own particular gifts.

Prodigies and Mature Talent

The emergence of a child demonstrating prodigious mastery is an unusual event – often a media event – which may inspire awe and disbelief in those of us possessing more mundane levels of talent. It represents the unlikely confluence of talent, the commitment to its development and an avenue for expression, and environmental support, all delicately intertwined and carefully timed. It does not, however, represent any guarantee that this confluence will continue in the future. Though the match between child and field is uncannily close, it is not necessarily robust, and the continued flourishing of the talent is not assured. It is important to recognize the phenomenon for what it is not, as well as for what it is.

During the 1920s and 1930s at least 70 musical prodigies hailed from San Francisco: more than one from every square mile of the city limits. Of these, all but five (Yehudi Menuhin, his sister Hephzibah, Ruggiero Ricci, Ruth Slenczynska, and Isaac Stern) have been virtually forgotten. The fate of this 'San Francisco cohort' is a sobering illustration of the long-term future of the prodigy. Rather than assuring continued future success in a field, the early, stunning achievements of child prodigies often represent the zenith of their achievements. Despite extraordinary talent, enormous discipline, and years of hard work, relatively few prodigies transform their talents into adult careers. Some find they cannot weather the transition between child star and mature (less adulated) adult practitioner; some find they are simply unable to develop their talents further; others in adolescence discover that their gifts have led to unwanted social isolation and sacrifice; some simply find their focus too limited and choose to abandon intensive study in favour of broader explorations.

Ironically, the 'goodness of fit' between child and domain may contribute in some cases to prodigies' decisions to cease further study. Prodigies are most noteworthy for their mastery of existing bodies of knowledge rather than for their original contributions to the field. Although they may eventually make outstanding contributions as adults (Mozart, Picasso, and Norbert Weiner are examples), and although the prodigy may aspire to such achievements, truly significant or creative accomplishments are not achieved by children, no matter how great their gifts. The match between child and field may encourage such aspirations despite the fact that they cannot reasonably be realized. The nature of many prodigies' talents may, in fact, lie in their ability to master the domain in its existing state rather than to break new ground. Their unique talents may be best for celebrating the current state of the art, not for transcending it.

Conversely, those who make the most singular contributions to a field may not be those who demonstrated the most precocious affinity for it as children (with the possible exception of music, where virtually every major performer has been a prodigy). The young Charles Darwin was a relatively indifferent student, demonstrating little of the brilliance and promise of his (now less famous) cousin Francis Galton; none of Marie Curie's teachers were likely to have suspected that their able, yet extremely shy pupil would win two Nobel Prizes. The prodigy's gifts are in part ones of anomalous timing: their talents assert themselves early and rapidly, while others' gifts require more seasoning and experience before they become apparent. Both have their time and place.

Prodigies and Evolution

It has been suggested elsewhere that the prodigy represents an evolutionary strategy that is based on behavioural specialization (Feldman with Goldsmith, 1986). As a species, humans easily move into a wide variety of environmental niches, altering their behaviour and their environment to maximize adaptation. Prodigies' unusual cognitive specialization indicates that there may be some benefit to an alternative adaptive strategy which emphasizes a preprogrammed, close fit between the individual and the environment, rather than the more common species strategy of flexibility and general adaptiveness. In this sense, the prodigy might be considered an evolutionary gambit: a less flexible organism, but one potentially exquisitely matched to certain environmental pressures.

If prodigies are subject to selection pressures for specialization rather than for generalized flexibility, must we assume a separate mechanism (such as mutation) to account for their existence in the population, or can the characteristics of the child prodigy be accounted for within the existing range of human variation? While prodigies' talents are indeed extraordinary they do not seem to be out of the bounds of expected variability. Though rare, they nonetheless occur with some regularity: each generation has its collection of extraordinary children to admire and amaze. In fact, the prodigy probably cannot be considered to possess high specialization at the expense of the generalized and flexible skills characteristic of people in general. While prodigies demonstrate a strong cognitive specialization, it is embedded within more or less 'normal' general functioning. It is true that some prodigies have been remarkable for eccentric or childish behaviour, but on the whole even these individuals negotiate the daily vicissitudes of life with little difficulty.

The domain specificity of prodigies' gifts would also seem to support the notion that their talents are underwritten by the existing gene pool rather than arising from new and rare mutations. Prodigies are found consistently in a small number of specific domains rather than demonstrating abilities in a wide and random array of fields. While prodigies may in some sense be anomalies of nature (and nurture), they are probably not totally fortuitous accidents.

It is also useful to ask what, specifically, is anomalous about prodigies' gifts, i.e. whether their abilities are extraordinary in some absolute sense, or merely in relation to the accomplishments of other children. It is clearly the speed of mastery which characterizes early prodigious achievement, and not the actual level of achievement: many adults master the domain more completely and make more original and lasting contributions. The prodigy's unusual abilities, then, would represent a case of cognitive heterochrony, or a change in the timing of development (Gould, 1977). To make a strong evolutionary argument about the specialized skills characteristic of child prodigies, one would have to argue for an adaptive advantage to the species of earlier and earlier acquisition of the abilities which prodigies demonstrate.

This, in turn, leads to more general issues about the possible biological advantage of the expression of such abilities. It could be argued that the fields which most often support early prodigious achievement are by definition 'discretionary' ones in that mastery of these domains is not necessary for effective functioning within the society. While it could be argued that literacy and 'numeracy' are requisite for full participation in late twentieth century societies, chess competence most clearly is not. Such optional fields probably confer little or no advantage (in evolutionary terms) on those who display strong talent for them. Those activities or disciplines which are (or have been) subject to strong selection pressures tend to show little variability and therefore would not support substantially accelerated acquisition. Thus one would have to make a prospective case for the future selective advantage of domains like music, chess, painting or literature, which support early prodigious achievement. This seems unlikely, although it is, of course, always possible.

A strict biological argument would also require that prodigies enjoy a selective advantage in terms of increased fecundity. Popular myth would have it that prodigies are significantly *less* likely to reproduce than the population at large. While this is probably not the case, there is no evidence to suggest that prodigies produce more children on average either.

Although there is no adequate way to address these issues at present, the questions framed above are among the ones that would have to be considered were one to make a strict case for the evolutionary value of the prodigy. On first impression, it would seem that such a case is not well supported.

The prodigy may yet bear a message about change and development, but it is likely to be one that pertains more to cultural rather than biological evolution. The vast majority of human activity occurs within environments which have been crafted by people and which 'evolve' through directed efforts to effect changes in the world (Bickhard, 1979; Campbell, 1975; Feldman, 1988). It is possible that the unusual gifts of child prodigies may play a special role in the evolution of human knowledge, if not in the evolution of the underlying genetic substrate.

Because prodigies begin to master their fields at such an early age, they potentially gain an extra 10 or 15 years in which to explore the more advanced and esoteric aspects of their fields. While early mastery does not necessarily guarantee that an individual will find the means to make significant and lasting contributions to a given discipline, this extra time does increase that probability. Prodigies' selective advantage (in the sense of cultural evolution) may be all in the timing: by dispensing with the preliminaries of learning a discipline long before others have even committed themselves to its study, the prodigy can proceed to explore the subtleties and intricacies of the domain while peers are still becoming acquainted with its basics.

Whether or not the phenomenon of the child prodigy is one with strong evolutionary underpinnings or implications, there are many lessons to be learned from its study. These are lessons about the identification, nurturance, and development of talent, and should apply to individuals at any level of ability, for they address issues of developing individual potential in general. The lessons emphasize the importance of diversity, persistence, environmental responsiveness, and active involvement in keeping the process of development on track.

Whether the product of serendipitous co-incidence or the result of evolutionary adaptation, the natural experiment which is the prodigy can help to answer questions about the optimization of talent and to frame new enquiries for future consideration.

Is the prodigy best described as a biological or a cultural phenomenon?

Do prodigies reflect random aberrations or do they offer a brief glance at a form of cognitive perfection?

How can we describe, and eventually explain, the nature of the prodigy's talent?

Does the awe and amazement we often feel at prodigious talent suggest that these children are, in some sense, freaks, or are these feelings due to the unusual opportunity to observe development in an exceedingly powerful form?

Perhaps these and other questions will occupy us in the future as we observe more closely prodigies occupied with the task of mastering their special fields.

Acknowledgement: I would like to thank Greg Ball and Mark Bickhard for earlier discussions about evolution and child prodigies. Greg was particularly helpful in clarifying issues of timing versus extent. I would also like to thank Rebecca B. Corwin, Ellen Winner and Arthur M. Wood for comments on earlier drafts of this chapter. Support for the preparation of this chapter came from the Exxon Education Foundation.

REFERENCES

ALBERT, R.S. (1978) Observations and suggestions regarding giftedness, familial influences, and the achievement of eminence. *Gifted Child Quarterly*, 22, 201–211.

ALBERT, R.S. and RUNCO, M.A. (1985) The achievement of eminence: A model of exceptionally gifted boys and their families. In R.J. Sternberg & J.E. Davidson (Eds), *Conceptions of Giftedness*. Cambridge: Cambridge University Press.

BALDWIN, A.Y. (1985) Programs for the gifted and talented: Issues concerning minority populations. In F.D. Horowitz and M.O'Brien (Eds), *The Gifted and Talented: Developmental Perspectives*. Washington, DC: American Psychological Association.

BAMBERGER, J. (1982) Growing up prodigies: The mid-life crisis. In D.H. Feldman (Ed.), *Developmental Approaches to Giftedness and Creativity*. San Francisco: Jossey-Bass.

BAMBERGER, J. (in press) *The Mind Behind the Musical Ear*. Cambridge, Ma.: Harvard University Press.

BAUMGARTEN, F. (1930) *Wunderkinder Psychologische Untersuchungen*. Leipzig: Johann Amrosius Barth.

BICKHARD, M.H. (1979) On necessary and specific capabilities in evolution and development. *Human Development*, 22, 217–224.

BLOOM, B. (1985) *Developing Talent in Young Children*. New York: Ballantine.

CAVALLI-SFORZA, L. and FELDMAN, M.W. (1981) *Cultural Transmission and Evolution: A Quantitative Approach*. Princeton, NJ: Princeton University Press.

CAMPBELL, D. (1975) On the conflict between biological and social evolution and between psychology and moral traditions. *American Psychologist*, 30, 1103–1126.

COLLINS, J. (1974) *My Seven Chess Prodigies*. New York: Simon & Schuster.

ECCLES, J.S. (1985) Why doesn't Jane run? Sex differences in educational and occupational patterns. In F.D. Horowitz & M.O'Brien (Eds), *The Gifted and Talented: Developmental Perspectives*. Washington, D.C.: American Psychological Association.

FELDMAN, D.H. (1979) The mysterious case of extreme giftedness. In A.H. Passow (Ed.), *The Gifted and the Talented: Their Education and Development*. Chicago: National Society for the Study of Education.

FELDMAN, D.H. (1980) *Beyond Universals in Cognitive Development*. Norwood, NJ: Ablex.

FELDMAN, D.H. (1988) Universal to unique: Toward a cultural genetic epistemology. *Archives de Psychologie*, 56, 271–279.

FELDMAN, D.H. with GOLDSMITH, L.T. (1986) *Nature's Gambit: Child Prodigies and the Development of Human Potential*. New York: Basic Books.

FELDMAN, D.H. and GOLDSMITH, L.T. (1986) Transgenerational influences in the development of early prodigious behaviour: A case study approach. In W. Fowler (Ed.), *Early Experience and Competence Development*. San Francisco: Jossey-Bass.

FELDMAN, D.H. and GOLDSMITH, L.T. (1989) Child prodigies straddling two worlds. *Medical and Health Annual*. Chicago: Encyclopedia Brittanica.

GARDNER, H. (1975) *The Shattered Mind*. New York: Knopf.

GARDNER, H. (1982) Giftedness: Speculations from a biological perspective. In D.H. Feldman (Ed.), *Developmental Approaches to Giftedness and Creativity*. San Francisco: Jossey-Bass.

GARDNER, H. (1983) *Frames of Mind*. New York: Basic Books.

GARDNER, H. and KRECHEVSKY, M. (in press) Nurturance of multiple intelligences. In M.J.A. Howe (Ed.), *Encouraging the Development of Exceptional Abilities and Talents*. Leicester, UK: British Psychological Society.

GARDNER, H. and HATCH, T. (in press) Multiple intelligences go to school. *Educational Researcher*.

GOLDSMITH, L.T. (1987) Girl prodigies: Some evidence and some speculations. *Roeper Review*, 10(2), 74–81.

GOULD, S.J. (1977) *Ontogeny and Phylogeny*. Cambridge, Ma.: Harvard University Press.

HOROWITZ, F.D. (1987) *Exploring Developmental Theories: Toward a Structural/Behavioral Model of Development*. Hillsdale, NJ: Erlbaum.

HOROWITZ, F.D. and O'BRIEN, M. (1985) Epilogue. Perspectives in research and development. In F.D. Horowitz and M.O'Brien (Eds), *The Gifted and Talented: Developmental Perspectives*. Washington, DC: American Psychological Association.

LEVI-STRAUSS, C. (1969) *The Raw and the Cooked*. New York: Simon & Schuster.

MILLER, L.K. (1989) *Musical Savants: Exceptional Skill in the Mentally Retarded*. Hillsdale, NJ: Erlbaum.

MISTRY, J. and ROGOFF, B. (1985) A cultural perspective in the development of talent. In F.D. Horowitz and M.O'Brien (Eds), *The Gifted and Talented: Developmental Perspectives*. Washington, DC: American Psychological Association.

RUNCO, M. and ALBERT, R.S. (1986) Exceptional giftedness in early adolescence and intrafamilial divergent thinking. *Journal of Youth and Adolescence*, 15(4), 335–344.

SACKS, O. (1987) *The Man who Mistook His Wife for a Hat*. New York: Harper & Row.

THE PROBLEM OF THE PRODIGY

John Radford

'LAUNDRETTE BANS CHILD GENIUS' DAD' runs a tabloid head-line (*The Sun* newspaper, 20 May 1989). The child turns out to be Ruth Lawrence, who has been in the news since she emerged as a math-ematical prodigy when she passed 'O' level mathematics in the General Certificate of Education (usually taken at 16), at the age of eight in 1980. In 1989 she can hardly still be considered a child, but labels stick.

The same page of *The Sun* carries an unrelated item that £11,000 had been paid at Sotheby's for a lock of Mozart's hair. Mozart's is perhaps the name that comes most readily to mind when the term 'child prodigy' is mentioned. Other media at the time of writing are full of the autobiography of Shirley Temple Black, *Child Star*. Shirley Temple remains the youngest ever winner of an Oscar, at six, by which age she had already made 27 films.

'Prodigy' and 'child prodigy' are popular rather than technical terms. I have elsewhere (Radford, 1990) glossed them with the phrase 'exceptional early achievers'. By 'achievers' I mean to indicate actual performance rather than potential, although a high score on an intelligence test could be an ambiguous case. The words 'exceptional' and 'early' both indicate some position on a dimension or dimen-sions, but like most human measurements they are relative rather than absolute. Ruth Lawrence's achievement in obtaining her GCE 'A' level at ten was surpassed by John Adams, who did it with a grade C at nine in 1987, and then by Ganesh Sittampalam who gained a grade A in 1988 a few months younger. An 'A' grade in mathematics at the normal age of eighteen is outside the reach of most of the population, but would hardly qualify as prodigious. At nine, or ten, it does, though any generally agreed cut-off point could only be estab-lished by enquiry. Achievement, like other human activities, can only be exceptional in relation to a norm, as has been apparent since Galton. A norm implies a reference group, and the question arises as to what this is. A GCE in anything would be as exceptional among the !Kung-San of the Kalahari (Blurton-Jones and Konner, 1976), as their tracking abilities would be in British schoolchildren. This of course says nothing about potential for either activity.

As it happens, the tracking abilities will shortly disappear, if they have not done so already, since the !Kung are currently being driven from their homelands in the interests of development. This is not irrelevant; it is an example of the increasing domination of (broadly-speaking) one culture, the same culture within which psychology and related studies have developed, and which has thus defined the nature of abilities. Even when this culture finally becomes universal it will not provide universally valid norms, since other standards have prevailed and may do so in the future. An individual can only be exceptional in comparison to a group and that must be one to which he or she might otherwise be thought to belong.

Thus I would wish to argue that the 'idiots savants' who have recently generated so much interest (e.g. Howe, 1989; Treffert, 1989) are clearly exceptional in relation to the variously retarded groups of which they otherwise seem to be part. Young 'idiots savants' could justifiably be called 'child prodigies', even though their abilities may not surpass those of averagely gifted 'normals'. I shall not have very much to say about them here, however.

The *Concise Oxford Dictionary* defines 'prodigy' as: 'Marvellous thing, esp. one out of the course of nature; wonderful example of (some quality); person endowed with surprising qualities, esp. precocious child'. The problem is that we do not know what the course of nature is; or, if nature is defined more narrowly, it is only one side of the equation that produces human behaviour. David Feldman is almost the only recent author who has tried to say something specific about prodigies as such, rather than gifted children in general. Notably in *Nature's Gambit* (1986), he presented case studies of six most exceptional children (see also Goldsmith, this volume). Feldman argues that the concept of a prodigy has been 'assimilated into the peculiarly American notion of the "intellectually gifted", or high-IQ, child'. A prodigy is considered to be a child of exceptionally high general intelligence, focused on one particular field. There is clearly much truth in this, and the tradition can be traced back through the work of McCurdy (1957), Cox (1926), Ellis (1904) and others, and ultimately to Galton.

Feldman and Goldsmith wish rather to revive some of the older 'out of the usual course of nature' meaning. This is partly because high IQ 'or any other relatively simple explanation' does not account for very exceptional performance. This is correct, but it requires qualification in two ways. First, very little if any human behaviour has a simple explanation. Second, high intelligence does not explain the prodigy because intelligence in itself is not an explanation, as Howe (1988) points out, and indeed as Ryle (1949) pointed out. It does not necessarily follow however that prodigies are not highly intelligent (though further confusion arises from lack of agreement as to what intelligence means).

Another part of the argument is that 'the prodigy seems to be unique in having an extremely specialized gift that is expressed only under very specific, culturally evolved environmental conditions'. Again there is much in this, yet it does not seem entirely apt even for Feldman's own subjects. Thus 'Ricky Velazquez' (all the names are pseudonyms) emerged as a chess genius at four, but is described as good all round, at first at sport but also gifted academically; Adam Konatowski excelled at languages, mathematics and music; Franklin Montana is described as liking to get very good at something and then leave it.

A third aspect of the argument, on which less weight is placed, is that some child prodigies seem to display something akin to extrasensory perception. Apart from all the usual difficulties surrounding this phenomenon, reports of it in children do not generally seem to have any systematic relationship to other 'prodigious' qualities.

Historical examples of extrasensory powers of perception are in fact a useful illustration of giftedness in young people. Modern spiritualism began with the young Fox sisters in 1848 in Hydesville, Connecticut (Brandon, 1983), and poltergeist phenomena have been associated with adolescents (Gauld and Cornell, 1979) since well before Dr Johnson debunked the Cock Lane Ghost in 1762. Now either such children have some peculiar gift, or they are remarkably adept at deceit or just possibly both. They may or may not have other talents. Currently the unitary view of intellectual capacity is less popular than a modular one (Fodor, 1987) exemplified in theories such as that of Gardner (1983) of multiple and relatively independent 'intelligences' (see Chapter 12, this volume). While this is no doubt to some extent a matter of fashion, it does make it easier to accommodate within a general framework both idiots savants and specialized geniuses in any field. This indeed is what Feldman wishes to do, since he remarks that the prodigy 'exhibits the very same kinds of developmental processes that we do'.

No one has ever doubted that human beings can excel at a variety of activities. Indeed this is almost tautologous, since given any distribution of performance, some individuals must come at the top end of it. The more different activities there are, the more geniuses there will be. The argument is over how closely performances in different activities correlate, and the likelihood is that they form clusters of varying degrees of size, cohesion and exclusivity. The pattern depends on which performances are selected for comparison, and this in turn on which are possible, or favoured, in a particular society. Within it, individual variations are often found. Galton, in *Hereditary*

Genius (1869), considered the relatively diverse talents of judges, statesmen, commanders, literary men, men of science, poets, musicians, painters, divines, mathematicians, oarsmen and wrestlers. His main purpose was to demonstrate first the range of achievement, by a quantifiable criterion of eminence, and then a common cause, heredity. He was less concerned with the analysis of ability (a term he preferred, in the second edition of 1892, to genius). Genius was as defined by Johnson, 'mental power or faculties', and implied to Galton independence of education, which ability did not. It is however the earlier version that became dominant.

Currently there is far more emphasis on education, or more broadly on the cultural environment. Here too there is a modular approach, since the interest is very much in specific factors that seem to mesh with particular modes of behaviour (Lave, 1988; Greeno, 1989). Much of this relates to a discovery or re-discovery of the ideas of L.S. Vygotsky (Wertsch, 1985; Belmont, 1989). A particular aspect is perhaps the stress laid by K.A. Ericsson in particular on the role of learning and memory (Ericsson and Faivre, 1988; Ericsson, Tesch-Römer and Krampe, this volume). Here we almost return to a pre-Galton concept; the hypothesis, with which he had 'no patience', that 'the sole agencies in creating differences between boy and boy, and man and man, are steady application and moral effort'. In the same way, as Fodor points out, the modular view constitutes a partial return to faculty psychology. Moral effort has not yet made a comeback. In reality, effort, or practice, would appear to be a necessary but not a sufficient condition of achievement. Dr Johnson (who seems to be becoming the patron of this chapter) explained his loss of interest in the violin with the remark: 'I found that to fiddle well, I must fiddle all my life; and I thought I could do something better'. It is extremely rare to find great achievement without effort, and apparent cases often turn out to be false (Howe, 1990); but it is not at all uncommon to see prolonged effort result in orfly mediocre achievement.

Johnson was himself a fair specimen of a prodigy as appears from Boswell's famous anecdotes: the infant learning the collect for the day in a couple of readings, the schoolboy whose superiority was consistently acknowledged by his fellows; and not least the short-sighted child, determined to get home alone, kneeling down to see his way across the gutter, and berating his careful schoolmistress for following him (Boswell, 1792). He also came under the influence of an unusual teacher, the scholarly but cruel Joseph Hunter, whose habit was to beat his pupils when they failed to answer, however unreasonable the question: 'He would call a boy up, and ask him Latin for a candlestick, which the boy could not expect to be asked. Now, Sir, if a boy could answer every question, there were no need of a master to teach him.' It is reminiscent of the insoluble problems with which so many classic experiments have confronted rats and dogs. The technique has been used to induce extreme motivation in 'thought reform', and in Zen, perhaps without the benefit of psychological theory. A master is quoted thus: 'If you answer wrongly I will give you forty blows. If you answer correctly I will give you forty blows. Speak!'

Less physically violent were the methods of James Mill, but like the thought reformers he practised 'milieu control' (Lifton, 1961). 'He was earnestly bent upon my escaping not only the corrupting influence which boys exercise over boys, but the contagion of vulgar modes of thought and feeling; and for this he was willing that I should pay the price of inferiority in the accomplishments which schoolboys in all countries chiefly cultivate' (JS Mill, 1873). In their place was perhaps the most extraordinary academic regime ever recorded, based for the first few years entirely on classical Greek (started so early that the boy later had no recollection of when he began), plus arithmetic. James Mill's methods, for example going straight to translation rather than grammar, were effective but also undoubtedly psychologically traumatic: 'My father, in all his teaching, demanded of me not only the utmost that I could do, but much that I could by no possibility have done . . . I was always too much in awe of him to be otherwise than extremely subdued and quiet in his presence'. This resulted in exceptional attainments, but also in markedly low self-esteem, since the boy had no one but his demanding father with whom to compare himself. Later in his autobiography Mill describes the severe crisis and overwhelming sense of hopelessness that came upon him at the age of 20, and from which he emerged only slowly and with difficulty.

John Stuart Mill stands at the head of the list of child geniuses compiled by Catherine Cox (1926). This appeared in the second volume of Terman's massive *Genetic Studies of Genius*, and was based on estimating the early intelligence of eminent persons of the past by comparing their childhood achievements with those of contemporary children from whom test norms were derived. Cox was careful to state that this provided 'only an approximation to a true score', though the very concept of a 'true score' might today be questioned. Mill's estimated IQ was 190–200, and he was followed in the 180–190 range by Bentham, Macaulay, Pascal, Goethe, Grotius, and Leibnitz; with Chatterton, Leopardi, Voltaire, Coleridge, Von Haller and Schelling scoring between 170–180. From her total sample of around 300 Cox estimated the average early intelligence of groups according to primary field of achievement. Philosophers came first at 170, soldiers last at 125, with writers and revolutionary statesmen (160), scientists and other statesmen (155), religious leaders (150), musicians (145) and artists (140) in between. It is certainly tempting to conclude that soldiers are more stupid than philosophers, but it is at least possible that some talents tend to appear earlier than others, while it is certain that some (such as learning to read) correlate more highly with intelligence as measured by Terman's tests. On a modular view, there is presumably such a thing as 'military intelligence' (which the future Marshal Foch is said to have shown at the age of six).

McCurdy (1957) examined the lives of Cox's top 20 individuals in some detail (in addition to those mentioned, there were nine in the 160–170 group: Niebuhr, Mirabeau, John Quincey Adams, Wieland, Tasso, Pope, Pitt, Musset and Melancthon). Fourteen of the 20 showed a pattern of unusual parental attention, often due to birth order: being only children (Leibnitz, Pope) or first children (Mill, Grotius, Goethe, Macaulay, Bentham, Leopardi, Wieland, Melancthon) or unusually in the case of Pitt, the second child, which meant that he would not inherit his father's peerage and thus could follow him into politics by way of the House of Commons (a fact with which Pitt is said to have expressed satisfaction at the age of seven). Coleridge was the son of his father's old age; Voltaire was sickly. In a later study, Albert (1980) reported that 76 per cent of Nobel Prize winners had occupied some 'special' position in their families. Polit and Falbo (1987), reviewing 141 studies, found evidence for only children scoring significantly higher on achievement motivation. The birth order literature however is extensive and not entirely conclusive.

Goethe, Pascal, Niebuhr, Macaulay, Voltaire and Mirabeau showed an intense affection for a sister, in the last case apparently extending to incest. Musset was devoted to an older, and Leopardi to a younger, brother. Whether these strong attachments have any connection with the fact that 11 of the 20 never married remains speculative. Mill, Goethe, Pascal, Bentham, Niebuhr, Adams, Wieland, Tasso and Pitt were the subject of exceptional educational programmes. This and other factors tended to mean that many of the 20 were much, or mainly, in the company of adults, and cut off from other children.

This does not necessarily imply a regime of the Mill type. It is noticeable that Ruth Lawrence, John Adams and Ganesh Sittampalam were all coached by their fathers, though as far as can be seen with no suggestion of forcing. Torrance (e.g. Torrance, 1983) has stressed the role of 'mentors' in creative achievement. A mentor 'encourages and supports the other in expressing and testing his/her ideas and in thinking through things. He/she protects the individual from the reactions of peers and superiors long enough for the person to try out ideas and modify them . . . .'. Such a role can clearly be taken by parents. An extreme case of a supportive programme is described by Deakin (1973): three children of exceptional attainments brought up in relative isolation, by parents who for philosophical reasons devoted themselves almost exclusively to providing a stimulating yet non-threatening environment, using largely Montessori derived methods. I have not come across a later account of this experiment.

The mentor role can also be taken by a teacher or a coach. Hemery (1986) interviewed at length 63 of the world's top performers in a range of sports. Over two thirds considered that they would not have reached the top without the help of their coach, whose approaches varied widely; it is very much 'horses for courses'. An unusually detailed account of successful coaching is given by Boris Breskvar (1987), who taught both Boris Becker and Steffi Graf. Graf has achieved more adult dominance, but Becker perhaps was the greater child prodigy; at thirteen by far the youngest competitor in the German youth championships, and of course winning Wimbledon at seventeen. Breskvar coached him almost every day from the age of six until he signed with Ion Tiriac in the spring of 1984. What impresses in Breskvar's account is first of all Becker's personal qualities: one of the first things the coach noticed was his determination – at six – to reach every ball, as a last resort throwing himself to the ground like a goalkeeper; and second the skilful way in which Breskvar combines theory with intuition and individual variation to suit the particular player. It is a model of effective teaching.

Almost all of Hemery's respondents stressed the importance of general family support. His most exceptional early achiever, Shane Innes (neé Gould), who at just over fifteen held every world freestyle swimming record, in particular described how her parents encouraged all their children, not just herself, as the star performer. Fowler (1981) concludes from both investigative and case study literature that exceptional early (cognitive) abilities flourish in highly intellectual families who early involve their children in rational communication with adults and who intensively stimulate them cognitively during their early development. A series of Chicago-based studies initiated by Benjamin Bloom (1985) and conducted by Lauren Sosniak (Chapter 8, this volume), and a number of other researchers provide evidence in support of this view. They studied about twenty outstanding young people in each of six fields: pianists, sculptors, swimmers, tennis players, mathematicians and neurologists. They found typically that, first, abilities showed themselves early, but this was followed by a long period of hard, though not necessarily unpleasant work, with an emphasis on high standards and with especially appropriate learning experiences. Second, it was the home in which this took place; third, there was strong parental support, in fact fourth, the role of parents – and teachers – was crucial. Fifth the period of training and learning for fulfilment of potential was never less than ten years.

These authors also found that it was very rare for there to be more than one outstanding child in a family. This might be because of the special position effect or what has been called the 'Matthew effect': 'To him that hath shall be given, and he shall have abundance'. There are anecdotal and historical cases where several or all the children in a family seem to have similar environments and encouragement, yet only one achieves fame, for example Shane Gould. The Bach family produced many musicians who appear in standard reference books, but only one Johann Sebastian. Plomin and Daniels (1987) have shown, as perhaps most parents know intuitively, that apparently identical treatment produces a different environment for each child; see also Plomin (1989).

Families exist in a culture and a wider society, and these also influence early achievement (see Berry, this volume; Simonton, 1987). Most simply, at any one time and place some activities will be available, or favoured and rewarded, and others not. It is perhaps rare for such circumstances to favour precocity as such, as with child film stars, since the aim is generally to maximize performance, and this is not possible at very early ages. The aim of coaches is usually to produce champions, rather than young champions. The optimum age varies from one activity to another. Stanley (1977; Benbow and Stanley, 1983) has argued that there are advantages in bringing on young mathematicians, in that, apart from their own personal satisfaction, their careers are lengthened and thus likely to be more productive. At the very highest levels of achievement it is difficult to know if this is so. Kane and Fisher (1979) for example, consider that in general those who start very early in sport develop more slowly than those who start later, and thus reach their peak at about the same age.

More specifically, Feldman (1986) argues that domains of knowledge vary in their appropriateness for prodigious achievement, in that at different stages of development domains demand different patterns of ability. A rather similar point was made by Mitchell (1907) in discussing mathematical prodigies. He was concerned with mental arithmetic and mental algebra, which he suggested were particularly likely to produce child prodigies since they could be practised alone, with no equipment, and with relatively little instruction because they depend on simple basic principles.

Practice does seem to be an essential ingredient for prodigious achievement if not sufficient in the way Ericsson appears to imply. Hemery's respondents were virtually unanimous in reporting total dedication to their sport. Much the same is reported of chess prodigies, for example Nigel Short, one of the dozen or so earliest achievers in the game (Short, 1981). At the same time this can hardly account for Capablanca who is said to have beaten his father the first time he played him, which was two days after seeing his first game at the age of four. It is likely that the amount of practice necessary varies both with the activity and the individual. But it is difficult to be certain that any particular individual has engaged in the optimum pattern of practice. It may partly depend on the standard necessary to excel, and this in turn on the competition or on role models. Reg Hall, discussing the development of traditional musicians, referred to the importance of 'idols within touching distance' (Hall, 1969). The future Lord Curzon, while still an intellectual prodigy at Eton, invited the Prime Minister, Gladstone, to speak at the school. Following this up, being one day in London he called unannounced when the great man was at breakfast with guests. Gladstone nevertheless came out immediately to see him. Harold Wilson is said to have stood on the steps of No. 10 as a young boy. Today, it is forbidden even to enter Downing Street; with what effects on potential politicians one can only speculate. Perhaps a concrete exemplification of Vygotsky's 'zone of proximal development'.

Such chance factors probably play a role in igniting enthusiasm. Walters and Gardner (1986) have described the 'crystallising experience' which marks a turning point in the development of some outstanding individuals, particularly in music and mathematics: it 'occurs principally when circumstances combine inborn talent, self-teaching, and proper exposure to a set of materials in a particular way'. Bertrand Russell, who began studying Euclid at the age of eleven, with his brother as tutor, provides an example: 'This was one of the great events of my life, as dazzling as first love. I had not imagined that there was anything so delicious in the world' (Russell, 1967). Still it is not clear how far such experiences should be regarded as causal.

There is a vast literature on motivation, and it is well established that it is a central factor in learning (Dweck, 1986; Hunter, this volume), but there seems to be relatively little on the extremes of enthusiasm that are, at least at times, found in high achievers including very young ones. One suggestive approach comes from Piechowski and Colangelo (1984) who describe the phenomenon of 'overexcitability' or modes of enhanced mental functioning, in gifted adults and adolescents. They distinguish five modes, assumed to be genetically independent of one another: 'psychomotor', 'sensual', 'intellectual', 'imaginational' and 'emotional'. This is only a start; possibly the recent work of Csikszentmihalyi and Csikszentmihalyi (1988) points a way forward.

Waterhouse (1988) suggests, although very tentatively, that whereas general mechanisms of enhanced brain function may be causally related to better learning, memory, or association, different mechanisms may underlie special talents. These, she thinks, in many cases arise from the same set of skills, concerned with the ability to store and use representations. This involves some form of special organization of the sensory, or polymodal, cortex, and will not arise in areas of dedicated tissue. The potential for special talents is innate, while environment and practice are necessary but not causal. Such brain organization may be associated with unique patterns of internal reward. There have also been suggestions that particular talents are associated with development of one or other of the cerebral hemispheres. Thus Cranberg and Albert (1988) offer three arguments in support of right hemisphere specialization for chess. The first is the association of that hemisphere with visuo-spatial skills, the second the association with pattern recognition, and the third the fact that very few women have excelled at chess. Similarly Benbow (1988) suggests a right hemisphere role in mathematics. Both relate this to the hypothesis of Norman Geschwind that exposure in foetal life to high levels of testosterone slows the development of the left hemisphere. All this is clearly still a long way from a physiological account of very exceptional achievement.

The same can be said of the perpetual debate over the inheritance of 'intelligence', however that is interpreted. In view, for example, of the mass of familial data (Bouchard and McGue, 1981) it seems absurd to deny that at least a potential for general ability is inherited; and it may well be that this is true of more or less specialized abilities. Indeed if a modular view is adopted this distinction disappears. What is not clear is what particular combination of inherited and environmental elements is either necessary or sufficient to produce a specified pattern of achievement. Apart from definite cases of handicap this is as true of low as of high achievement. It is obvious that one cannot argue backwards from specific cases that the circumstances of their emergence were uniquely appropriate; theoretically the possibility remains that any variation might have produced any change, from zero to total. This theoretical range is restricted in practice, so that for example the infant Mozart, trepanned like a child of Hamelin into the Kalahari desert, could hardly have produced the music he did. But it does not follow that he could not have excelled over his new contemporaries by as much as, or even more than, he actually did, in music or some other activity. It is unlikely but without experiment it remains possible.

Experiment is not available either to answer questions as to the future progress of prodigies. Still, a general pattern does seem to emerge. Montour (1976, 1977) believes there is a widely held but false view that prodigies typically fail in later life – 'early ripe, early rot'. She thinks that this is largely due to one particular case, better known in the USA than elsewhere, that of William James Sidis, sometimes called with no real justification 'the world's greatest child prodigy' (Wallace, 1986). He was nevertheless sufficiently remarkable: he read in English by three, and by five also in Russian, French and German; before he was eight passed the entrance examination for

Massachusetts Institute of Technology; entered Harvard at eleven and the next year (1910) gave a lecture on the fourth dimension which Norbert Wiener (a contemporary prodigy almost as startling) later said 'would have done credit to . . . a graduate student of any age'. This was his high water mark; he subsequently failed to complete graduate work, could not hold a teaching post, and spent the rest of his life in menial work, dying at 46, unemployed and destitute. It is apparent that this sorry outcome was the result, not of his early achievement, but of emotional problems, the legacy of an affectionless and demanding childhood, exacerbated by press hounding, itself partly instigated by his publicity seeking father.

To counter this Montour cites several precocious students whose later careers were successful, and describes three boys in particular: L entered Harvard at 14, subsequently taking up the family profession of medicine and lecturing occasionally at Johns Hopkins; M entered Harvard at fifteen and became an academic but published little and made full professor only at 65; E went to Columbia at 12 and was later a minister of the Episcopalian church, theologian and writer. It is obvious that these three careers, while by no means failures, fall far short of the early promise. A positive, but less than complete, correlation between early and later achievement is what one would expect, and what is, in general, found. The largest cohort of gifted children in a longitudinal study remains that of Terman (1925). As is well known his sample of some 1,500 excelled over the general population in almost every respect and maintained this advantage throughout life. But they did become more heterogeneous, and they did not produce adult achievement of the very highest class, the Nobel prize level for example. Similarly with Cox's sample, even though they were actually selected for adult eminence in the first place. John Stuart Mill, who stands alone in her list, would hardly be said to be the greatest philosopher of the modern period, nor do the rest of the top 20 children correspond to the 20 most eminent adults. The course of development varies from a straight line for many reasons. Illness or misfortune may supervene; motivation may change; the ideal combination of endowment and circumstance may not last; and the talents and behaviour that are appropriate for an exceptional child may not be so for an adult.

It is very rare for a child, or even an adolescent to produce work that matches the highest adult achievement (Goldsmith, this volume; Simonton, 1988). Where the work of children remains of interest it is usually either because of the later history of the individual, which may be fulfilled as for example Mozart or Picasso, or cut short as in the case of Thomas Chatterton; or on the other hand because of its frankly childish qualities, as with precocious film stars or with *The Young Visiters*, the masterpiece of nine year old Daisy Ashford.

Nevertheless there have been attempts, usually by parents, deliberately to produce child prodigies, and there has been quite a widespread movement, the so-called 'hothousing', to bring on children's talents earlier than might otherwise be the case. Both James Mill and Leopold Mozart could be said to exemplify this, and they perhaps represent the two main reasons: either to produce a remarkable child, possibly for personal gain or gratification, or to develop an exceptional adult. Boris Sidis set out deliberately to demonstrate his educational theories in the person of his son. Terman (1918) reported an interesting case of a father who, purely as an experiment, determined to teach his infant daughter to read. Without specialized knowledge, he developed many modern-seeming techniques, depending essentially on principles of operant conditioning, to such effect that Martha had at 24 months a reading vocabulary of 200 words, and at 26½ months, 700 words. A contemporary example is that of the Polgar sisters, Zsusza, Zsofia and Judit. Their father Laszlo Polgar reportedly set out to produce exceptional chess players, it seems by immersing them in a constantly encouraging though chess-dominated world. The results so far are that the two older girls are 'normally strong prodigies', expected to become grandmasters, while Judit is, extraordinarily, two full years ahead of any previously recorded chess prodigy (Reuben, 1988; press reports).

Such dramatic examples have suggested to some that any child can be a genius, but this is clearly an unjustified conclusion to draw from highly uncontrolled experiments. The likelihood is that the performance of many children can be enhanced, and that of some will be exceptional, given suitable circumstances. What these are, in general, probably is much as described by Pressey (1955) in his discussion of precocious athletes and musicians: early opportunities and encouragement; superior early and continuing opportunity to practise and extend abilities; close association with others in the field, fostering abilities and providing stimulation; many and increasing experiences of success with general acclaim.

Forcing and extreme 'hothousing' are less likely to produce good results, at any rate in the long term, and there is something of a reaction against such methods. For example Gallagher and Coché (1987) suggest that many parents may overstructure infant learning because of their own inadequacy and guilt, making their children into symbols of achievement (especially academic), and increasing anxiety in both their children and themselves. Furthermore spending increased time on purely academic development may reduce opportunity for exploratory play which is perhaps important for later intellectual achievements. In an extreme case such as Boris Sidis, or even James Mill, parental behaviour is reminiscent of those who actually abuse children, as described for example by Steele and

Pollock (1978): ' . . . they expect and demand a great deal from their infants and children. Not only is the demand for performance great, but it is premature, clearly beyond the ability of the infant to comprehend what is wanted and to respond appropriately'. Far different are the attitudes of the parents of Deakin's 'children on the hill' or, as far as one can tell, those of the various contemporary prodigies I have mentioned. Nevertheless in each case children will respond, and in some cases do so with exceptional achievement.

Despite the growth in 'hothousing' it is well known that, in the UK (Freeman, 1986) and even in the USA (Reis, 1989), research into and provision for able children lag far behind work for the handicapped, who themselves come fairly well down on the list of national priorities. 'Special educational needs' refers normally to deficit rather than to gifts; in the USA it is possible to refer to a child as 'severely gifted', almost suggesting an attempt to assimilate the two. The elaborate selective systems of other countries such as East Germany and the USSR are too complex to describe here (e.g. Dunstan, 1987).

The question arises as to whether prodigies should be considered as the extreme end of some dimension, or as in some way unique. The general view taken here is that both are true. The late John Paul Getty was asked in an interview to what he attributed his immense wealth. His reply was along the lines of: 'I had ability, but others had ability; I was lucky, but others had luck; I was hard working but so were many more. It was the particular combination of a high level of these and other factors that was crucial'. In essence, this is much like Feldman's concept of 'co-incidence' (see Goldsmith, this volume) which he invokes in explaining prodigies. It is suggested here that precisely the same concept must apply to every individual. Each constitutes the intersection of a vast number of dimensions. In that sense, genius is rare but not peculiar.

There are at least two ways in which this account might be inadequate. It might be that more, or different, dimensions are necessary to describe some individuals, especially those of great ability. This too has been proposed by Feldman (e.g. 1980). He argues that prodigious achievement is in some respects like all other development, in some like some other, and in some like none. Prodigious development is unique for the following reasons: it is not a universally occurring phenomenon (though it does depend on certain universally occurring thought processes); it is not 'spontaneous' in Piaget's sense and will not occur without specialized resources and instruction; and it 'represents an unusual (but not altogether discrepant) form of idiosyncratic expression', typified by the selection of a disciplined body of knowledge much earlier than is usual. While this may well be accurate as a description of certain individual children, it is less clear that the argument implies a unique sort of explanation. The thought that every individual is in some ways like all men, in some like some, and in some like none, goes back at least to Kluckhohn and Murray (1953).

The second line of argument is a statistical one. Since Galton it has been generally assumed that dimensions on which human beings can be measured will tend to be normally distributed. This assumption has been questioned, for example by Walberg. Walberg *et al.* (1984) quote many examples of positive-skew distributions, such as the fact that 15 per cent of scientists account for 85 per cent of publications, and that the best colleges produce four times as many PhDs as the average. Thus it might be argued that a position on a normal distribution can adequately describe the average child of 12 who speaks one language, occasionally one and a bit or even two; but not the future Sir William Hamilton who, at the same age, had Hebrew, Latin, Greek, French, German, Italian, Spanish, Syriac, Persian, Arabic, Sanskrit, Hindi and Malay besides his native English. He also competed in public 'not without honour', against the calculating prodigy Zerah Colburn. But it does not follow that because performance may be skewed, the factors producing it are necessarily so. It might be that more factors are involved, or that the factors have to mesh more exactly; and, as noted, there may be further circumstances such as the Matthew effect. A somewhat similar argument applies to the question of continuity versus discontinuity. In a football crowd Robert Pershing Wadlow, the tallest reliably recorded man at 8 feet 11 inches, would appear to be, indeed would actually be, in a class of his own. Another nine men are known, as of 1989, to have exceeded eight feet. Clearly others may have occurred, or will occur in the future, and the larger the population the more the distribution is likely to appear continuous. Similarly the achievement of Ganesh Sittampalam, extraordinary in average terms, was only fractionally separated from that of John Adams.

The existence of children who do exceptional things and are loosely labelled 'child prodigies' points up many issues in the explanation of behaviour, but there is no reason to think them beyond explanation.

REFERENCES

ALBERT, R.S. (1980) Family positions and the attainment of eminence. *Gifted Child Quarterly*, 24, 87–95.

BELMONT, J.M. (1989) Cognitive strategies and strategic learning: The socio-instructional approach. *American Psychologist*, 44, 142–148.

BENBOW, C.P. (1988) Neuropsychological perspectives on mathematical talent. In L.K. Obler and D. Fein (eds), *The Exceptional Brain*. NY: Guilford Press.

BENBOW, C.P. and STANLEY, J.C. (1983) *Academic Precocity: Aspects of Its Development*. Baltimore: Johns Hopkins University Press.

BLACK, S.T. (1989) *Child Star*. London: Headline.
BLOOM, B.S. (1985) *Developing Talent in Young People*. NY: Ballantine Books.
BLURTON-JONES, N. and KONNER, M.J. (1976) !Kung knowledge of animal behaviour. In R.B. Lee and I. Devore (Eds), *Kalahari Hunter-Gatherers: Studies of the !Kung and their Neighbours*. Cambridge, Mass: Harvard University Press.
BOSWELL, J. (1792) *The Life of Samuel Johnson LL.D* repr. London: Dent 1906.
BOUCHARD, T.J. and McGUE, M. (1981) Familial studies of intelligence: A review. *Science, 212*, 1055–1058.
BRANDON, R. (1983) *The Spiritualists*. London: Weidenfeld and Nicolson.
BRESKVAR, B. (1987) *Boris Becker's Tennis: The Making of a Champion*. London: Springfield Books.
COX, C.M. (1926) *Genetic Studies of Genius, Vol 2: The Early Mental Traits of Three Hundred Geniuses*. Stanford, CA: Stanford University Press.
CRANBERG, L.D. and ALBERT, M.L. (1988) The chess mind. In L.K. Obler and D. Fein (eds) *The Exceptional Brain*. NY: Guilford Press.
CSIKSZENTMIHALYI, M. and CSIKSZENTMIHALYI, I.S. (1988) *Optimal Experience: Psychological Studies of Flow in Consciousness*. Cambridge: CUP.
DEAKIN, M. (1973) *The Children on the Hill: The story of an extraordinary family*. London: Quartet Books.
DUNSTAN, J. (ed) (1987) *Soviet Education Under Scrutiny*. Glasgow: Jordanhill College Publications.
DWECK, C.S. (1986) Motivational processes affecting learning. *American Psychologist, 41*, 1040–1048.
ELLIS, H. (1904) *A Study of British Genius*, London: Hurst and Blackett.
ERICSSON, K.A. and FAIVRE, I.A. (1988) What's exceptional about exceptional abilities? In L.K. Obler and D. Fein (eds) *The Exceptional Brain*. NY: Guilford Press.
FELDMAN, D.H. (1980) *Beyond Universals in Cognitive Development*. Norwood, NJ: Ablex.
FELDMAN, D.H. (1986) *Nature's Gambit: Child Prodigies and the Development of Human Potential*. NY: Basic Books.
FODOR, J.A. (1987) *The Modularity of Mind*. Cambridge, Mass: M.I.T. Press.
FOWLER, W. (1981) Case studies of cognitive precocity. *Journal of Applied Developmental Psychology, 2*, 319–367.
FREEMAN, J. (ed.) (1986) *The Psychology of Gifted Children: Perspectives on development and education*. Chichester: Wiley.
GALLAGHER, J.M. and COCHE, J. (1987) Hothousing: The clinical and educational concern over pressurising young children. *Early Childhood Research Quarterly, 2*, 203–210.
GALTON, F. (1869) *Hereditary Genius*. London: Macmillan.
GARDNER, H. (1983) *Frames of Mind: The Theory of Multiple Intelligences*. London: Paladin.
GAULD, A. and CORNELL, A.D. (1979) *Poltergeists*. London: Routledge and Kegan Paul.
GREENO, J.G. (1989) A perspective on thinking. *American Psychologist, 44*, 134–141.
HALL, R. (1969) Sleeve note to *Masters of Irish Music: Martyn Byrnes,* London: Leader Sound Ltd.
HEMERY, D. (1986) *Sporting Excellence: A study of sport's highest achievers*. London: Collins (Willow Books).

HOWE, M.J.A. (1988) Intelligence as an explanation. *British Journal of Psychology*, 79, 349–360

HOWE, M.J.A. (1989) *Fragments of Genius: the Strange Achievements of Idiot Savants*. London: Routledge.

HOWE, M.J.A. (1990) *The Origins of Genius: The Psychology of Exceptional Ability*. Oxford: Blackwell.

KLUCKHOHN, C. and MURRAY, H.A. (1953) *Personality in Nature, Society and Culture*. London: Cape.

LAVE, J. (1988) *Cognition in Practice: Mind, Mathematics and Culture in Everyday Life*. Cambridge: Cambridge University Press.

LIFTON, R.J. (1961) *Thought Reform and the Psychology of Totalism: A Study of "Brainwashing"*. London: Gollancz.

McCURDY, H.G. (1957) The childhood pattern of genius. *Journal of the Elena Mitchell Society*, 73, 448–462.

MILL, J.S. (1873) *Autobiography*. Oxford: Oxford University Press, repr. 1924.

MITCHELL, F.D. (1907) Mathematical prodigies. *American Journal of Psychology*, 18, 61–143.

MONTOUR, K. (1976) Three precocious boys: What happened to them? *Gifted Child Quarterly*, 20, 173–179.

MONTOUR, K. (1977) William James Sidis, the broken twig. *American Psychologist*, 32, 265–279.

PIECHOWSKI, M.M. and COLANGELO, N. (1984) Developmental potential of the gifted. *Gifted Child Quarterly*, 28, 80–88.

PLOMIN, R. (1989) Environment and genes: determinants of behavior. *American Psychologist*, 44, 105–111.

PLOMIN, R. and DANIELS, D. (1987) Why are children in the same family so different from one another? *Behavioral and Brain Science*, 10, 1–16.

POLIT, D. and FALBO, T. (1987) Only children and personality development: A quantitative review. *Journal of Marriage and the Family*, 19, 309–325.

PRESSEY, S.L. (1955) Concerning the nature and nurture of genius. *Scientific Monthly*, 81, 123–129.

RADFORD, J. (1990) *Child Prodigies and Exceptional Early Achievers*. London: Harvester Wheatsheaf.

REIS, S.M. (1989) Reflections on policy affecting the education of gifted and talented students. *American Psychologist*, 44, 399–408.

REUBEN, S. (1988) The Polgar sisters. *Personal communication*.

RUSSELL, B. (1967) *Autobiography*. London: Allen and Unwin.

RYLE, G. (1949) *The Concept of Mind*. London: Hutchinson.

SHORT, D. (1981) *Nigel Short: Chess Prodigy*. London: Faber.

SIMONTON, D.K. (1987) Developmental antecedents of achieved eminence. *Annals of Child Development*, 4, 131–169.

SIMONTON, D.K. (1988) Age and outstanding achievement: What do we know after a century of research? *Psychological Bulletin*, 104, 252–267.

STANLEY, J.C. (1977) Rationale of the study of mathematically precocious youth (SMPY) during its first five years promoting educational acceleration. In J.C. Stanley, W.C. George and C.H. Solano (eds) *The Gifted and the Creative: A fifty-year perspective*. Baltimore: Johns Hopkins University Press.

STEELE, B.F. and POLLOCK, C.B. (1978) General characteristics of abusing parents. In C.M. Lee (ed.), *Child Abuse: A reader and source book*. Milton Keynes: Open University Press.

TERMAN, L.M. (1918) An experiment in infant education. *Journal of Applied Psychology, 2,* 219–228.

TERMAN, L.M. (1925) *Genetic Studies of Genius, Vol I: Mental and physical traits of a thousand gifted children.* Stanford, CA: Stanford University Press.

TORRANCE, E.P. (1983) Role of mentors in creative achievement. *Gifted Child and Adult Quarterly, 8,* 8–16.

TREFFERT, D.A. (1989) *Extraordinary People: An Exploration of the Savant Syndrome.* London: Bantam Press.

WALBERG, H.J. STRYKOWSKI, B.F. ROVAI, E. and HUNG, S.S. (1984) Exceptional performance. *Review of Educational Research, 54,* 87–112.

WALLACE, A. (1986) *The Prodigy: A biography of William James Sidis, the world's greatest child prodigy.* London: Macmillan.

WALTERS, J. and GARDNER, H. (1986) The crystallising experience: discovering an intellectual gift. In R.J. Sternberg and J. Davidson (eds), *Conceptions of Giftedness.* Cambridge: CUP.

WATERHOUSE, L. (1988) Speculations on the neuroanatomical substrate of special talents. In L.K. Obler and D. Fein (eds), *The Exceptional Brain.* NY: Guilford Press.

WERTSCH, J.V. (1985) *Vygotsky and the Social Formation of Mind.* Cambridge, Mass: Harvard University Press.

ON THE ORIGINS OF EXCEPTIONAL INTELLECTUAL AND CULTURAL ACHIEVEMENT

Colin Berry

Despite evidence that special programmes for the intellectually gifted can be successful (Tannenbaum, 1986), decisions in implementing such provision cannot yet draw on much knowledge about factors which commute early promise into later achievement. It often seems to be assumed *faute de mieux* that these factors do not vary much according to the individual or to the type of talent an individual possesses or which it is wished to promote. In fact this is unlikely to be the case. Since meeting the needs of the gifted is very expensive of resources, evidence on this issue may eventually help maximize returns on the investment.

This prospect is some way off. Much thinking about provision for the gifted remains impaired by uncritically accepted assumptions and hostile popular images. In Britain, despite acceptance of special provision for those gifted in music, dance or sport, widespread resistance persists to the notion that the intellectually talented warrant, and can even benefit from, enrichment or early promotion. Educators and laypersons often invoke negative stereotypes ('burning out', 'early to ripen, early to rot', etc), and assert that precocious talent is paid for in personal maladjustment, ignoring evidence that this is no more common in gifted than in other groups (Janos and Robinson, 1985), and overlooking the likelihood that such problems result from lack of suitable provision.

Negative folk beliefs are reinforced by ideological attitudes of the political Left and Right. Ironically, both tend to policies of neglect: one rejects the enhancement by social policy of inequalities to be deplored in Nature; the other relishes the romantic notion of the gifted triumphing by will over adversity (while saving taxpayers' money).

Adherents of the latter view, most notably Margaret Thatcher, the British Prime Minister at the time of writing, have accorded Michael

Faraday the status of heroic role model. His qualification is apparently his lack of formal educational opportunity and the unusually obvious practical relevance of his theoretical discoveries. But, as the President of the Royal Society pointed out in his Dimbleby Lecture (Porter, 1988), the example of Faraday is problematic in several ways. For one thing, though the practical utility of his work on electromagnetism is obvious in retrospect, it was by no means obvious to the Prime Minister of his day. It is also problematic in that, while disadvantaged, Faraday also enjoyed unusually *privileged* special provision in the support of a sympathetic patron and in a close association with one of the outstanding scientists of his era. The conclusion that even talent as exceptional as Faraday's may surmount educational adversity unaided is thus unsafe unless it can be shown that many other major contributors to scientific and industrial advance have overcome lack of normal education without his advantages. If not, evidence of other common features of their early lives may aid understanding of institutional and personal factors promoting exceptional attainment.

This chapter seeks consistent patterns in biographical data bases to test hypotheses about high achievers and to provide clues to conditions tending to develop creative potential. The hypotheses derive from views which, if not always sharply formulated, are widely held in various forms. One such view is that some national groups have a greater aptitude for certain activities than for others. Another, common among many educators, is that individuals of high intellectual potential appear very rarely and more or less at random. Many argue, furthermore, that when they do appear, special resources, at least before secondary education, are not important since, if as children they are brighter than their teachers, they can educate themselves. In view of what follows, I propose to term this the *Myth of the Nobel Savage*.

Two specific hypotheses can be extracted for testing from this complex of views:

1. that there is a random distribution of attainment within nations;

2. that non-random differences exist between nations.

A conclusion of this chapter will be that, although there are apparent national differences in science achievement, these are largely an artefact of demographic structures and of the non-randomness of the origins of achievers within them.

Since the nineteenth century, scholars have found evidence of non-randomness in the socio-economic origins and religious backgrounds of eminent scientists. Galton's *English Men of Science* (1874), a study of Fellows of the Royal Society, described them as marked by steady perseverance and a home background of independent spirit, often of a non-dogmatic reformed church tradition, and coming most frequently from the urban upper class. This mid-Victorian sample may be untypical of eminent scientists elsewhere or at other times, but about the same time de Candolle (1873; 1885) studied the backgrounds of several European samples, finding few Catholics among foreign associates of the Paris Academy between 1666 and 1883, and a sevenfold over-representation of Protestants. He noted also that the Royal Society of London and the Berlin Academy had almost no English, Irish or Swiss Catholic members, and that French Protestants were members of the Royal Society as often as Catholics despite being a minority in the population.

Twentieth century evidence has shown similarly disproportionate involvement among American scientists of those from backgrounds of Protestant tradition, a similar and growing Jewish over-representation, and a near total absence of any Catholic contribution (Roe, 1952; Datta, 1967; Zuckerman, 1977).

Sociological theory has linked this evidence to religious core values, ascribing a key role to the psychology of ascetic Protestantism in science (Merton, 1973; Zuckerman, 1977) and pointing to the congruence of post-ghetto Jewish norms with the values of science (Singer, 1960). Alternative hypotheses (Datta, 1967) stress 'liberality' of religious tradition (Lehmann and Witty, 1931) and a 'hedonist-libertarian' ethic of some Protestant groups and post-ghetto Jews, 'inconsistent with the ascetic-masochistic elements of both Calvinism and Catholicism' (Feuer, 1963). These interpretations rest on the empirical observation of a rich contribution to science by Jewish and Protestant traditions and a meagre one by the Catholic tradition. However, stress on psychological values in interpreting these observations draws attention to large differences in fruitfulness among Protestant groups (Datta, 1967; Hardy, 1974).

Striking agreement on the socio-economic origins of scientists is found in American studies at different time periods. Cattell and Brimhall (1921) found that 51 per cent of the fathers of leading scientists were professional men, although this group formed only about 3 per cent of the male work force in 1910, and thirty years later Roe (1952) found a figure of 53 per cent. However consistent within the United States, this picture may not hold world-wide. The provincial middle class origins of many American scientists seem at odds both with Galton's description of eminent British scientists as coming typically from the urban upper class, and with Raskin's (1936) report that about a third of the most eminent international scientists of the nineteenth century came from the lowest two social classes, in contrast with eminent writers, who more often came from the upper and merchant classes.

More agreement exists about personality features of scientists.

There is evidence that they are characterized by strong perseverance, low social dependence needs, introspectiveness and marked self-sufficiency (Raskin, 1936; Cattell and Drevdahl, 1955), and that more successful scientists have stronger traits of dominance and initiative than less successful ones (Chambers, 1964). Uncertainties exist about common early life experiences, however. Some writers (see Simonton, 1989) have linked typical personality features to experiences such as early loss of a parent, childhood illness or disability. Roe (1952) is often cited on the characteristics of eminent scientists, despite the fact that her sample numbered only 64, all from the United States. A high proportion of these had lost a parent early and the physical scientists in particular had suffered serious childhood illness or disability. Twenty-five per cent of Roe's biologists, 13 per cent of physical scientists and 9 per cent of social scientists had lost a parent by age 10, compared with an estimated 6 per cent for college students. A number of other studies suggest that many scientists have lost a parent in childhood (Krohn, 1971; Silverman, 1974; Woodward, 1974; Mansfield and Busse, 1981). This seems also to hold for eminent mathematicians (Bell, 1937). Rates of early loss in mixed samples of eminent individuals have been reported to be in the range of 25–45 per cent (Eisenstadt, 1978; Albert, 1971; Walberg, Rasher and Parkerson, 1980).

Evidence supporting Roe's finding on early illness is scanty, although Eiduson (1962) points out that a number of prominent scientists were sickly as children. As with early bereavement, it is hard to be sure how typical these cases were of all countries and time periods, and what the psychological consequences may have been for the individuals in question. There is again the problem of small samples: Roe had twelve cases of childhood health problems among her 64 scientists. It can only be concluded that further study is warranted.

Another focus of research on eminent scientists has been their higher education and research histories. Highly successful and creative scientists in Britain and America are very likely both to have been associated at an early stage in their careers with one of a handful of 'élite' universities such as Harvard (Zuckerman, 1977) or Cambridge (Hudson, 1958), and to have had close contact with a previous winner or 'prizeworthy' figure in their field. Zuckerman (1977) reported that of 84 American laureates she studied, 44 had earlier worked under 63 older laureates, and Krebs (1961) pointed to an 'apostolic succession' of supervision and association running back from himself to Lavoisier in the eighteenth century. Although this points to a mechanism of advantage among the scientific élite (Merton, 1973; Zuckerman, 1977), it remains to clarify what characterizes those who obtain access to such advantage. It is essentially this question which the major part of this chapter addresses.

Several problems beset most data bases of high achievers. Most are very restricted by the region and time period considered; criteria for inclusion are problematic; and information may be incomplete and subject to bias. Biographical notes seem more apt to mention a subject's father if he was an undistinguished surgeon than if he were a successful shopkeeper.

The Nobel scientists offer a base which partly avoids such problems, and minimizes possible distortion of patterns by national or regional peculiarities. The laureates form a large heterogeneous international sample of outstanding contributors to a wide range of science (physics, chemistry and medicine and physiology), and over a long period of modern science. Of those given the prize by 1988, the earliest born winner was born in 1836, the most recent in 1946. Also, the problem of selection has been tackled by others with a success that has given the Prize unusual prestige among scientists. Although many scientists generally deemed worthy of it have not won the Nobel Prize, few winners have been contentious or seen in retrospect as undeserving of the award.

The expectation that information on laureates' lives is readily available, however, is in fact only partly fulfilled. Even outline information on the childhood and youth of many older laureates is often hard to find, and for a long time much biographical data on recent laureates, now usually included in the Nobel Yearbooks, did not become available for some years. For this reason, an earlier effort to use Nobel scientists as a data base (Moulin, 1955), besides the very much smaller sample size at the time, was hampered by very incomplete data, leaving open the possibility of non-random omissions, and consequently misleading data on fathers' occupations.

Using a base of around 300 Nobel scientists in the late 70s, I made a lengthy search for missing details. With some regret, I abandoned the richness of literary biography for basic data on birthplace and education, father's occupation and family religious tradition. A standard proforma sent to living laureates for whom such information was missing contained an open-ended question, asking to what they were inclined to attribute their achievement. This prompted enough variety and humour to add to my misgivings about the dry course I had chosen, especially as some laureates went on to provide personal accounts of fascinating and often touching human interest. My formal analysis (Berry, 1981) focused on the early family and school milieux of future laureates, not from any belief that later experiences are unimportant in creative science, but because those of childhood and youth are basic and less idiosyncratic. For this reason, attention was given to the national and regional setting of laureates' childhood rather than to where laureates were based when they did their prize-winning work. Laureates were thus attributed to a country or region if they were born there and received the major part of their secondary education there, as long as at least one parent was a national of the country. National and regional 'productivity' was calculated on the basis of the 1900 population figures (1910 for the USA) and estimated as number of laureates per million.

The results, almost complete for at least a small number of standard biographical details, confirmed that earlier work had indeed given a rather misleading impression of Nobel scientists' social backgrounds. For example, it was apparent that the occupations of fathers of higher professional status tended to be more likely to be reported in biographical notes. The data confirmed, however, that Nobel laureates tended to have rather specific social origins and early experience, and had very frequently worked early in their careers at one or more of a handful of 'élite' institutions. There were few reports of serious childhood illness, and early loss of a parent was rarer than the literature had suggested.

There were large differences between Jewish and Gentile productivity. With Jewish and Gentile data analysed separately, most 'Protestant' countries were found to have rather similar productivity. 'Catholic' countries also resembled one another in productivity, but at a considerably lower level. In other words, religious differences in productivity appeared to be more important than national differences *per se*.

To extend the base, and to allow more precise testing of hypotheses about the origins of eminent scientists, I have now undertaken new analyses based on biographical information on all the 393 Nobel Science winners up to 1988. Besides using a data base enlarged by about 30 per cent over the previous one, this re-analysis incorporates a number of modifications. The first concerns the reliability of the data. The biographical data were reviewed and corrected on the basis of subsequently published details. Also, new population statistics were employed, using the reference year 1910 for all countries as far as possible, and were based on improved estimates published in the second edition of Mitchell's *Historical Statistics* (1978).

NATIONAL ORIGINS OF NOBEL SCIENTISTS

To make national comparisons taking account of the international mobility of laureates' families, productivity calculations were based on native country, defined by the territory in which laureates were born (as long as at least one parent was a national of that country) or, if the birth occurred abroad, that in which the parents were citizens and normally resident. Where frontier changes applied from 1918, attribution was made to the emergent state. For Poland, Czechoslovakia, Trianon Hungary, the Austrian Republic, Yugoslavia and the

Table 1.   Distribution of origins of Nobel laureates in science by religious tradition

| | GENTILE LAUREATES | | | | JEWISH LAUREATES | | | |
	Physics	Chemistry	Medicine	Total	Physics	Chemistry	Medicine	Total
Protestant countries	77	74	80	231	22	12	26	60
Catholic countries	14	11	25	50	4	7	11	21
Rest of world	15	4	3	22	3	0	1	4
Unclassified	1	1	0	2	1	1	0	2
	Gentile total			304	Jewish total			89

Baltic States, the criterion used was that at least one parent was a subject of the original state and became, or would have been likely to become, a citizen of its successor. Thus, Austrian laureates were those reared and receiving secondary education in the territory of the post-1918 Austrian Republic, with at least one parent who was previously a subject of the Habsburg Monarchy. An exception was Alsace-Lorraine, whose winners were allocated neither to France nor Germany. On the above basis, only 10 of the 393 laureates could not be attributed to a country.

To refine estimates of sub-populations and to avoid inflation of the Jewish productivity indices based on estimates of Jewish population sizes, a sharper criterion for classification into Gentiles and Jews was adopted. Children with one Gentile parent and one parent indicated by biographical sources as half Jewish were classified as Gentiles. Finally, estimates were made for each country of the number of inhabitants in Protestant and Catholic traditions.

Table 1, which shows 'productivity' of countries in the main western religious traditions, makes clear the disproportionate Jewish contribution world-wide and the predominance of the 'Protestant' countries. The greater Jewish contribution to physics and medicine than to chemistry should also be noted; likewise the concentration of the Asian contribution on physics.

The Jewish and Protestant predominance is evident also from the more detailed, country by country figures of Table 2, which shows Gentile and Jewish 'productivity indices' per million of the 1910 population fractions, lumping Gentiles of all western Christian traditions together.

Table 2. Number of future laureates born as citizens of the country (1910 or 1911 figures)

	GENTILE LAUREATES		JEWISH LAUREATES	
	Prizes	Gentile index	Prizes	Jewish index
Switzerland	10	2.7	1	71.3
Denmark	4	2.2	1	166.7
Sweden	12	2.2	1	100.0
Netherlands	12	2.1	0	0.0
Norway	3	1.3	0	—
United Kingdom	49	1.2	1	5.0
New Zealand	1	0.9	0	—
Australia	4	0.9	0	—
Germany*	45	0.8	19	35.2
United States	70	0.8	35	28.9
Finland	2	0.7	0	—
Canada	4	0.6	0	0.0
Rest of Protestant world	14		3	
Austria*	6	0.9	4	26.7
Belgium	4	0.5	0	0.0
France (minus Alsace)	17	0.4	3	35.3
Czechoslovakia*	4	0.3	1	2.9
Hungary*	2	0.4	2	5.3
Ireland	1	0.2	0	—
Portugal	1	0.2	0	—
Italy	6	0.2	3	81.1
Argentina	1	0.2	1	20.8
Spain	2	0.1	0	—
Poland*	1	0.1	0	—
Rest of Catholic world	1	0.0	1	0.4
Yugoslavia	3	0.8	0	0.0
Romania	1	0.1	0	0.0
Russia*	7	0.1	4	0.8
Asia	14		0	
Totals	304		89	

* indicates that census figures refer to population figures within post World War I boundaries.

As in the first study, Gentile rates differed between those countries with substantial Protestant populations and those without. Comparing countries in the western Christian traditions, a Mann-Whitney test yielded U = 5 for N_1 = 12, N_2 = 11, p(1-tailed) <0.001. Jewish productivity was higher than Gentile across countries with a Jewish population of over 5,000 in 1910 (Sign test: N = 16, x = 3, p = 0.011). The tendency for Jewish productivity to be greater in Protestant than in Catholic countries did not reach significance (Mann-Whitney, U = 21 for N_1 = N_2 = 8, p (1-tailed) = 0.139).

A problem with the above analysis is that the distinction between 'Protestant' and 'Catholic' countries is a crude one. It is also misleading since Switzerland and Germany have roughly equal proportions of their populations in the two main branches of the western Christian tradition. If religious traditions vary in production of notable scientists, account should be taken of the varying proportions of the respective fractions in the Gentile population. The next refinement was therefore to derive *quantitative predictions* of national performance from data on population fractions. This should permit assessment of hypotheses about cultural and national differences, such as the frequent suggestion that Britain is 'particularly good' at producing Nobel scientists (and thus, perhaps, can afford to reduce her national investment in 'pure' science) can be put to quantitative test, with the null hypothesis that its 'performance' is simply what would be expected for a country of its size and population structure.

The question of 'expected' numbers of prizes can be approached using the technique of multiple regression (Pedhazur, 1982). Multiple regression allows coefficient values to be calculated which measure how far national totals generally depend on the separate religious group sizes. Expressing these sizes in millions, or proportions of millions, provides a general estimate of the number of prizes per million for each group across all countries. These values furnish a 'regression equation', from which expected prize totals can then be calculated for each country by substituting its demographic particulars.

The regression statistics can also be expressed in standard form, ß-weights, which do not depend on the way the predictor scores are expressed. They have a theoretical maximum of 1, and are estimates of the relative importance of the predictors. Their statistical significance is assessed, like that of non-standard regression coefficients, by computing the probability of the null hypothesis that their true value is zero. A significant p-value indicates that a variable can be taken to have a material influence on the number of prizes won.

Regression equations were computed for Nobel laureates born in 'western' countries who met similar criteria to those above: one for overall national totals predicted from total population size and the fraction sizes for the three main religious traditions, and one for national Gentile totals predicted from the estimated Protestant and Catholic fraction sizes in 1910 or the first year after this for which statistics were available (usually 1911). Solutions were computed for regression through the origin so that the best fit was obtained that would predict zero for a hypothetical country of zero population. By substituting values for the sizes of the fractions in each case, predicted values were obtained for each country from the two main regression equations. Table 3 shows a series of observed totals and estimates from alternative sets of predictors.

The most immediately obvious correlate of the number of prizes won by a country is total population size, with which it has a simple correlation of 0.927. However, the correlation with Protestant sub-population total, at 0.970, is even higher. Moreover, this variable has an effect over and above that of raw population total. Adding the Protestant sub-population variable to the total population factor in the initial regression set raised the adjusted 'explained' variance from 85.57 per cent to 97.22 per cent, leaving the regression of prize totals on both factors highly significant ($\beta = 0.355$ and 0.664, respectively, $p < 0.0001$). Since this means that the size of the Protestant fraction and the total population size with the Protestant contribution discounted both significantly influence the prize totals, I next examined the success of the separate sub-population sizes in accounting for the variance in prize totals.

The solution for the regression of overall national totals on the sizes of the three main religious groups showed that both Protestant and Catholic population sizes were significant factors ($\beta = 0.857$ and 0.210 respectively, $p < 0.0001$), but that Jewish was not ($\beta = 0.004$, $p = 0.942$). This undoubtedly reflects many disturbing factors: great variations in opportunities open to Jews, especially restricted opportunities among the large Jewish communities of eastern Europe, where population estimates were least reliable, and where the Polish, Russian, Romanian, Yugoslav and Lithuanian communities suffered near extinction in the Holocaust. In addition, the reader will have noted in Table 2 the absence of a contribution to the ranks of Nobel scientists from the large and important Jewish community of the Netherlands, a successful Nobel prize-winning country with little anti-Jewish discrimination.

A further feature of the general regression solution for overall national totals is that the United Kingdom, although doing rather well in terms of what would be predicted from its population size alone, has a total well below that predicted from its demographic composition. France, on the other hand, although achieving much below the prediction from population size, does much better than its religious composition would suggest. At the same time, Austria,

Table 3. Predicted and observed numbers of future laureates for western countries (1910 or 1911 census figures)

| | TOTAL PRIZES Predicted from: | | | GENTILES PRIZE TOTALS | |
	Gross population	Religious fractions	Actual	Predicted from religious fractions	Actual
Switzerland	4	4	11	3	10
Denmark	3	3	5	2	4
Sweden	5	9	13	7	12
Netherlands	6	7	12	5	12
Norway	2	4	3	3	3
United Kingdom	40	61	50	46	49
New Zealand	1	1	1	1	1
Australia	4	6	5	5	5
Germany	58	64	65	47	45
United States	86	98	106	72	71
Finland	3	5	2	5	2
Canada	7	7	4	5	4
Latvia	2	2	1	3	1
Estonia	1	1	0	1	0
Austria	7	3	10	2	6
Belgium	7	5	4	3	4
France	39	16	20	9	17
Czechoslovakia	13	8	4	6	3
Hungary	8	6	4	4	2
Ireland	4	2	1	1	1
Portugal	6	2	1	1	1
Italy	34	14	9	8	6
Argentina	8	3	3	2	2
Spain	20	8	2	5	2
Poland	25	10	7	6	1
Lithuania	2	2	2	1	0
Venezuela	2	1	1	1	0
Chile	3	1	0	1	0
Uruguay	1	1	0	0	0
Luxembourg	0	0	1	0	0
Yugoslavia	8	2	3	1	3
Romania	7	2	1	1	1

Switzerland, The Netherlands and Sweden do a good deal better than predicted on either basis.

Given the insignificant regression on Jewish population size, predictions were re-calculated by regressing Gentile totals on Protestant and Catholic population sizes only. The new solution again shows highly significant regression on these factors (ß = 0.887 and 0.167 respectively, p <0.0001 in both cases) and an adjusted proportion of 'explained' variance of 0.972 ($F_{2,30}$ = 563.642, p <0.0001). The generally better numerical predictions for Gentile laureates do not suggest 'under-performance' of the United Kingdom, but confirm the suggestion that the other countries mentioned strikingly 'over-perform'.

In general, these results suggest that national differences as such matter little compared with the composition of each national group by religious tradition. Success in accounting for national productivity from these variables encourages the view that substantial quantitative departures from predicted values should be amenable to meaningful interpretation.

But could the basic data be influenced by the nature of the selection process of potential Nobel prize-winners? And would this necessarily invalidate the present results? Bias could only produce the pattern of overall findings if the three separate Nobel committees colluded by collating obscure demographic information on large numbers of nominees, including religious background, much of it not readily available. This makes little sense, and would seem unlikely to have escaped notice for 90 years. Bias against the Soviet Union has occasionally been suggested, but this would not affect findings on groups in the western Christian traditions, and would be unlikely to affect overall findings on social background. An unwitting source of bias could lie in the provisions for nominating candidates. While the three Nobel Science committees invite nominations from about a thousand scientists a year from minor and major research centres around the world on a shifting basis, permanent rights of nomination, besides those of existing laureates, belong to members of the Swedish Academy of Sciences, the Karolinska Institute and the relevant faculties of the eight oldest Scandinavian universities. No one would suggest that Scandinavian laureates are generally less worthy than others, but it is possible that these provisions produce more thorough scouring of local institutions for prize worthy nominees than elsewhere, and that this could partly explain the relatively high number of Nobel prizes won by Scandinavians.

Returning, then, to the departures from predicted totals noted above, we can now ask whether large apparent over- or under-performance is fortuitous, or reflects systematic patterns. As even casual inspection of the basic data indicated that a very high proportion of Austrian and French laureates were born or educated in

Vienna and Paris, sources of apparent over- and under-achievement were examined, distinguishing large metropolitan centres from the provincial regions around them. The former have generally been found to have markedly higher productivity (Berry, 1971; Simonton, 1989).

REGIONAL DIFFERENCES IN PRODUCTIVITY

Table 4 shows 'productivity' of metropolitan and provincial places of secondary education, subject to the national attributions described earlier. It is clear that the over-performance of France and Austria is not a nationwide phenomenon, but results from the high productivity of the capital cities. Catholic Bavaria shows a similar pattern, affording the prime example of a major centre out-performing its hinterland. Munich, a town of only half a million in 1900, was the birthplace of three Nobel laureates and the place where a further six (including Einstein, much as he hated it) received secondary education. By contrast, the provinces in all three cases show the low productivity typical of Catholic regions everywhere. Differences between 'Protestant' and 'Catholic' countries are thus primarily a provincial phenomenon. Most Protestant regions are fairly productive, ranging from c. 0.6 to over 2 for the highest achieving regions, whereas no Catholic province has a productivity index above 0.3. Unlike the capitals of the strongly centralized Catholic states, the major cities in Protestant countries generally contribute little to national totals because of their small size or, in the case of London and Chicago, their low 'per capita' productivity.

In short, Catholic and Protestant countries that 'do well', do so in different ways. Protestant countries usually have nationwide sources of achievement in science. Catholic countries sometimes enhance what would otherwise be very low national totals by high metropolitan output. When they do this, what is happening? And who contributes?

Who Contributes to National Achievement in Science?

Most of the high-performing cities are ones that have enjoyed a traditional reputation for excellent *lycées* and *Gymnasien*. But have these promoted attainment in science in all groups? If Catholics do as well as Protestants here, it can be argued that differences elsewhere may be due to poor facilities in Catholic provinces, which might be overcome by better provision. If not, it would seem that differences in religious traditions are so profound, even in secularized modern societies, that they, rather than differences in facilities, determine the non-randomness observed.

Table 4.   Regional indices: provinces vs metropolitan centres by place of secondary education (Gentiles only)

PROVINCES		METROPOLITAN CENTRES	
Protestant			
Sweden	2.0	Stockholm	6.6
Switzerland	2.7		—
Netherlands	2.1	Amsterdam	2.2
Norway & Denmark	0.9	Oslo/Copenhagen	4.8
United Kingdom: South	2.2	London	1.1
Midlands & North	0.7	Birmingham/Manchester/Liverpool	2.9
United States: East	0.8	New York/Boston	2.1
Mid-West	0.9	Chicago	0.6
West	1.8		—
Germany: North	0.6	Berlin	3.2
		Hamburg/Frankfurt	4.2
Catholic			
Germany: South	0.3	Stuttgart/Cologne/Breslau	4.2
		Munich	16.0
France	0.2	Paris	4.2
Austria	0.2	Vienna	3.3
Hungary & Czechoslovakia	0.1	Budapest/Prague	4.0
Belgium	0.3	Brussels	3.3
Italy	0.2	Rome	2.2
Spain & Portugal	0.1	Madrid/Lisbon	0.0
Poland	0.0	Warsaw	3.0

One way to examine the metropolitan factor is to ask whether in Catholic areas, any benefits offered by the major centres extend to the majority group or are confined to minorities who may be over-represented in an administrative and educational élite. Information on families of Gentile laureates from Paris, Vienna and Budapest is unfortunately incomplete. The religious origins of 12 of the 20 Gentile laureates educated in these cities are unknown: two are known to have been Catholic, three Protestant and three of mixed Protestant-Catholic background. We have a clear picture for Munich, however. Of the nine German laureates educated there, one is known to have been Jewish, one Catholic and six Protestant. The Protestant contri-bution is that of an 'élite' group: four of the fathers were university professors (as was the father of the one Catholic), one a senior military officer and one a manufacturing director. This hardly sug-gests an impact of superior opportunities on the population at large. Nor is there evidence of democratization in terms of a raised inci-dence of laureates with fathers of lower occupational status in any of the cities mentioned.

This cannot be explained simply by the lower occupational pos-itions being held by Catholics, since the occupations of fathers of Gentile laureates educated in 'successful' Protestant cities like Ham-burg, Frankfurt and Berlin provide a similar picture; these fathers were mostly senior academics, administrators, prosperous merchants and businessmen, with only a few instances of more humble origins. Table 5 shows, for metropolitan centres and their provinces separ-ately, the distribution of fathers' occupations in three types of region: predominantly Catholic (France, South Germany, Austria, Hungary and Czechoslovakia); predominantly Lutheran (North Germany and Scandinavia); and regions with large radical Protestant (Calvinist and other ascetic Protestant) communities (Switzerland, the Nether-lands, the United Kingdom and the United States).

The table shows little variation in distribution of occupational backgrounds between metropolitan centres and provinces, so that, despite being generally more productive, the major cities do not seem to produce a 'democratization' of achievement in science. What does seem a factor in 'democratization' to some extent, however, is the religious character of the region. Thus, university professors figure less prominently in both kinds of Protestant area, and school teacher fathers are almost as frequent as university professors in the 'radical' areas. All Protestant areas, but especially 'Calvinist' provinces, pro-duce a few laureates from modest social backgrounds. Even here, as elsewhere, however, those who benefit are clearly not drawn from the population at large.

The data on the social origins of Nobel scientists world-wide (Table 6) confirm that eminent scientists come disproportionately from pro-

Table 5. Occupations of Nobel science laureates' fathers in different metropolitan regions by secondary education. Figures are expressed as percentages

| | CENTRAL AND NORTHERN EUROPE | | | | EUROPE AND USA | |
| | 'Catholic' | | 'Lutheran' | | 'Calvinist' | |
	Metropolitan	Provinces	Metropolitan	Provinces	Metropolitan	Provinces
Academic professionals						
university staff	36.9	33.3	20.0	14.0	10.2	14.7
school teachers	0.0	0.0	6.7	9.3	10.2	11.9
Other professionals	24.6	25.0	40.0	41.8	37.2	33.0
Business	32.3	33.3	26.7	20.9	27.1	26.2
Employees	0.0	0.0	6.7	4.7	6.8	10.5
Others	6.2	8.3	0.0	9.3	8.5	6.8

Table 6. Origins of exceptional achievers in various areas by occupational category of father, expressed as percentages.

| NOBEL LAUREATES | | | | | | |
	Physics	Chemistry	Medicine	Literature	Engineering	Mathematics	Music
Academic professionals							
university staff	25.5	16.5	14.1	3.8	7.7	10.0	1.7
school teachers	5.1	4.1	9.8	11.5	0.0	0.0	4.3
Other professionals	20.9	30.6	36.4	40.4	38.5	28.0	54.8
Business	17.9	30.0	20.7	8.7	0.0	24.0	14.8
Employees	9.7	4.7	4.3	7.7	7.7	2.0	1.7
Others	20.9	14.1	14.7	33.7	46.2	36.0	22.6

fessional, as opposed to non-professional, backgrounds. Less than 10 per cent of the fathers of science laureates were employees, most of these being white rather than blue collar. Across all the science prizes, professional men made up at least half the total, and businessmen 20 to 30 per cent. University professors and researchers are notable among the professional group, especially in physics.

The table omits data on Jewish laureates, who have distinct and changing patterns of socio-economic class of fathers, but the same general pattern for laureates born since 1914 (Berry, 1981). After that date, the socio-economic status of fathers of American Jewish laureates tends to resemble that of Gentile communities, except for a higher proportion of independent businessmen. A comparable shift in the social pattern of family occupational backgrounds of notable Gentile scientists may have occurred before the Nobel period, reflecting rising prosperity and increasing industrialization in the nineteenth century, bearing in mind that among Gentiles, besides association with education and scholarship, a common feature of the occupations of future laureates' fathers was an involvement with technology, whether at the craft skill level, as a large manufacturer, or as manager or director of technically oriented businesses.

CONTRASTS BETWEEN ACHIEVERS IN SCIENCE AND OTHER AREAS

It is apparent from Table 6 that the generally similar patterns in the father's occupational background among Nobel scientists differ radically from that of Nobel literature laureates. Although professionals are again well represented among the fathers of laureates, university staff and businessmen are not. Moreover, the professional fathers are more often from traditional professions, for example, law, medicine and journalism.

Another difference between science and literature winners is in the higher incidence among the latter of disruption in childhood, notably the higher presence of bereavement, separation, abandonment and impoverishment. Thus, the percentage of laureates who have lost a parent in childhood or youth is 7.5 per cent or less in physics and medicine winners, about 12 per cent among chemistry winners and 20 per cent among literature laureates. These rates compare with estimates that 6 per cent of American college students have lost a parent (Gregory, 1965) and 10 per cent of US children live in homes where the father is absent.

As already noted, there are problems in drawing inferences from samples from various time periods selected on different criteria. It is especially hard to establish a basis for expected rates of early parental loss in the Nobel laureates. However, the figures do not suggest strong evidence of an enhanced rate of loss among Nobel scientists. This accords with Woodward's (1974) conclusion that though many historically notable scientists lost at least one parent early in their lives, no evidence can be adduced for an enhanced rate of loss among twentieth century scientists of eminence. The Nobel data do, however, indicate a rather high rate of early bereavement for literature prize-winners, consonant with evidence of high incidence of early loss for writers generally (Brown, 1968; Martindale, 1972).

One cannot be certain that all information on early loss of parents through death, separation, abandonment or divorce is complete, though the data represent the best that can be done by consulting readily available biographical information. Assuming that any omissions are random, it can be said that literature and science winners contrast greatly in the general incidence of family tribulation and disaster. Besides losing parents before adulthood less often, science winners are hardly ever reported as experiencing separation or divorce of parents.

The typical picture of the early lives of Nobel scientists seems one of untroubled progress. Future laureates travel, as it were, through a series of green lights. I shall present an account elsewhere of exceptional cases of slow or 'false' starts and disruption by external adversity. For the present, we may note that singleness of purpose and absence of external adversity are very much the norm in the development of exceptional scientific talent – in striking contrast to the literature laureates, among whom, besides the high incidence of family disruption referred to, failure to complete higher education is the rule rather than the exception.

The usual image of the 'great scientist' as a genius overcoming unhappy and disrupted education like Einstein, or social and financial disadvantage and poor schooling, like Faraday, is very unrepresentative of notable scientists, although it seems to typify eminent writers. It is an unhappy irony that these untypical cases exemplify successful scientists for the public at large, and perhaps mediate reactions to those who show promise in science. Both Einstein and Faraday, like other exceptions to the modal picture, nevertheless share many other common features of leading scientists. Einstein, besides being Jewish and having a father engaged in a modern technical industry, was unhappy at the same Munich school that produced several other Nobel scientists. Faraday belonged to a radical Protestant sect, had early access to books (through his benefactor), and worked alongside one of the most creative scientists of his generation.

How do the characteristics of scientists on the one hand and writers on the other compare with those of achievers in other fields? To answer this, I have begun an analysis of data on the lives of 111 eminent mathematicians, 123 engineers and 212 composers selected on the basis of major entries in works of reference for these respective fields from the seventeenth century onwards. The data should be treated with caution at present, but analysis suggests that the background characteristics and early life experiences of eminent achievers in these fields differ markedly from those of Nobel scientists.

Two areas have now been identified where the Catholic contributions are strong (literature and music) and one where the Jewish is low (engineering). To explain briefly, evidence is emerging of characteristic and contrasting patterns to background and early experience in different areas of intellectual achievement. This, along with evidence that outstanding achievers in different fields have quite distinct personality characteristics (Raskin, 1936; Cattell and Drevdahl, 1955), suggests *prima facie* that the idea that the same treatment will benefit them all is rather implausible.

Evidence on the educational careers of the eminent achievers studied is particularly interesting, and bears on current attitudes in policy making. As noted already, Faraday does *not* represent a significant group of scientists who have overcome adverse circumstances by sheer will-power or brilliance. The Nobel scientists, a group containing many of the most important contributors to technological and economic advance in the last hundred years, show smooth progress through conventional basic and higher education. The most successful institutions and regions are those which allow accelerated progress or which provide stimulation tailored to individuals' needs by outstanding teachers or researchers. This is not to say that a few rare individuals do not overcome great adversity, but this fact would be a foolish basis for public policy. Nor does it mean that there is not a large autodidactic and independent element in the development of scientists. Tannenbaum suggests that a pattern of withdrawal from the world and grappling with it is characteristic for them and the balance of these elements may well vary with different areas of work.

Though outstanding mathematicians and engineers show at least equal intellectual precocity to Nobel scientists, their contact with unique individuals and other opportunities is less often within conventional institutional settings and their educational progress is more fitful and idiosyncratic. Indeed, many great mathematicians have been largely self-taught, and many eminent engineers of the past have lacked higher education, or have not even completed primary education. This fact is informative if we see the aim of special provision within formal education to be to plan as far as possible for events which historically have usually come about by happy accident. It is not evidence that the gifted can generally best be left to their own devices. Moreover, enthusiasm for the idea that they would

Table 7.   Formal education level reached by eminent engineers

Date of birth	Not completing education to 16	Completing higher education
Before 1840	20	9
1841–1890	6	12
Since 1890	1	7

necessarily be beneficially stimulated by being pitched into the 'real world' of industry and commerce at the earliest opportunity, should be dampened by examining Table 7. It shows that although a large proportion of the eminent engineers left school very early, usually going into a mechanical trade or apprenticeship, this phenomenon occurred almost entirely before the latter part of the last century.

A basic implication seems to emerge that the educational motives, personalities and requirements of potential achievers in different fields vary greatly. Efficient provision for the intellectually talented requires further challenging of folk myths and of ideologically motivated policy decisions, and clarification of how the differing needs may be met in schools and colleges.

REFERENCES

ALBERT, R.S. (1971) Cognitive development and parental loss among the gifted, the exceptionally gifted and the creative. *Psychological Reports, 29*, 19–26.

BELL, E.T. (1937) *Men of Mathematics*. New York: Simon & Schuster.

BERRY, C. (1981) The Nobel scientists and the origins of scientific achievement. *British Journal of Sociology, 32*, 381–391.

BROWN, F. (1968) Bereavement and lack of a parent in childhood. In E. Miller (Ed.) *Foundations of Child Psychiatry*. Oxford: Pergamon.

DE CANDOLLE, A. (1873) *Histoire des Sciences et des Savants depuis Deux Siècles*. 2nd edition 1885. Geneva: H. Georg.

CATTELL, J.M. and BRIMHALL, D.R. (1921) *American Men of Science*. Garrison, NM: Science.

CATTELL, R.B. and DREVDAHL, J.E. (1955) A comparison of the personality profile of (16 P.F.) of eminent researchers with that of eminent teachers and administrators, and of the general population. *British Journal of Psychology, 46*, 248–261.

CHAMBERS, J.A. (1964) Relating personality and biographical factors to scientific creativity. *Psychological Monographs, 78*, 12–20.

DATTA, L.E. (1967) Family religious background and early scientific creativity. *American Sociological Review, 32*, 626–635.

EIDUSON, B.T. (1962) *Scientists: Their psychological world*. New York: Basic Books.

EISENSTADT, J.M. (1978) Parental loss and genius. *American Psychologist, 33,* 211–223.

FEUER, L.S. (1963) *The scientific intellectual.* New York: Basic Books.

GALTON, F. (1874) *English Men of Science.* London: MacMillan.

GREGORY, J. (1965) Anterospective data following childhood loss of a parent. *Archives of General Psychiatry, 13,* 99–120.

HARDY, K.R. (1974) Social origins of American scientists and scholars. *Science, 185,* 497–506.

HUDSON, L. (1958) Undergraduate academic record of Fellows of the Royal Society. *Nature, 182,* 1326.

JANOS, P.M. and ROBINSON, N.N. (1985) In Horowitz, F.D. and O'Brien, M. (Eds) *The Gifted and Talented: Developmental Perspectives.* Washington, D.C.: American Psychological Association.

KNAPP, R.H. (1963) Demographic, cultural and personality attributes of scientists. In Taylor, C.W. and Barron, F. (Eds) *Scientific Creativity: Its Recognition and Development.* New York: Wiley Science Editions.

KNAPP, R.H. and GOODRICH, H.B. (1952) *Origins of American Scientists.* University of Chicago Press.

KREBS, H. (1961) The making of a scientist. *Nature, 215,* 1441–1445.

KROHN, R.G. (1971) *The Social Shaping of Science: Institutions, Ideology and Careers in Science.* Westport, Conn: Greenwood.

LEHMANN, H.C. and WITTY, P.A. (1931) Scientific eminence and church membership. *Scientific Monthly, 33,* 544–549.

MANSFIELD, R.S. and BUSSE, T.V. (1981) *The Psychology of Creativity and Discovery.* Chicago: Nelson-Hall.

MARTINDALE, C. (1972) Father absence, psychopathology and poetic eminence. *Psychological Reports, 31,* 843–847.

MERTON, R. (1973) *The Sociology of Science: Theoretical and Empirical Investigations.* Chicago: University of Chicago Press.

MITCHELL, B.R. (1978) *European historical statistics 1790–1975. 2nd edition.* London: MacMillan.

MITCHELL, B.R. (1983) *International historical statistics: The Americas and Australasia.* London: MacMillan.

MOULIN, L. (1955) The Nobel prizes for the sciences from 1901–1950 – An essay in sociological analysis. *British Journal of Sociology, 6,* 246–263.

PEDHAZUR, E.J. (1982) *Multiple Regression in Behavioral Research: Explanation and Prediction. 2nd edition.* New York: Holt, Rinehart & Winston.

PORTER, G. (1988) *Knowledge Itself is Power.* The 1988 Dimbleby lecture. London: BBC Publications.

RASKIN, E. (1936) Comparison of scientific and literary ability: A biographical study of eminent scientists and men of letters of the nineteenth century. *Journal of Abnormal and Social Psychology, 31,* 20–35.

ROE, A.A. (1952) *The making of a scientist.* New York: Dodd Mead.

SILVERMAN, S.M. (1974) Parental loss and scientists. *Science Studies, 4,* 259–264.

SIMONTON, D.K. (1989) *Scientific Genius.* Cambridge: Cambridge University Press.

SINGER, C. (1960) Science and Judaism. In Finkelstein, L. (Ed.) *The Jews.* New York: Harper Brothers.

STRODTBECK, F.L. (1958) Jewish and Italian immigration and subsequent status mobility. In McClelland, D.C., Baldwin, A.L., Bronfenbrenner, U.

and Strodtbeck, F.L. *Talent and Society: New Perspectives in the Identification of Talent*. Princeton, NJ: van Nostrand.

TANNENBAUM, A.J. (1986) Giftedness: A psychosocial approach. In Sternberg, R.J. & Davidson, J.E. (Eds) *Conceptions of giftedness*. Cambridge: Cambridge University Press.

WALBERG, H.J., RASHER, S.P. and PARKERSON, J. (1980) Childhood and eminence. *Journal of Creative Behavior*, 13, 225–231.

WOODWARD, W.R. (1974) Scientific genius and loss of a parent. *Science Studies*, 4, 265–277.

ZUCKERMAN, H. (1977) *Scientific Elite*. New York: Free Press.

SIBLING RELATIONSHIPS IN CREATIVE LIVES

Doris B. Wallace

In our studies of the creative person using the *evolving systems approach* (Wallace and Gruber, 1989; Wallace, 1989; Gruber, 1981), we have emphasized that creative moments are embedded in creative work which is, in turn, embedded in a creative *life*. The person's life outside the work, such as domestic arrangements and the network of family and social relationships does not consist of givens to which the person adapts, but is constructed and fashioned by the creative person to enhance and facilitate the work (Wallace, 1985).

In this essay I attempt to bring together recent psychological research on sibling relationships with the notion of collaboration in creative work. I examine one set of siblings, William and Dorothy Wordsworth, and their particular form of creative partnership in some detail. Collaboration will be seen to have a direct bearing on the social nature of creative work.

SIBLING COLLABORATION IN CREATIVE WORK

Sometimes, a creative life includes a relationship with a sibling that is central in the development of the creative work. The sibling may be a teacher, a collaborator, a mentor, or a supporter. The relationship may be active for some particular period, may last a lifetime, or may change over the over the siblings' lives. Vincent Van Gogh's younger brother Theo, a remarkable man, supported Vincent financially while the latter was struggling to become a painter. All Van Gogh's paintings – about 1,800 of them – were created in a ten year period of incredible fecundity which ended with his suicide in 1890. Theo, who worked for an art dealer, believed in Vincent and introduced him to Toulouse-Lautrec and some of the Impressionist painters. For many years, Theo was also Vincent's main correspondent and, while only Vincent's letters to Theo have survived (New York Graphic Society,

1978), they show how crucial the brothers' relationship must have been to Vincent. It was to Theo that he expressed his ideas and feelings about his work, what he wanted to paint, his struggles to master his craft, his triumphs, loneliness and despair. Thus Theo filled several roles for his brother: he represented a practical connection to the world of art, he provided money, and he never failed to give Vincent emotional support, even when other members of the family had given up.

The Social Nature of Creative Work

Creative work is both individual and social. The creative person orchestrates the movement of his or her activity between these modes. Van Gogh is a case in point. He worked alone, but he needed to discuss his work and could do so with his brother who was an art dealer in Paris. Vincent at one point hoped to start an artists' colony in Arles in the South of France and he invited Gauguin to come and work there. But a few weeks after Gauguin's arrival, the two men quarrelled and Gauguin left. However difficult it was for Van Gogh to be with people for any sustained period, he still had an intense need to turn to a professional milieu (as well as for a wider world to which he longed to sell his paintings). Various artists figured in his life as mentors, collaborators, critics, and supportive friends and correspondents.

The duration of the creative life leaves room for mixed patterns of work alone and work with others. Some individuals may need to work alone for prolonged periods and then work collaboratively. For others, solitary and collaborative work may alternate in a different rhythm.

The social nature of creative work takes many forms: Darwin kept up a voluminous correspondence in which he exchanged information with botanists and biologists all over the world. He also gave papers to various learned societies, enabling him to air his ideas and listen to those of others. Darwin was also a member of a local pigeon fanciers' club, learning there much about animal breeding (Gruber, 1981).

Social relationships begin in the family. In psychology, recognition of this point has led to an overemphasis on the parent–child relationship and on the family as a fixed structure whose primary function is caretaking and socialization – by parents of children. In its application to the study of creativity, this approach has led to emphasis on authority relations between the generations and on heredity.

This picture of the family has been shifting. Nowadays, the family is seen more as a developing system in which relationships change over time (Grotevant and Cooper, 1983; Minuchin, 1985). Moreover, because of the longstanding exclusive emphasis on parent–child relations, the child system in the family, that is, the sibling system, has only recently been given serious attention. Harlow (1971), in his seminal studies of monkeys' relationships with their mothers and peers, argued that peer relationships, for humans as well as for monkeys, are essential for the discovery and utilization of social and cultural patterns and for later heterosexual love. But Harlow studied peers, not siblings, and makes no mention of siblings. It may be that the distinction is unimportant in non-human primate families. Many children, however, have their first experience of age-mate social relations with a brother or sister and learn these same patterns first in their own families.

SIBLINGS: NOT ONLY RIVALRY

Brothers and sisters are handed to you. There is no choice. Furthermore, the sibling relationship may be the longest in life, outlasting parent–child and spousal relationships. But even in the family, personal relationships are constructed. Siblings can murder each other as Cain did Abel; they can love each other against all odds (Bank and Kahn, 1982); they can guide and cooperate with each other at an early age (Dunn and Kendrick, 1982) as well as in adolescence (Shapiro and Wallace, 1987); and they can support each other in adversity (Wallerstein and Kelly, 1980). What is quite clear is that siblinghood evokes more than mere rivalry.

Moreover, the sibling relationship involves more than similarity, modelling, and emulation. In general, siblings work out differentiated or complementary roles and relationships. This complementarity can encourage collaboration. It can counteract and even preclude rivalry. For a considerable portion of their lives, siblings are in a position of enforced proximity and intimacy. People need to understand how they differ from their siblings in the course of developing their own identity, as well as how alike they may be. They tend to believe that they are more unlike than like each other (Shapiro and Wallace, 1987), they typically differentiate themselves from their siblings and carve out different roles (Schachter, 1982), and they experience an apparently common family environment differently (Daniels and Plomin, 1985). Thus, siblings themselves emphasize their differences and complementarity rather than their similarity. At the same time, they have an enormous reservoir of shared experiences, built up over many years.

Collaborative relationships between siblings in the interests of creative work are not uncommon: Darwin and his brother Erasmus, the Wright Brothers, the Grimm Brothers, the Brontë children, William and Henry James, to name a few, all exhibited important work relationships between siblings. But as a topic in its own right, siblings and creativity has had little attention. Freud did not say very much about siblings, but his notion that they are locked in a fundamental conflict of competition for the love of the parents has deeply penetrated our thinking. Adler's notion of the power struggle between siblings based on ordinal family position did little to change this basic orientation. This emphasis on rivalry combines readily with a bias towards seeing creative work as something carried on by the lonely genius working mysteriously in self-inflicted solitude.

SIBLING CREATIVITY: WILLIAM AND DOROTHY WORDSWORTH

I turn now to a discussion of the collaboration of one famous sibling pair: William and Dorothy Wordsworth. William Wordsworth, one of the great Romantic poets, had an intense emotional relationship as well as a work relationship with his sister Dorothy. Dorothy Wordsworth was recognized, long after her death, for the journals she kept of daily life in the countryside, of tours undertaken with her brother, for example, to Scotland, and of sensitive descriptions of nature.

William Wordsworth's most recent biographer, Stephen Gill (1989), spends relatively little time on the relationship and tends to reduce Dorothy's significance. For example, in describing Dorothy and William's tour of Scotland in 1803, Gill presents a passage from Dorothy's *Recollections* of the tour and then makes this statement:

> [Dorothy's] sustained work of ordering and reflection, the *Recollections*, occupied her, in distinct phases, until the end of May 1805. As usual Wordsworth dealt with his experiences in a different way. Episodes and images were allowed to seep through to the deep strata of his imagination. (Gill, 1989, pp.215–6)

The implication is that episodes and images were not allowed to seep through to the deep strata of Dorothy's imagination. This is especially arguable since Gill has just quoted from an entry in Dorothy's *Recollections* that flatly contradicts this idea.

The Wordsworths' collaborative relationship is of interest for a number of reasons. First, after a separation of more than ten years they made an explicit *decision* to pool their resources and share their lives. There was a longstanding affinity and love between them, which both recognized long before they decided to live together. Second, the duration of their close relationship was very long. After William married Dorothy's close friend Mary Hutchinson, the three continued living together. William and Mary had several children. Dorothy continued as a member of this household until William died.

Towards the end of her life, she became physically, and then mentally, ill. She died in 1855, outliving her brother by several years. This sibling bond was purposefully lifelong. Third, Dorothy and William clearly played different roles in their work and life together. These were finely articulated and dovetailed. Fourth, their relationship was marked by mutual security rather than rivalry. Theirs is a pure case of mutual aid. Finally, their creative life and work, and its fusion in William's poetry, clearly bring out the three systems of knowledge, purpose, and affect, that make up the evolving systems approach to creative work (Gruber, 1980).

The Decision to be Together

William and Dorothy Wordsworth were both born in the Lake District (in Cockermouth) and eventually settled there together. Their feeling for this countryside, and its significance in their lives, is evident in all their writing. They spent a considerable portion of their childhood and youth living apart, due in part to the deaths of their parents when they were very young. Their mother died in 1778, when Dorothy (1771–1855) was six and William (1770–1850) almost eight. Dorothy was sent to live with her mother's cousin in Halifax, Yorkshire, and spent the rest of her childhood there. She would not see her brothers again for nine years. The following year, 1779, William and his brother Richard went to boarding school in Hawkshead, Lancashire (Gill, 1989). Unlike her brothers, Dorothy never went home again and she did not see her father before he died in 1783 (Gittings and Manton, 1985). After her father's death, Dorothy was sent to live with her maternal grandparents. Whereas she had been very happy in Halifax with her second cousin, who became a surrogate mother, Dorothy disliked her grandparents and felt alien and unwelcome in their house. For Dorothy, therefore, the loss of her mother was associated with separation from her brothers, her father and her home. This may, to some extent, account for the strength of her affection for her brothers, most intensely expressed towards William, the closest to her in age.

Eleven years after their father's death, in 1794, William and Dorothy visited the Lake District together. They had spent time together before this, mostly when William visited Dorothy during the long vacation while he was at Cambridge. They decided to pool their small respective capitals in order to live together. The following year they lived in Dorset and then in Alfoxden in West Somerset. Dorothy began to write her first journal, the Alfoxden Journal, in 1798. It was here, too, that Wordsworth and Coleridge began the highly creative association that led, among other works, to the *Lyrical Ballads*, first published in 1798.

In December of 1799, William and Dorothy settled in their own cottage in Grasmere in the Lake District. He was 29, she 28. They were to live together, although not alone after 1802 when William married, until William died in 1850.

Mutual Love and Solidarity

Each has left a record of their affectional and working relationship. Dorothy's record is found in her journals and letters, William's in his poetry and letters. Their love and admiration for each other are well known and figure in the commentaries of their contemporaries (in particular, Coleridge, de Quincey), as well as in biographies and literary criticism. Their private and personal relationship was deeply intertwined with their intellectual work together. They led a creative life that was extraordinarily harmonious and, before Wordsworth's marriage, extraordinarily intimate. In his long, unfinished poem, 'The Recluse', which William began during the Alfoxden year and continued to work on for more than 15 years (Gill, 1989), he described their journey to Grasmere 'side by side', the wind driving them onward:

> like two Ships at sea,
> Or like two Birds, companions in mid-air,
> Parted and reunited by the blast.
>
> (Darlington, 1977, MS B p.51)

These lines describe the two in completely egalitarian terms, simply as two members of the same genus – ship or bird – 'parted and reunited by the blast'. 'The blast' is also a metaphor for the loss of their parents which had separated them physically but united them spiritually. In the same poem, William referred to Dorothy as a 'younger orphan of a home extinct', indicating the powerful *mutuality* of their loss of parents and home, and its role in forming their sibling equality and solidarity. In the same poem he described his sister's importance in his thoughts, and her presence in his *mind*:

> Mine eyes did ne'er
> Fix on a lovely object, nor my mind
> Take pleasure in the midst of happy thoughts,
> But either She whom now I have, who now
> Divides with me this loved abode, was there,
> Or not far off. Where'er my footsteps turned,
> Her voice was like a hidden Bird that sang.
>
> (Darlington, 1977, MS B 109–10)

Among many expressions of his love for her are these lines in a fragment composed about 1800:

My dear companion of my lonely walk,
My hope, my joy, my sister, and my friend,
Or something dearer still, if reason knows
A dearer thought, or in the heart of love
There be a dearer name.[1]

For her part, Dorothy, in the letters of her young adulthood, described herself as most closely tied to her brother William. But this relationship was embedded in a general feeling of warmth towards all her four brothers, united by their early misfortune.

In these adolescent letters, and in spite of being orphaned, Dorothy wrote often of missing her brothers but hardly ever of missing her parents. Though she had close women friends, the sibling relationship was the most important and enduring one in her life. William was her favourite. In another letter, she admitted that half the virtues she saw in him were created by her love and *by his for her*:

> he was never tired of comforting his sister, he never left her in anger, he always met her with joy, he preferred her society to every other pleasure, or rather when we were so happy as to be within each other's reach he had no pleasure when we were compelled to be divided. (Letter to Jane Pollard, July 10, 1793, de Selincourt, 1935, p.98)

The kind of security each felt in the other's love is most fully realized, usually, in the love of parents. Dorothy and William gave each other the security of parental love.

De Selincourt (1933) has suggested that Dorothy's love for William was so intense that it prevented her from having a love relationship with someone else. Herbert Read, in his Wordsworth biography, maintained that the relationship between William and Dorothy was 'not a normal one' (1930, p.90) and that Dorothy was a neurotic who, 'finding no outlet for her excessive sensibility, the repression became too much for her and she finally went insane' (p.91). We do not know what the mental affliction was that struck Dorothy in her sixties until her death at 84. But mental problems in the sixties do not necessarily flow from a lifetime neurosis. She could, indeed, have been suffering from senile dementia in her later years, whose onset in the sixties is by no means unusual. A recent biography by Gittings and Manton (1985) makes this suggestion.

The extent and intensity of Dorothy's love for William is reflected, more than anywhere else, in her journals. Dorothy was a great and eloquent recorder. The *Grasmere Journals*, which I draw on in this essay, were begun on 14 May 1800 *for William*. On that day, William and their younger brother John (of whom they were especially fond) left Grasmere for Yorkshire.

My heart was so full that I could hardly speak to W. when I gave him a farewell kiss. I sate a long time upon a stone at the margin of the lake, and after a flood of tears my heart was easier . . . I resolved to write a journal of the time till W. and J. return, and I set about keeping my resolve . . . because I shall give W. Pleasure by it when he comes home again. (Moorman, 1971, pp.15–16)[2]

Her journals are transparent concerning her feelings about William. On those occasions when he is away, she thinks about him constantly, tidies his things, keeps herself busy. Her language is frequently extravagant enough to suggest that their love may have bordered on the erotic. For example, on one occasion when William was away for a day or two, she records 'I *will* be busy, I *will* look well and be well when he comes back to me'. She continues:

Thursday [4th March, 1802]. I walked round the two Lakes crossed the stepping stones at Tydale Foot. Sate down where we always sit. I was full of thoughts about my darling. Blessings on him. (Moorman, 1971, p.97)

Wordsworth's contemporary Shelley suggested that the Lucy poems are really about Dorothy (J. Wordsworth, Jaye and Woof, 1987). But although the Lucy poems are love poems, Lucy is idealized, almost mythical, and not at all erotic. While one may be struck by words in the *Journal* that, in their current usage, describe heterosexual love, their naïve, transparent innocence contradicts that idea. Gittings and Manton (1985) maintain that, even as a young girl, Dorothy had no interest in sexual love. Bateson (1963), on the other hand, believed that William and Dorothy were in love without physical consummation, unconsciously 'infatuated' (p.144), and that William's poetry written in the years immediately following 1798 reflect it. Gittings and Manton (1985) present some evidence that there was local gossip that William was intimate with his sister (pp.105–6). In the absence of definitive evidence in either direction the issue must remain unresolved. In general, however, the biographical literature during the last ten years, in contrast to earlier works, has given less credence to the idea of an incestuous relationship between William and Dorothy.

The intimate life together that William and Dorothy described was, in any case, often shared, for example, with Coleridge. It was a collaborative life. They walked together in their beloved landscape and Wordsworth's poetry and Dorothy's journal were part of their shared daily activities. It is from Dorothy's journals that we get a sense of this joint life. She described their domestic activities, like picking vegetables from the garden, cooking, sewing, fishing; social activities, such as writing and receiving letters, visiting and receiving visitors; frequent accounts of being unwell – with headaches and colds – that seemed to afflict both William and Dorothy. Dorothy took, and was given, the major role of being in charge of the domestic arrangements for their life. These arrangements gave fullest play to Wordsworth's work.

Also recorded in the journals is William at work – composing poetry, reading it to Dorothy – and Dorothy writing it out. On a given day, the journal might record that William was composing a poem, Dorothy might walk with him while he read the poem to her, she would cook lunch, a neighbour might come to tea. Towards evening, there would be a walk to a neighbouring village to see if there was any mail. In the evening more writing and reading separately and together, sometimes into the night. Here is the description of the end of such a day:

> *Wednesday [17th March, 1802].* A sweet Evening as it had been a sweet day, a grey evening, and I walked quietly along the side of Rydale Lake with quiet thoughts. . . . Thus I was going on when I saw the shape of my Beloved in the Road at a little distance – we turned back to see the light but it was fading – almost gone. . . . When we came in sight of our own dear Grasmere, the Vale looked fair and quiet in the moonshine. . . . There were high slow travelling clouds in the sky that threw large masses of Shade upon some of the Mountains. We walked backwards and forwards between home and Oliffs till I was tired. William kindled and began to write the poem. We carried cloaks into the orchard and sate a while there, I left him and he nearly finished the poem. I was tired to death and went to bed before him – he came down to me and read the Poem to me in bed. – A sailor begged here today going to Glasgow he spoke chearfully in a sweet tone. (Moorman, 1971, p.103)

The journals contain Dorothy's descriptions of the surrounding landscape. Her observations during the daily or nightly walks, taken alone or with her brother are fine-grained and sensitive. And the weather and seasons, which so powerfully govern the impact of landscape in the Lake District, are never forgotten:

> *Friday [31st October 1800].* The moon shone like herrings in the water. (Moorman, 1971, p.49)
> *1st March [1798].* The shapes of the mist, slowly moving along, exquisitely beautiful; passing over the sheep they almost seemed to have more of life than those quiet creatures. The unseen birds singing in the mist. (Moorman, 1971, p.9)
> *Tuesday 24th [November, 1801].* It [our favorite birch tree] was yielding to the gusty wind with all its tender twigs, the sun shone upon it and it glanced in the wind like a flying sunshiny shower. It was a tree in shape with stem and branches but it was like a Spirit of water. (Moorman, 1971, p.61)

Dorothy Wordsworth's talent as an observer and writer of prose are well recognized (de Selincourt, 1933; Moorman, 1971; Clark, 1978). Coleridge wrote of 'her eye watchful in minutest observation of nature' (Coleridge, 1797); and de Quincey noted that:

> the pulses of light are not more quick or more inevitable in their flow and undulation, than were the answering and echoing movements of her sympathizing attention. (1862–63)

How these talents were mingled with her brother's poetry is the topic I turn to now.

Collaboration: Complementary Roles

Dorothy Wordsworth's first journal was the record she kept for some months in Alfoxden where she and William lived in 1798. Alfoxden marked the beginning of one of the most fruitful periods in Wordsworth's poetic composition. In that year he and Coleridge produced the *Lyrical Ballads*. The following year, during a stay in Germany in 1799, Wordsworth composed the first drafts of *The Prelude* (Jeffrey, 1989), the Lucy poems, and other important works. Upon their return from Germany, he and Dorothy settled in Grasmere. The next few years saw an outpouring of some of Wordsworth's best poetry. During this same period, 1800 to 1803, Dorothy kept her Grasmere journals.

In the Preface to the second edition of the *Lyrical Ballads* (1800), Wordsworth made several statements about what poetry is. First, he said that 'all good poetry is the spontaneous overflow of powerful feelings', but he added that poems with any value are produced by someone who has also 'thought long and deeply' – thoughts that modify the feelings (1800; 1962, p.139). Later in the Preface, he elaborated this idea into a more deliberate developmental sequence which begins with the sentence that 'poetry takes its origin from emotion recollected in tranquillity'. This amputated sentence is widely cited as Wordsworth's famous definition of poetry. In fact it is not only inaccurate but a real falsification of what he actually said, to wit:

> [poetry] takes its origin from emotion recollected in tranquillity: the emotion is contemplated till, by a species of reaction, the tranquillity gradually disappears, and an emotion, kindred to that which was before the subject of contemplation, is gradually produced, and does itself actually exist in the mind. In this mood successful composition generally begins. (1800; 1962, p.154)

Thus did Wordsworth, writing on the process of making poetry, insist on the close relationship between cognition and affect.

Similarly, in Wordsworth's poetry, the impact of thought, or reflection, is almost always added to the affect laden descriptions of events or perceptions of nature. In 'Tintern Abbey', written in 1798, Wordsworth reflects on how he has changed since he last visited the same place in 1793. Central to this change is the idea of reflection or contemplation of remembered experience. He remembers how he used to be, how perception *alone* of the objects of nature used to be his passion:

> Their colours and their forms, were then to me
> An appetite; a feeling and a love,
> That had no need of a remoter charm,
> By thought supplied, or any interest
> Unborrowed from the eye.

> (1798 text, Gill, 1975, p.133)

Now the role of nature had deepened and expanded for him, far beyond the enjoyment of its sensory messages, to include his mind and spirit. Aware of his own development, Wordsworth made a profound commitment as a poet to an all-encompassing nature:

> well pleased to recognize
> In nature and the language of the sense,
> The anchor of my purest thoughts, the nurse,
> The guide, the guardian of my heart, and soul
> Of all my moral being.

> (Gill, 1975, op.cit.)

Wordsworth went on to contemplate Dorothy. He melded his past self with her, describing her as he once was, the pure untrammelled lover of nature:

> For thou art with me here upon the banks
> Of this fair river; thou my dearest friend,
> My dear, dear friend; and in thy voice I catch
> The language of my former heart, and read
> My former pleasures in the shooting lights
> Of thy wild eyes. Oh! yet a little while
> May I behold in thee what I was once,
> My dear, dear sister!

> (Gill, 1975, op.cit.)

William looked at nature for the sake of the mind and attributed to Dorothy looking at nature for its own sake (Homans, 1980). But he identified Dorothy with his former self. There is a mixture of feelings here: on the one hand Wordsworth made a continuity between Dorothy and himself because she was the way he used to be, and through her, not only through his own memory, he could recapture his former self and its joys; on the other hand, he had left this former self behind and its irretrievable loss also meant a kind of separation between him and his sister. In typical sibling fashion (Shapiro and Wallace, 1987) he is both differentiating himself from his sister and conveying their likeness.

With these lines from 'Tintern Abbey', Wordsworth described what would be the complementarity of their collaboration. In the body of Wordsworth's poetry in which he draws on Dorothy's journal entries, their emotional symbiosis and the synthesis of their two points of view appear. Dorothy's compelling descriptions of what her sensitive eye and ear had perceived were the raw material that William mined, transformed into poetry and embellished with reflective commentary. She pointed the way for him (Gittings and Manton, 1985) in her own prose. But just as he was guided by her, her eye was also guided by him in a recursive process. In some instances, a word or phrase in her journal also appears as a word or phrase in his poetry, but it is not clear whether hers came first or his. A clear sequence is apparent in 'The Daffodils' – one of the best known instances of their collaborations. Dorothy and William saw the daffodils on a windy walk in April 1802. Here is Dorothy's journal entry.

> *Thursday, 15th [April, 1802].* When we were in the woods . . . we saw a few daffodils close to the water side . . . as we went along there were more and yet more and at last under the boughs of the trees, we saw that there was a long belt of them along the shore, about the breadth of a country turnpike road. I never saw daffodils so beautiful they grew among the mossy stones about and about them some rested their heads upon these stones as on a pillow for weariness and the rest tossed and reeled and danced and seemed as if they verily laughed with the wind that blew upon them over the lake, they looked so gay ever glancing ever changing. There were here and there a few stragglers a few yards higher up but they were so few as not to disturb the simplicity and unity and life of that one busy highway. (Moorman, 1971, p.109)

Dorothy's metaphor was of the daffodils as travellers on (life's?) highway, some weary and resting, some dancing. She did not 'merely' describe nature.

Wordsworth's poem, written later, in 1804, exactly caught this mood in his description of the daffodils. But he added a powerful frame, first by introducing an *observing* self:

> I wandered lonely as a cloud
> That floats on high o'er Vales and Hills,
> When all at once I saw a crowd,
> A host, of dancing Daffodils;

He then described the daffodils:

Along the Lake, beneath the trees,
Ten thousand dancing in the breeze.

The waves beside them danced, but they
Outdid the sparkling waves in glee:–
A Poet could not but be gay
In such a laughing company:

Wordsworth closed the poem with the *contemplative* 'I', and closing the frame:

I gaz'd – and gaz'd – but little thought
What wealth the show to me had brought:

For oft, when on my couch I lie
In vacant or in pensive mood,
They flash upon that inward eye
Which is the bliss of solitude;
And then my heart with pleasure fills,
And dances with the Daffodils.

(Curtis, 1983, pp.330–2)

Dorothy's metaphor of travelling along a road was transformed into William's, of wandering above the countryside. For her, it was the daffodils that were travelling; for him 'I'. In 'Tintern Abbey', as Gill points out (1989), Wordsworth was not concerned so much with what is seen but with the eye that sees. In 'The Daffodils', there is a hierarchy in which the seen is the aliment of the mind and the mind's eye.

'The Daffodils' exemplifies a complex, long term collaborative manifold (Jeffrey, 1989). William and Dorothy both see the daffodils. Dorothy records her experience of them. Much later, William uses her description and presumably his own memory in the poem. He injects himself, first as the observing, then the reflecting poet, ending with a contemplation of the memory of the daffodils. His mastery was not only in transforming Dorothy's prose into poetry but in taking the poem over and making it his by introducing the masterful 'I'.

A different kind of connection between journal and poem is evident in the case of 'The Butterfly'. One Sunday morning at breakfast in 1802 (March 14), Dorothy and William's reminiscences triggered this poem. William had woken early and before rising had finished a poem 'The Beggar Boys'. He came down to breakfast. The idea for the poem, so we learn from Dorothy's journal, first occurred to him as they were talking about

the pleasure we both always feel at the sight of a butterfly. I told him that I used to chase them a little, but that I was afraid of brushing the dust off their wings, and did not catch them. (Moorman, 1971, p.101)

This single memory – not brushing the dust off their wings – caps the poem. Wordsworth went to write the poem immediately, though it was not published until 1807, five years later. Here are the last few lines, which again emphasize the different temperaments of William and Dorothy:

> Oh! pleasant, pleasant were the days,
> The time, when in our childish plays
> My sister Emmeline and I
> Together chased the Butterfly!
> A very hunter did I rush
> Upon the prey: – with leaps and springs
> I follow'd on from brake to bush;
> But She, God love her! feared to brush
> The dust from off its wings.

(Curtis, 1983, pp.203–4)

Their conversation about the butterfly provided the occasion for William to celebrate their early childhood, always overshadowed by the death of their parents (in lines not quoted). He contrasts his own careless, boyish pursuit of the butterfly with his sister's, giving her protective and loving interest the last word. Again, the Wordsworthian 'I' is in charge of the narrative.

The day that had begun with the breakfast conversation and the composition of the poem, continued with Dorothy writing the poem out and reading it to William. That night the process of composition continued, as recorded in her journal:

> Wm went to bed. I lay upon the fur gown before the fire, but I could not sleep – I lay there a long time. It is now half past 5 – I am going to write letters – I began to write to Mrs Rawson. William rose without having slept – we sate comfortably by the fire till he began to try to alter 'The Butterfly', and tired himself – he went to bed tired. (Moorman, 1971, p.101)

The journal records were not always of events experienced together. The longer poem 'Beggars' was based on a long, complex journal entry (27 May 1800). It describes a series of events which began at Dove Cottage, when a beggar woman came to the door, and continues when Dorothy later, on her way to Ambleside (a neighbouring village), saw what she thought were the husband and children of this woman. Two years later (13 March 1802), Dorothy records that William 'wrote the Poem of the Beggar woman taken from a Woman whom I had seen May – (now nearly 2 years ago)' (Moorman, 1971, p.100).

We can draw several conclusions from the evolution of 'Beggars'. William must have habitually examined his sister's journal for material for his poetry, both to add to and stimulate his own memory of events experienced with her, and to search for material from her experiences. In other words, he felt a basic trust in what she recorded. This is important because he was following certain principles in his poetry which he had made explicit in the Preface to the second edition of the *Lyrical Ballads* (1800; 1962). He wanted to 'choose incidents and situations from common life', describe them in 'language really used by men' (as opposed to traditional flowery and formal language), and he also often chose to write poetry about 'humble and rustic life' because 'in that condition, the essential passions of the heart find a better soil' (1800; 1962, p.138). Dorothy's journals were written in a simple language that accurately described and powerfully communicated experiences of such a life. One of the striking themes in the *Grasmere Journal* is beggars – the men, women, and children, who often came to the cottage to beg and who roamed the countryside. Wordsworth used this content several times in his poetry. It fitted with his desire to include humanity in a holistic view of nature.

It is important not to forget as well Wordsworth's basic criterion for what a poet is: someone who has thought long and deeply about the things he writes about. The deceptively simple poems I have quoted here should not obscure this point. Indeed, the long lag between some journal entries and the beginning of poetic composition suggests that this was also true of short individual poems.

These aspects of their work point up the purposefulness of Wordsworth's writing, both of the process, through recollection, and the content. His trust in Dorothy's journal was based on shared values: she recorded in limpid language the events and experiences that struck her and among them were those that he wanted to describe and think about in his poetry.

Their collaboration blended the sensuous and the intellectual. Dorothy selected the content to record, an intellectual task, and described it as she had perceived it, sensuously and thoughtfully. His transformation of this sensuous experience into poetry, often adding intellectual commentary, was an integrative process, drawing into a coherent whole his purposes as a poet, his interest in recording affect, and his deep knowledge of what he wrote about and of his craft.

Conclusion

The long-continued collaboration of Dorothy and William Wordsworth may be rare, but is by no means singular. The Wright brothers, the brothers Grimm, and the Mongolfier brothers, for example, also had long and continuous collaborative creative lives.

But how does this collaborative spirit develop? William and

Dorothy's early life together, in a larger web of loving sibling relationships, and the loss of their parents and home drew them closely together. Their long separation served to cement rather than dilute their affection. By explicitly renewing their commitment to each other and emphasizing their emotional ties they could strengthen the family that had been driven apart. These attitudes and feelings were especially strong for Dorothy and William who had always shared the same values, especially a love of nature.

A striking feature of the Wordsworths' relationship *is* that they were brother and sister. The closeness of their life together before William's marriage gave it a completeness that is probably seen more often in childhood with its special proximity and shared experience. Professional collaborations begun later in life do not have this background. Although the Wordsworths were together during their early formative years, they were separated for a significant period of their childhood and youth. This separation may have opened the way to their joint exploration of experiences which, had they lived together all their lives, would have seemed merely commonplace.

At the same time, their relationship was not exclusive. Other people were taken into their life and work, notably Coleridge. With William's marriage to Mary Hutchinson, a different series of assimilative shifts took place.

This collaborative relationship, like others, was one with many different functions and roles interwoven. It should be clear that it was asymmetrical in that Dorothy was helping William with his work and not he with hers. She did this both in her nurturing role as a woman and as an intellectual companion in a variety of ways. As her letters and journals show, she was often the first reader, sounding board and critic of Wordsworth's poetry. She was the housekeeper and manager of their domestic life. When he was away, she was the absent companion with whom William wanted to share his thoughts. She was the recorder of primary experience, ordering the record of their daily life, giving status to humble events. Finally, when needed, Dorothy was the transducer of experience for William's poetry.

Notes

1. According to Beer (1978), this fragment was extracted from Dorothy's journal by Professor Knight. Its source, cited in Beer, is de Selincourt and Darbyshire (1940–49).

2. All quotations from Dorothy Wordsworth's *Grasmere Journal* are from this Moorman (1971) edition.

Acknowledgement: I want to thank Lucy Wallace and Margery B. Franklin for their thoughtful and useful comments on earlier drafts of this chapter. My special thanks go to Howard E. Gruber for his care and suggestions.

REFERENCES

BANK, S., and KAHN, M.D. (1982) *The Sibling Bond*. New York: Basic Books.
BATESON, F.W. (1963) *Wordsworth, a re-interpretation*. 2nd ed. London: Longmans.
BEER, J. (1978) *Wordsworth and the Human Heart*. London: Macmillan.
CLARK, C. (Ed.), (1978) *Home at Grasmere*. Harmondsworth: Penguin.
COLERIDGE, S.T. (1797) In E.L. Griggs (Ed.), *Collected Letters of Samuel Taylor Coleridge*, 1, 330–1 Oxford. Cited in Beer (1978, p.140).
CURTIS, J. (Ed.) (1983) Poems, in two volumes, and other poems, 1800–1807. *The Cornell Wordsworth*. Ithaca: Cornell University Press.
DANIELS, D., and PLOMIN, R. (1985) Differential experience of siblings in the same family. *Development Psychology, 21*, 747–760.
DARLINGTON, B. (Ed.) (1977) Home at Grasmere, Part first, book first, of 'The Recluse'. *The Cornell Wordsworth*. Ithaca: Cornell University Press.
DUNN, J., and KENDRICK, C. (1982) *Siblings: love, envy and understanding*. Cambridge, MA: Harvard University Press.
GILL, S. (Ed.) (1975) The Salisbury Plain poems. *The Cornell Wordsworth*. Ithaca: Cornell University Press.
GILL, S. (1989) *Wordsworth, a life*. Oxford: Clarendon Press.
GITTINGS, R., and MANTON, J. (1985) *Dorothy Wordsworth*. Oxford: Clarendon Press.
GROTEVANT, H.D., and COOPER, C.R. (Eds) (1983) Adolescent development in the family. *New Directions for Child Development, No.22*. San Francisco: Jossey-Bass.
GRUBER, H.E. (1980) The evolving systems approach to creativity. In S. Modgil and C. Modgil (Eds), *Toward a theory of psychological development*. Windsor, UK: NFER Publishing.
GRUBER, H.E. (1981) *Darwin on Man: a psychological study of scientific creativity*. Chicago: University of Chicago Press.
HARLOW, H.F. (1971) *Learning to Love*. San Francisco: Albion Publishing Co.
HOMANS, M. (1980) *Women Writers and Poetic Identity*. Princeton: Princeton University Press.
JEFFREY, L.R. (1989) Writing and rewriting poetry: William Wordsworth. In D.B. Wallace and H.E. Gruber (Eds), *Creative people at work: 12 cognitive case studies*. New York: Oxford University Press.
MINUCHIN, P. (1985) Families and individual development: Provocations from the field of family therapy. *Child Development, 56*, pp.289–302.
MOORMAN, M. (Ed.), (1971) *Journals of Dorothy Wordsworth*. New York: Oxford University Press.
NEW YORK GRAPHIC SOCIETY (1978) *The Complete Letters of Vincent Van Gogh*, 3 vols. Boston: Little, Brown & Co.
DE QUINCEY, T. (1862–63) Recollections of the Lakes and the Lake Poets. *Works*, 15 vols. Edinburgh, Cited in Beer (1978, p.140).

READ, H. (1930) *Wordsworth*. London: Faber & Faber.

SCHACHTER, F.F. (1982) Sibling deidentification and split-parent identification: a family tetrad. In M.E. Lamb and B. Sutton-Smith (Eds), *Sibling relationships: their nature and significance across the lifespan*. Hillsdale, NJ: Erlbaum.

DE SELINCOURT, E. (1933) *Dorothy Wordsworth, a biography*. Oxford: Clarendon Press.

DE SELINCOURT, E. (1935) *The Early Letters of William and Dorothy Wordsworth (1787–1805)*. Oxford: Clarendon Press.

DE SELINCOURT, E. and DARBYSHIRE, H. (Eds.) (1940–49) *The Poetical Works of William Wordsworth*, 5 vols. Oxford: Oxford University Press.

SHAPIRO, E.K., and WALLACE, D.B. (1987) Siblings and parents in one-parent families. In F.F. Schachter and R.K. Stone (Eds), *Practical concerns about siblings: bridging the research-practice gap*. New York: The Haworth Press.

WALLACE, D.B. and GRUBER, H.E. (Eds) (1989) *Creative people at work: 12 cognitive case studies*. New York: Oxford University Press.

WALLACE, D.B. (1989) Studying the individual: the case study method and other genres. In Wallace, D.B., and Gruber, H.E. (Eds), *Creative people at work: 12 cognitive case studies*. New York: Oxford University Press.

WALLACE, D.B. (1985) Giftedness and the construction of a creative life. In F.D. Horowitz and M. O'Brien (Eds), *The gifted and talented: developmental perspectives*. Washington, DC: American Psychological Association.

WALLERSTEIN, J.S., and KELLY, J.B. (1980) *Surviving the breakup: how children and parent cope with divorce*. New York: Basic Books.

WORDSWORTH, J., JAYE, M.C. and WOOF, R. (1987) *William Wordsworth and the Age of English Romanticism*. New Brunswick, N.J.: Rutgers University Press, co-published with The Wordsworth Trust, Dove Cottage, Grasmere, UK.

WORDSWORTH, W. (1962) *Preface to the second edition of Lyrical Ballads*. In C. Norman (Ed.), *Poets on poetry*. New York: Collier. (Original work published in 1800.)

THE INTELLECTUALLY GIFTED ADOLESCENT

Joan Freeman

It is a truism to say that all intellectual development takes place in a social context. To live comfortably in any social group means adjusting one's behaviour to some extent. This implies the ability to assess the capacities and predict the behaviour of other people, which is an important part of early intellectual development. The capacity for behavioural adjustment is shown in the way an individual tackles an intellectual problem, which may change considerably with time and place. Little children, for example, can often think better at home than they do at school (Tizard, 1985).

Because intelligence always functions in the real world, it must be affected by what is valued there. But as these values inevitably change, and the individual continues to develop, the demands upon and exercise of his or her gifts can be very different at different times. One should not seek to understand giftedness in adults by viewing intellectual development as coming to a halt, say, in late adolescence: passing exams is not the same as making a business deal. It is important to track children's development for as long as possible to see whether the gifted are different in their continued development, and if so, to find out ways in which they are different. It is the only way to question Shakespeare's commonly accepted dictum: 'Early ripe, early rot'.

Certainly in the developed world over the past three generations there has been an enormous improvement in opportunities for people to develop and use their talents. The more complex the society in which people live, the more intelligent they must be to exploit the opportunities available, and to adjust their own behaviour to that of others in a continuous calculation of the balance of profit and loss. What individuals actually accomplish in our potentially limitless society can now provide some evidence both about their cognitive capacities, and the outside social factors (such as social class, gender, parents' qualifications) which may affect them.

ADOLESCENCE IN A LIFE-SPAN PERSPECTIVE

Adolescence is the time of transition between puberty and adulthood, when novel and often strong behaviour patterns emerge. Its major psychological characteristic is the refinement of accumulated personal identity, particularly self-esteem, via cognitive and social transformations. It is out of these changes that patterns of thought, social and moral values, and a deeper understanding of one's own abilities and interests evolve which will define the self for the rest of the relatively stable time of adulthood. These processes are partly due to external life changes, such as child-parent power shifts in the family, and peer influences, as well as to individual biological changes. However, the young person is not of course a passive recipient, but has a distinct influence on events and outcomes.

Adolescence is a time for a developmental shift in cognitive abilities, which for most means a move into higher levels of reflective thinking. The gifted, though, may have reached that stage already, maybe even by late childhood. It is for the very reason of their different abilities that the gifted find themselves subject to particular stresses and vulnerabilities as they go through adolescence, which may affect them emotionally, and so alter the path of their cognitive functioning.

Academically highly able adolescents may be under extra emotional pressure from expectations both for short-term achievement, notably in exams, and beyond that, for future careers. They are not only expected to do well, but to be keenly motivated to reach those high standards. Because of the heavy study load, gifted adolescents have to stay longer in a child-like state, in which growing personal autonomy has to be reined in. Consequently, they may experience this time as one of greater than average frustration and compromise, being obliged more than most of their age-peers to balance present preferences against future orientated constraints.

The highly able are far more likely to suffer from the secondary effects of other people's reactions to them, such as stereotyping. Distorting myths about the gifted vary considerably with the culture which carries them: the youngsters are then faced with either attempting to fit in with the prevailing stereotype or rejecting it. They may, for example, be expected to be top of the class all the time: as a result they may either strive constantly to please or mentally drop out. This kind of experience affects the development of personal relationships, which become more apparent in the adolescent years, and through these relationships, self-concept.

The 'little professor' syndrome is a typical loading on to a gifted child, normally a boy. Teachers and parents find him 'cute', apparently absorbed in his own thoughts about the universe, and making pronouncements in a childish treble. It is perhaps a little worrying to them that he has few friends, but it is accepted that this is an outcome of his superior thinking abilities, and perhaps he will make some later at university. But by the age of 15, with few developed social skills at making or keeping friends, and plagued with the normal spots and yearnings of adolescence, the gifted youth may well be on the way to a life of loneliness, peering down a microscope away from people and emotional comfort. One of the major opportunities for growth in adolescence is to learn how to use solitude. But their loneliness is more extreme than the normal adolescent search for respite from the pressure of adult demands, which sends them to their bedrooms for hours.

Yet friends are usually the best part of a teenager's life. It is mostly through them, and the unbiased feedback they provide, that they develop a sense of who they are. Adolescents, including gifted ones, talk at length and with great intensity to others of their own age, reinterpreting their experiences to facilitate their integration and development. The gifted, though, may have to cope with a distinction between age- and ability-peers for different aspects of their development.

THE EFFECTS OF SELF-CONCEPT ON ACHIEVEMENT

Adolescents finding their way into adulthood are disruptive in almost all communities to a greater or lesser extent, and each culture has ways of handling it. Since the dawn of the written word, we know that the young have taken issue with the way their elders have run the world, and the elders have complained about the behaviour of the young. Margaret Mead pointed out the conflicting messages given to young people in Western society: that they should be responsible yet fun-loving, childlike yet mature. Though conflict is usually considered a necessary condition of growth, it is also difficult to live with. Many highly achieving people had early years which were very difficult, for example, Thomas Edison, Eleanor Roosevelt, Albert Einstein. This was true for William Sidis (Wallace, 1986), whose father's craving for public attention for his genius son became particularly devastating to the boy's self-concept during his adolescence.

The difference between adolescence and adult life is not that moods change, but they do so very quickly and to greater extremes of dejection and exhilaration. Unlike adults, they are less protected by the accumulation of experiences. A sensitive adolescent's autonomy in learning can be very distorted when he or she is overconcerned about what others think of them. They may put all their energy into themselves and their social relationships, to the detriment of their study, or retreat from the threat of unpopularity by immersing themselves in study.

School underachievement in the gifted is mostly due to the same emotional problems as in other children, such as disruption at home. But for some, the effects of functioning at an unnaturally low level may be stress and anxiety – even today, a particular feature of gifted girls. But there are other difficulties, directly related to the gifts, which can operate in all learning circumstances. A common one is that a fine awareness of what can be achieved can set self-expectations too high, from which might follow perceived failure, producing real failure.

The effects of a school's influence on its pupils' achievements is well recognised (Rutter *et al.*, 1979). Yet teenagers only spend a third of their time there, and underachievement – the gap between potential and production – is at least as much due to non-school emotional factors (Butler-Por, 1987). The gifted youngster can get into the double bind of both 'fear of failure' and 'fear of success': the first, because of the threat failure poses to the self-image of being gifted and thus special; the second is pertinent to girls because of the pressure to achieve constant high grades and still to appear feminine. The major factor in adolescent achievement is the home atmosphere, in that adolescents who are happy at home tend to be happier and do better at school. This is enhanced, of course, by congruence of the parents' and the children's goals.

Although not working specifically with the highly able, Csikszentmihalyi and Larson (1984) have made valuable inroads into understanding (American) adolescents. They used an experience sampling method, in which 75 teenagers described into tape-recorders precisely what they were doing at regular intervals from early morning to late at night, as well as having several interviews. Interestingly, almost all their preferred activities were for leisure, which was the opposite for the high achievers described below, who mostly gave achievement as their greatest pleasure. Csikszentmihalyi and Larson used the term 'flow' to describe deep involvement in any activity which brings reward, such as a career, sport, or hobby. When the flow is going well you can feel the harmony between dimensions of consciousness, between goals, thoughts, emotions and activation. Your psychic energy is focused, and your being functions as an efficient whole. For any activity to have flow, its complexity must increase over time to provide a challenge on which to exercise growing skills. This concept fits the highly able adolescent particularly well, for whom skills are quickly learned, and boredom lurks, especially at school.

COGNITIVE PROCESSING IN THE GIFTED

In its broadest sense, intelligence is a purposive adaptation to that real world which is relevant to one's life. It makes an assessment of what is available and sorts out appropriate actions to be taken. There are two generally recognized ways of cognitive processing in which this works (Luria, 1982). Simultaneous – where relationships between elements are seen together in a holistic manner – and successive – where information is organized in a temporal sequence. This seems to parallel the functions of the two cerebral hemispheres. The difference is between looking deeply for meaning and purpose in the material to be learned, or staying on the surface and simply memorizing. Simultaneous processing is the more powerful discriminator of cognitive maturity. It functions at the highest levels of such skills as reading and comprehension (Das and Heemsbergen, 1983), and is essential for the highest levels of cognition.

Metacognition is a person's awareness of his or her own cognitive machinery. It is crucial in the choice of high level problem-solving strategies, and in putting them to work; the more accurate it is the more effectively intelligence can be used. A strategy is a plan, an integrated sequence of procedures, selected with a goal in view. Generally, the better the mental strategies employed in learning and making decisions, the better the result. Planning how they learn is what children should, but rarely do, learn in school. But it is what the intellectually gifted often do so well.

Those who do exceptionally well in examinations are a particular group with specific mental skills. They must have the ability to concentrate, to remember considerable amounts of material, as well as to access the higher mental skills necessary to draw ideas together during the examination. Those mental skills are linked with the whole child in his or her life circumstances, particularly in such matters as feelings of competence and the freedom to experiment. The links are noticeable in an individual's cognitive style – the manner in which a learner takes up the material to be learned. Cognitive style includes preferences for a personal psychological-environmental learning set-up, motivating factors, working alone or with others, dominant sense modality, autonomy in choice of what to learn, persistence, length of concentration, memory span, and the way those means are used.

Competition can be a strategic way of finding and defining your own capabilities, whether against others or your own best performance. Many highly able children (see page 100) used it quite consciously to improve their skills, because of the reward it offered them. But they knew that in order to be effective, the comparison had to be meaningful, as well as part of the process of getting to the top, which is not the same as the simple thrill of winning.

Sternberg and Davidson (1986) consider style of processing to sort the gifted from the non-gifted. It shows in the way an individual tackles novel tasks, which demand speedy formulation of an overall plan to produce effective strategies, execution of the task, and self-monitoring of performance. In Australia, Schofield and Ashman (1987) found that the dual model worked well with young teenagers identified as gifted by IQs of 124 plus on the WISC-R. Though the gifted scored much the same as their above-average controls on tasks of successive processing and low-level planning, they did significantly better with tasks of simultaneous processing and high-level planning.

There is now sufficient evidence from research, using tests of memory span and scanning, to conclude that learning efficiency in children improves with age and IQ. Because high IQ scorers would be expected to have a broader knowledge base than others (as the IQ test is somewhat dependent on its acquisition), they should thus be more efficient at swift and effective integration of new information with existing knowledge and long-term memory; a great learning advantage.

However, though speed of processing seems to be a probable differentiation in the way the intellectually gifted function, in spite of great efforts to find a biological basis for intelligence by associating speed of mental action with measured IQ, high correlations have been found only with samples containing disproportionately high numbers of retarded subjects. For modest correlations (0.2–0.4), the results are not reliable and may simply reflect differences in sustained attention (Mackintosh, 1986).

The very highest level of planning is broad, with numerous sub-plans ready to cover possibilities, and the building up of those sub-components can be taught. Working initially with disturbed children, Feuerstein (1980) has designed a scheme to bring about holistic type thinking. In this, a mediator enables the child to relate and co-ordinate his or her experiences, however disparate, in a meaningful way. He says that, without that mediation, even highly intelligent children with problems can be cognitively deprived.

Bastick (1982), in his work on intuition, proposed a system which takes account of the interactions between emotional states and cognitive processes. He sees a continuum of cognitive functions, ranging from intuitive to analytical, most being a mixture. Towards the analytical end thinking is slow, with a limited range of information and high degree of awareness. When wrong, it produces large errors because of its linear nature – even one small contradicting detail can foul up an argument. But at the intuitive end, thinking is fast, with a low degree of awareness, and is seldom precisely correct or drastically wrong.

New information is incorporated according to the subjective associations of the thinker, and emotional sets then act as memory 'hooks', so that people can evoke these feelings to recall the information. In a situation of threat, anxiety inhibits these intuitive powers, which thrive better in an environment which is permissive and game-like. The emotional content is evident from the rewarding feeling of satisfaction and the reduction in tension that accompany an insight in, for example, resolving cognitive dissonance. It is possible that people may deliberately create a mild form of dissonance (as in competition) in order to get that satisfying reward which is the basis of curiosity and the need for the stimulation of variety.

From this and other evidence (including my own described here) it seems that where the intellectually gifted really excel is in simultaneous processing functions and higher level metacognition. Even young gifted children show a distinctly more mature and more expert competence in information processing than their age-peers.

Creativity

However, the outstanding expertise of a gifted intelligence is not only to absorb information (which it does extremely well) but to find and solve problems. In this respect, both intellectual and creative activity grow from the same roots, the nourishing experience common to both being children's play. Both are aspects of intelligence in action, but each implies a somewhat different personal approach.

It is because highly able adolescents are often in a situation of facing more and more conventional exams that they run the risk of getting into a rut of reproducing their accumulating information, and losing their creative edge. There is also a danger in too much patterning, in that having found a cognitive procedure that works well, one can become mentally lazy. It can happen at all levels of intelligence, such as the regular way home which we may take without conscious awareness. Even though some of these patterns may become very refined, unless they remain flexible and open, they cannot accept new information and new ideas. It is often when one familiar idea is put unexpectedly against another that a moment of creative insight can occur. So, patterns used sensibly can save energy for creative endeavour, but used all the time they are bad for creativity.

Excellence can be taught. Bloom and his colleagues (1985), spent four years taking a retrospective look at 120 young people who were extremely successful as pianists, research mathematicians, Olympic swimmers, etc. He found that no matter what the initial characteristics (or gifts) of the individuals, unless there had been a long and intensive process of encouragement, nurturance, education and training, they did not reach extreme levels of capability. Few of these high achievers had been child prodigies. The parents said (by phone) that they had set high standards for their children and saw that they were met. One did not idle in those homes. Though the children had begun with pleasurable play, they had moved on to spend years in serious practice. Bloom concluded that almost anyone can learn anything, given the time and the appropriate conditions of learning. However, he did not compare those young people's lifestyles with a control group with similar upbringing, even with the siblings of the successful. Nor do we know whether the young people were able to keep the flame of originality and creativity alive, or whether they were merely supremely competent.

Years of research by many have shown that the creative individual is usually highly intelligent and also intellectual. Such people think about problems and issues. Perkins (1981) sees creative work as a function of values and beliefs, and Albert and Runco (1985) say that it is made up of a particular sensitivity and orientation to problems, through which individuals attempt to define themselves. Practising creativity appears to call for some personal discontent and disapproval of the state of things – the grain of sand in the oyster – as well as a need to right it, which demands some social independence, a trait all creative persons share. It means being aware of, but not enthralled by, others or their work, and it all has to happen in the right place and time.

An alternative proposition from Howard Gardner (1983) is his theory of at least seven relatively autonomous intelligences. Though he does not deal directly with the cognitive structures of the gifted, such as a general problem-solving ability, his theory would explain exceptionality such as 'idiots savants' and prodigies. Some cultures, he says, favour one kind of intelligence over another, which can promote particular bias in development and creativity.

Motivation

Learning style is distinctly affected by the motivation to learn, which is of course founded on each person's personal outlook. In fact, motivational considerations seem to be more important than the technical aspects of instruction in successful learning (Entwistle and Ramsden, 1983). The ease and depth of concentration will obviously affect the way of learning, and those who manage the most effective concentration also have the highest intrinsic motivation for it. The deepest levels of learning and thinking come with clearly relevant goals, such as a career or a genuine interest in the subject. It can have a spiral effect. Students who use a deep approach become more interested, and they not only spend more time at it, but are better organized to produce the greatest pay-off. But when the driving force is fear of failure, the surface route is often chosen, and interest fades.

Yet because intellectual activity has a social implication, concepts and goals are often similar, and problems can arise for the creative individual whose perceptions do not fit with those around. They have the options of altering them, moving to a different environment where possible, or battling on alone.

Intrinsic motivation cannot be imposed, but comes when a person sees him or herself as effective and also challenged. Everyone needs some challenge of risk and failure, and even some negative feedback, to feel that they are truly effective. For the highly able, for whom many things come easily, the feedback often runs to extremes, so that they may be given praise too readily, which may make them feel that they are simply doing the bidding of the teacher, or they get very little because a good performance is expected of them all the time. Too much supervision can also work against intrinsic motivation, because autonomy becomes a psychological impossibility. This can happen to the highly able learner in the pressured, controlled atmosphere of a high-powered academic school, where the received goal is only university entrance.

Life choices become acute for adolescents when they have to decide what they might do from the range of what is available to them. An activity which makes teenagers happy and cheerful, which is beneficial and exciting and provides the opportunity for growth, will most likely keep them active and alert. One of the reasons for boredom, at any ability level, is a lack of aims. Without goals there is no motivation, and without motivation, no chance to follow a route of anything which they would consider worthwhile. Either being underwhelmed or overwhelmed, the balance is not right.

THE GULBENKIAN RESEARCH PROJECT

In spite of the recognized social aspect of learning, much of our psychological understanding of how it happens has come from detailed studies of the processes, often in laboratories and with animals. In the Gulbenkian study of highly able youngsters, I chose to take a broader and more unusual view. This was to include both the social context in which the young people grew up and formed their study habits, and also the way they perceived their own behaviour. As well as measuring with psychological tests, I interviewed in depth all the subjects and their parents in their homes. It became clear that the more successful the learners, the more insightful and competent they were at choosing their personal learning methods, that is to say, at metacognition. The study threw valuable light on specific matters affecting the highly able learner at school, and provides information as to how this could be generally applied to all learners.

The First Part: 1974–1979

To start with, 70 children aged 5 to 14, who had been suggested as gifted by their parents, were each compared with two control children. Both the controls were matched for age, sex, socioeconomic status and school class, but only one was matched for intelligence (with 'Raven's Matrices'), the other being taken at random in that respect. All 210 children and their families were visited in their homes, and 60 class- and 60 head-teachers were interviewed in their schools (Freeman, 1979).

It was evident then that the brightest children were also the most sensitive and responsive to their general educational environment, in that poor circumstances appeared to be relatively more damaging to them than to average ability children. The effect was seen in their IQ scores, which are to some extent an achievement measure dependent on the educational environment. For all those in poor settings, the children within the top 1 per cent on the Raven's Matrices pattern test of general intelligence, scored relatively lower (1 per cent significance) on the Stanford-Binet IQ test, whereas bright children in good circumstances showed no differences. However, the average ability children living in either poor or good circumstances showed insignificant differences in their scores on the two types of test (Freeman, 1983; 1985).

The Follow-up Study: 1984–1986

In the follow-up study, 81 per cent (N=169) of the original sample of families (both children and parents) were interviewed, now often living separately, making about 350 interviews. The young people were aged 14 to 23, 60 girls and 109 boys, spread across Britain, with mean Stanford-Binet IQ 135, SD 19.9. Though the sample did have a middle-class bias, it included the full spread of economic levels, from dire poverty to great wealth.

The semi open-ended interviews averaged about four hours. The questions were asked privately in the families' homes, and each answered without knowledge of the others' responses. Yet many statistically significant pointers emerged from their answers, about the relationships between the young people's circumstances and the way they function intellectually. All the verbal material was audio-taped and analysed in detail.

The IQ Groups

It was not possible to measure the young people's learning by their examination results because they were at different stages and at different types of school. However, as the Stanford-Binet Intelligence Test is known to correlate highly with school success (for which it was of course designed), the IQ scores did provide a reliable, ordered indicator of their potential for passing exams. The sample was sorted into three IQ groups:

Table 1.   The IQ groups

IQ group	IQ Range	Percentage of sample
high IQ	140–170	44
above average IQ	120–139	31
average IQ	92–119	25

IQ and type of school. There was a distinct relationship between the pupil's IQ and the type of school he or she attended. The High IQ group were far more likely to go to selective schools (private or state), and the less intelligent to mixed ability schools. Considering the learning potential of their pupils, along with the schools' academic bias, it was really not surprising that the selective schools produced an overall higher level of examination success than the other less examination orientated schools.

There was no direct questioning of teachers in the follow-up – not least because by then many of the young people had left school. However, teachers appeared to be good judges of the examination ability of their highly able pupils, as was shown in three ways:

- by putting them in for public examinations.
- by accelerating them within the school system. Of the High IQ group, 23 per cent were either accelerated, or young for their school class.
- in the spoken and non-spoken messages given by teachers to the pupils themselves. Subjects were asked how they thought their teachers rated their ability in school. Their answers corresponded well with the IQ measure.

Study Preferences at School

In line with their IQ, significantly different styles of teaching were sought by the pupils.

Table 2.   Preferences for study alone

Prefer to work with teacher	
high IQ	87%
above average IQ	68%
average IQ	68%

Communication. Having a high IQ did not indicate a desire to work independently at school, as is often said of the gifted. In fact, those with the highest IQs much preferred to work with and bounce their ideas off the teacher.

David A. (IQ 159):   *'I talk to the teacher a lot about what I think, and what's going on in the world, and the actual theory that he's teaching us. I find talking to a teacher much more fun than talking to my peer group because teachers know so much.'*

Mixed ability. Nearly all the subjects preferred to have a say in how they would be taught, especially with regard to selection by ability.

Table 3.   Preference for selection or not

Prefer selective classes	
high IQ	80%
above average IQ	68%
average IQ	41%

Most of the High IQ group preferred to be taught in classes pre-selected by ability, rather than in mixed ability groups – even at university:

Lois A. (IQ 170): *'At university it's "mixed ability" – everybody in one class. Personally though, I prefer to be in a group where everybody wants to work quickly.'*

Reported Learning Facilities

In their self-descriptions the High IQ high achievers were significantly different from the rest in a mixture of intellectual and personal qualities.

Memory. The most useful intellectual asset appeared to be a good memory. The higher the IQ, the better the memory, which tied in closely with examination results. Yet the High IQ group, who had outstandingly good memories, did not have identical types of memory. Those who said they remembered facts best had IQs which were more than a standard deviation higher than those with other kinds of memories, such as for people. Some described highly tuned visual or auditory memory, which they could access during examinations to scrape extra marks.

Simon W. (IQ 163): *'Machine code – I could remember all of about sixty-odd totally abstract numbers all in hexi-decimal – that's to base 16 – and I could remember pairs of those as operational. I have a good memory like that. I was terribly upset, though, when I had to ask a girl what her name was, and I'd known her a year.'*

Table 4. Memory

Type of memory	Good	Facts	People	General
high IQ	84%	46%	8%	45%
above average IQ	66%	23%	15%	62%
average IQ	57%	17%	14%	69%
mean IQ	—	143	131	132

Understanding the material. The higher the IQ the more likely the young people were to look for principles, that is to use strategic thinking, and less likely to study by rote.

Jeremy S. (IQ 170): *'When I understand the principles I understand the subject, even before I start working for it. If I didn't understand them, then I'd really start worrying.'*

Concentration. The higher the IQ, the longer the concentration span the subjects claimed, though some gifted youngsters chose to use much shorter spans of as little as five or ten minutes, with constant little breaks.

Table 5. Concentration

mean IQ	Concentration
144	Many hours
138	Three hours
131	Two hours
124	One hour

Danny R. (IQ 156): *'Once, I worked from four o'clock when I got home, till half-past one in the morning, and then had my break for tea. I concentrated totally. It was just something that had to be done.'*

Multi-attentiveness. The higher the IQ the more likely the young person was to claim to be able to give attention to more than one thing at a time, and to be able to process more than one thing at once. This is the facility spotted by Schofield and Ashman (1987) as distinguishing the highly intelligent.

Dominic A. (IQ 165): *'When two people are talking to me at once, I'll understand both, rather than listening to one and understanding that, then listening to the other. So I process them together, but still holding different bits of information in my mind.'*

Motivation to study

Table 6. Pressure to achieve

Strong pressure to achieve	
high IQ	64%
above average IQ	28%
average IQ	21%

Table 7. Perceived laziness

IQ group	Parents say lazy	Subject says lazy
high IQ	6.8%	20.3%
above average IQ	13.2%	9.4%
average IQ	14.3%	—

Parental influence. In general, the higher the parents' occupational group, the higher the young person's IQ. This was also true for the levels of education of both parents, but especially of fathers. Parental occupation and education were also directly related to pressure and expectation placed on the young person to be academically successful.

Self motivation. However, the high achievers were much harder on themselves than were their parents. Considerably more of them spontaneously described themselves as lazy than in the other groups. This was not in response to questioning, but emerged so frequently that it had to be taken into account. It seemed that the gifted young people could perceive better the way that they should go and found it frustrating and blamed themselves when they were not getting there fast enough. Both the gifted and their parents were able to judge what they were capable of academically. Overall, there was a distinct relationship between academic potential and the drive to realize it, from parents, children and teachers – a powerful trio.

DISCUSSION

For anyone who is exceptional in any way, their difference from other people is bound to affect them, both in how they see life and in how life treats them. This is true for those who grow up with an exceptionally high level of intellectual ability. It affects the way each individual will experience, select and store input from the environment, though of course this is also affected by personality and social values. The highly able do have the capacity to extract more from the same educational provision than the less able (Freeman, 1983), but they cannot do their best without specific teaching and understanding of the way they function. There has to be a fit between high ability and the child's circumstances, for the exceptional really to flower.

There were several clear indictors from the Gulbenkian Research as to why some adolescents had done outstandingly better than others at their studies. The major one was their higher academic potential – sheer ability – as measured by the IQ. This included a better memory, especially long-term, and an excellent ability to concentrate. School success was greatly enhanced when the educational environment, whether of school or home, included provision of both material and good communication. Both were important, in the sense that one cannot play a violin without a violin, no more than one can learn chemistry without tuition. Unlike the conclusions drawn from other work (e.g. Fox, 1981; Tannenbaum, 1983), this research was encouraging in that both teachers and parents seemed to be competent judges of pupil potential, and made efforts to provide adequately for its growth.

As teachers always say, however, hard work is a great equalizer in school: it can substitute for talent and produce good marks. A notable proportion of the average and above average pupils had, in fact, acquired very good examination results by unstinting labour. But on balance the motivation to work was very much stronger for the gifted, who more often saw themselves as lazy, and tried to overcome this perceived deficiency. They also recognized their high level abilities, which they saw as marking them off from their age peers. The alliance of ability, hard work, provision and compatible goals for youngsters and adults is a sure recipe for success in education.

To be aware how one is thinking, planning and learning makes a sophisticated set of skills. Only those of the very highest ability and achievements in this study had accomplished it so that it was reliable and could run smoothly at will. They described insight into their mental procedures, so that they could function more nearly at their best for more time than others. This meant giving greater consideration to the substance of the material they were learning, such as looking for underlying principles, using personalized schemata, and metacognitive and simultaneous processing functions. The less successful used significantly more rote learning, and usually only from their lesson notes.

Metacognition is what children should, but do not normally, learn in school. It does not come naturally to most children to be aware of how they are thinking, planning and learning. Schools vary, of course, and a few pupils in this sample were lucky to be taught how to learn and to be aware of their learning. But there is no getting away from involvement of the whole self in learning. Everyone has to do their own learning; the teacher or parent cannot learn for the child. Usually, children do this on a fairly *ad hoc* basis, according to what they can pick up from those around them, but they need teachers who are sufficiently aware, and who are able to help them develop their exceptional potential to its fullest extent, including the highly able. At times, though, in the panic of revising for exams, even those who had found excellent learning procedures often set their metacognitive skills to one side, and dabbled higgledy-piggledy among the material they were setting out to learn. For the highly successful, as well as the less successful, rote learning is always boring, tiring and off-putting.

Although in this chapter high ability has been discussed in cognitive-intellectual, IQ terms, the Gulbenkian Project was very concerned with a more all-round view of giftedness, particularly the concepts of creativity and task commitment in the context of socio-emotional development. By including these less easily measurable aspects, it meant that their estimations had to make use of relatively subjective procedures, such as rating scales, but that is the price to be paid for more valid criteria of the identification of giftedness.

It is precisely because of their powerful learning potential, and of other people's reactions to it, that the intellectually gifted adolescent needs some extra emotional safeguards. It is important for teachers and parents to avoid too much emphasis on the development of exam passing abilities at the cost of emotional, creative and physical needs. Motivation and adjustment are equally important determinants of achievement as ability, and are also basic to the child's happiness.

The gifted adolescents in this sample were very appreciative of skilled teaching and genuine feedback on their work. They responded well to teachers who were prepared to work with them, rather than for them; teachers who were concerned with the structure of their pupils' learning and how each one could cope. In addition, for a balanced life, the highly able do need to enjoy the stimulation of like-minds from time to time, not just from the company of their teachers, but also of their contemporaries. They thrive on honest communication, the opportunity to follow their interests, and acceptance as all-round people, which is just what friends provide.

Education for the highly able should not be merely a matter of achievement, of acquiring exam successes early, culminating in a PhD at 20. It should encourage a feeling for consideration and stimulate curiosity. The highly able, at least as much as any others, should be practised at analysis and evaluation. Practically, this would involve immersing them in ideas which are complex, sophisticated and stimulating.

Separate education for the highly able has its good and bad points, but there are ways of avoiding it altogether by dovetailing some differentiation for them into normal school timetables by means of both vertical and horizontal school streaming. A great deal of school learning revolves around acquiring content, and it is not only the highly able who find this inadequate. There is a need to enrich or even completely abandon this aim for a more stimulating and cognitively demanding one. Enrichment within the normal classroom is a valuable help with many of these problems, in that those who are advanced can move on to more interesting work rather than either more of the same or escaping into day-dreaming. Special curricular materials could be shared by a group of schools, or housed in the school library for the child to go to, out of the classroom. In fact, that sort of reward, implying work well done and responsibility for oneself, also provides valuable motivation for a child with learning difficulties, who may actually be gifted. Bright children like a challenge, and they usually enjoy education which encourages creativity, a little on the wild side.

Acceleration, administratively the easiest way out for the precocious learner, was not found to be generally successful in this study, where 17 youngsters had been moved up a year or two. It seemed to work well enough in childhood, but in adolescence the gap in maturation between for example a 15 year old and a 17 year old, could be decidedly detrimental to the young person's self-concept and to family harmony. Several of those accelerated had done less well in their school leaving exams than might have been expected, and almost all the parents and the young people regretted the move.

The highly able can be expected to be as well balanced as any others, but they are also vulnerable in special ways because of their exceptionality. Poor adjustment, due to those special vulnerabilities, may result in a low self-concept, inhibited creativity due to anxiety, and scholastic underachievement, especially in gifted girls. In addition, the gifted often seem to have a heightened sensitivity, so that they can appear to over-react. Though these problems are delicate, they can be resolved with sensitive handling, maybe including counselling.

The best conditions for growth clearly involve maximizing harmony in all dimensions of consciousness. This means not allowing disorder to disrupt emotion, cognition or motivation. If you sacrifice one, it is usually detrimental to the others. The question of how much energy young people put into education, and how much into outside activities, is crucial for the kind of adults they will become. So many of the highly able are obliged to put every ounce of energy into training for the future.

LESSONS FROM THE ADEPT LEARNERS – ADAPTABLE LEARNING

The methods used by the more successful learners in this sample, are not only applicable to them, but to all children, and can be taught. They are similar to what is recognized as good teaching, but they are different in that the highly able stand to gain most from getting hold of them.

1. Everyone can be helped to find ways of learning which are better for them, such as strengthening their personal, preferred style of learning imagery.

2. Closer and more personal communication with teachers is a priority in helping the pupils to know how they can learn best. It is not as difficult as it might seem – when asked, most children are able to tell the teacher how they like to learn, though some need a little help to find out. The problem of organizing a classroom to suit individual modes of learning is faced by all teachers, with more or less success, every school day.

3. The outstandingly strong motivation to study which the intellectually gifted described, is more likely to come about and also to be reinforced, because the goals their parents and teachers have for them are within their potential, i.e. higher education will mean more of the same. However, for the non-academic pupil, lessons at school are likely to appear much less appropriate to their immediate personal needs, as well as less relevant to their future lives. The answer is to make lessons seem more relevant, to be concerned about the pupil's reception of lessons. It means talking to them about it.

4. For any learner, expert action makes use of available schemas which evolve from accumulated experience, without recourse to the original separate bits of learning or chunks – the crucial components. Since schemas are so difficult to change, it is important to catch them as they are being formed, to stop them becoming rigid and inflexible. Flexibility not only offers students the facility to retain information better, but also a greater facility for using it creatively. The ability a teacher has to encourage this is largely dependent on his or her understanding of psychology, not the theoretical kind taught in so many teacher training courses around the world, but the applied kind.

The most effective teaching, at all levels, constantly seeks to develop insight, because it is basic to the learning process, and is part of it at all levels of learning and teaching. Highly able learners are capable of and want increased cognitive stimulation, which is somewhat dependent on teachers' task-setting abilities, including a problem-posing as well as a problem-solving approach to thinking. Teaching which uses that outlook is more likely to have an immediacy to learners, and would also be unlikely to result in simplistic classroom activities, such as copying, drawing, and passive listening or regurgitation. What is required is not a total rejection of the present content, but rather restructuring of the way it is organized and presented.

To improve methods of learning in schools, teaching methods have to change somewhat in both outlook and practice. For most young people, their gifts become canalized in one direction or another, and then it is hard to change route. For the highly able, as well as the less able, the goal is to help them learn in an adaptable way, so that they can use the abilities they were born with in many different situations. Flexibility in working with others, and in using what one has learned in a wide variety of places and problems, remains for life. The attitudes of each pupil to learning, and the nature of what he or she learns are fundamental to the way in which society operates, and the consequences range immensely wide.

REFERENCES

ALBERT, R.S. and RUNCO, M.A. (1985) The achievement of eminence: A model based on a longitudinal study of exceptionally gifted boys and their families. In R. Sternberg and J.E. Davidson (Eds) *Conceptions of Giftedness*. London: Cambridge University Press.
BASTICK, T. (1982) *Intuition: How we Think and Act*. Chichester: Wiley.
BLOOM, B.S. (1985) *Developing Talent in Young People*. New York: Ballantine Books.

BUTLER-POR, N. (1987) *Underachievers in School; Issues and Intervention*. London: Wiley.

CSIKSZENTMIHALYI, M. and LARSON, R. (1984) *Being Adolescent: Conflict and Growth in the Teenage Years*. New York: Basic Books.

DAS, J.P. and HEEMSBERGEN, D.B. (1983) Planning as a factor in the assessment of cognitive processes. *Journal of Psychoeducational Assessment, 1*, 1–15.

ENTWISTLE, N.J. and RAMSDEN, P. (1983) *Understanding Student Learning*. London: Croom Helm.

FEUERSTEIN, R. (1980) *Instrumental Enrichment*. Baltimore: University Park Press.

FREEMAN, J. (1979) *Gifted Children: Their Identification and Development in a Social Context*. Lancaster: Medical Technical Press; Baltimore: University Park Press.

FREEMAN, J. (1983) Environment and high IQ – a consideration of fluid and crystallised intelligence, *Personality and Individual Differences, 4*, 307–313.

FREEMAN, J. (Ed.) (1985) *The Psychology of Gifted Children*. Chichester: Wiley.

GARDNER, H. (1983) *Frames of Mind: the Theory of Multiple Intelligence*. New York: Basic Books.

LURIA, A.R. (1982) *Language and Cognition*. New York: Wiley.

MACKINTOSH, N.J. (1986) The biology of intelligence. *British Journal of Psychology, 77*, 1–18.

MEAD, M. (1954) The gifted child in the American culture of today. *Journal of Teacher Education, 5*, 211–214.

PERKINS, D.N. (1981) *The Mind's Best Work: a New Psychology of Creative Thinking*. Harvard: Harvard University Press.

ROSS, A. and PARKER, M. (1980) Academic social self concepts of the academically gifted. *Exceptional Children, 47*, 6–10.

RUTTER, M., MAUGHAM, B., MORTIMER, P. and OUSTON, J. (1979) *Fifteen Thousand Hours*. Open Books: London.

SCHOFIELD, N.J. and ASHMAN, A.F. (1987) The cognitive processing of gifted, high average, and low average ability students. *British Journal of Educational Psychology, 57*, 9–20.

STERNBERG, R.J. and DAVIDSON, J.E. (Eds) (1986) *Conceptions of Giftedness*. London: Cambridge University Press.

TANNENBAUM, A.J. (1983) *Gifted Children: Psychological and Educational Perspectives*. New York: Macmillan.

TIZARD, B. (1985) Social relationships between adults and young children, and their impact on intellectual functioning. In R.A. Hinde, A-N. Perret-Clermont and J. Stevenson-Hinde (Eds) *Social Relationships and Cognitive Development*. Oxford: Clarendon Press.

WALLACE, A. (1986) *The Prodigy. A Biography of William James Sidis, the World's Greatest Child Prodigy*. London: Macmillan.

THE ROLE OF PRACTICE AND MOTIVATION IN THE ACQUISITION OF EXPERT-LEVEL PERFORMANCE IN REAL LIFE: AN EMPIRICAL EVALUATION OF A THEORETICAL FRAMEWORK

K. Anders Ericsson, Clemens Tesch-Römer and Ralf Th. Krampe

Most of our firsthand knowledge about exceptional performance comes from public competitions and exhibitions of élite athletes, musicians and perhaps chess masters. In such public displays we can admire the excellent musical interpretation of a soloist, the amazing speed and skill of athletes and the rapid and seemingly effortless move selection by a chess grandmaster playing against a large number of opponents. The vastly superior performance which is displayed so smoothly and often without apparent effort continues to amaze us and compels us to attribute special talents to these individuals.

However, if we are seriously interested in understanding the structure and characteristics of the displayed performance, we need to study the relevant preceding activity and preparation and shouldn't limit our study to the public performance of fully accomplished individuals. In the study of exceptional performance, there are some possible parallels with phenomena in geology and evolutionary biology. Not too long ago, it was a common belief that the various species on earth had been created by divine powers and that canyons and other geological formations were similarly created. It was inconceivable that the small brook in the middle of the valley could have been responsible for the huge canyon. We now have ample evidence that slow changes accumulated over thousands and millions of years have profound effects, which are hardly noticeable within the life span of an individual. Whether the geological metaphor is applicable to the study of exceptional performance is a testable conjecture that can be evaluated empirically by a careful examination of the processes associated with the preparation and practice necessary to achieve exceptional performance.

Recent work on expertise and skills has demonstrated the essential role of acquired characteristics in expert-level performance in a wide range of domains (Chase and Simon, 1973; Chi et al. 1982; Lesgold, 1984). Careful examination of the cognitive processes mediating superior performance on representative tasks in the respective domains of expertise has revealed that experts rely on specific knowledge. The superior performance of experts appears to be predominantly due to rapid and efficient access to relevant previous experiences and knowledge stored in their memory, thus eliminating the need for time and effort consuming problem solving. Relevant studies indicate that expert-level performance requires a vast amount of knowledge. Hence, the mere acquisition of the extensive organized body of prerequisite knowledge is a time-consuming task requiring long periods of preparation and practice.

Laboratory research on the acquisition of knowledge and skill has shown that, across a wide range of tasks, the attained level of performance is a monotonic function of the amount of practice (Anderson, 1982; Newell and Rosenbloom, 1981).

In applying the skill acquisition framework to exceptional performance in real life, the simplest claim is that improved performance is primarily a function of the amount of practice. However, the estimated amount of practice for real life expertise would be several orders of magnitude (100 to 10,000 times) larger than that monitored in laboratory studies. Simon and Chase (1973, p.402) empirically support this claim by observing that in chess: 'There appears not to be on record any case (including Bobby Fischer) where a person has reached grandmaster level with less than about a decade's intense preoccupation with the game'. In a recent review of a large number of studies, Ericsson and Crutcher (1990) showed that about ten or more years of practice and preparation are required to attain an international level of performance in the arts and sciences, and in sports. Hence, there is compelling evidence for the necessity of practice in reaching exceptional levels of performance.

In this chapter, we describe a theoretical framework for the acquisition of expert-level performance in highly competitive real-life domains such as music, sports and chess. Based on this framework, we derive hypotheses about the developmental history and practice intensity of expert-level performers and evaluate these hypotheses against empirical evidence on international, national and regional level performances in these three domains.

A Theoretical Framework for Acquisition of Expert-level Performance in Real Life

If expert-level performance is the result of long and intensive practice, an adequate theoretical framework for its acquisition must account for how practice was originally initiated and then increased to the high levels observed in expert performers. In particular, how do the performers know what to do during practice? How do they find the time and energy required for intensive training? A complete description of the period of preparation essential to attaining exceptional performance will have to take into account the inevitable changes in the daily lives of the future exceptional performers, as they increase the necessary amount of practice.

We propose that the preparation period for reaching exceptional levels of performance can be represented as a sequence of states. Each state represents the stable characteristics for a time period in the individuals' lives, such as level of performance, and amount of practice. A sequence of the various stages of such states (extracted with slight modifications from Bloom, 1985) is illustrated in Figure 1, where the first stage corresponds to the playful introduction to the domain, the second to the start of systematic practice supervised by a teacher and a coach, and the third and critical stage to attaining expert levels of performance. During the extended period of preparation, the characteristics of the corresponding states are changed incrementally to gradually match the final state.

For each state we must examine how individuals cope with the demands of different practice activities in order to maximize the rate of improvement. At the start of regular practice, individuals receive detailed instruction from teachers and coaches regarding the goal of the practice activity. In that case, the practice activity resembles the conditions of laboratory research on skill acquisition, where the amount of practice has consistently been found to be closely related to the attained performance.

There are, however, important differences between skill acquisition under laboratory conditions and in real life. The amount and distribution of practice in laboratory studies are carefully controlled and, typically, subjects will only practise for one to two hours per day for two to four days a week. In real life, there are no experimentally imposed limits on how much practice an individual is allowed. Hence, the observed amounts of total practice time is one of several interesting dependent variables that we will examine in more detail later.

The amount of practice at a given state is limited by a number of factors. In order to be able to practise, individuals need to be able to allocate their time. Depending on the individual's age, activities,

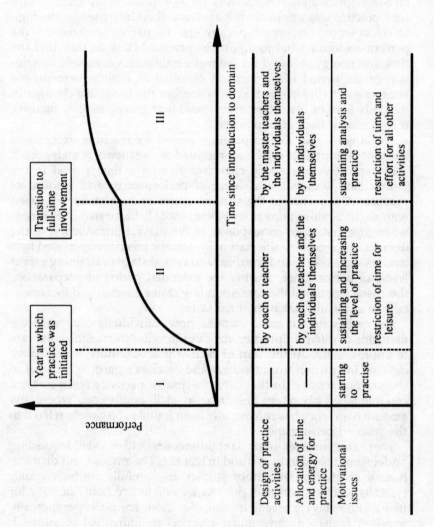

Figure 1.   Stages in the acquisition of expert level performance

school, homework or work may take priority over practice. The amount of time individuals can control and allocate to practice has to be negotiated, often at the expense of desirable leisure activities. Furthermore, the increased levels of practice have to be maintained during many years of preparation.

Practice activities, which involve careful analysis of one's performance, deliberate fine-tuning and acquisition of new procedures through massive repetition, are of a very different nature from spontaneously enjoyable activities within the domain. Examples of such spontaneously enjoyable activities are the play of children and the 'flow state', which is defined by Csikszentmihalyi (1975) as the optimal match between the individual's skill level and the demands of the chosen field, with the individual feeling fully consumed by the activity. In contrast, practice requires deliberate control and effort, which most people, especially children, find unpleasant, particularly as it is extended over longer periods of time.

Since practice activities are not spontaneously enjoyable, it is important to find out why individuals engage in practice and why they continue and even increase their efforts over extended periods of time. Hunter (this volume), in an excellent review of case studies, found that social recognition awarded to exceptional performers motivates further practice to maintain and increase the level of performance. In highly competitive domains, however, such as music and sports, with millions of motivated individuals, an explanation based on practice and motivation alone seems to be insufficient. There must be additional factors and constraints. In the following, we shall discuss developmental aspects and competition for limited resources as potential factors accounting for marked individual differences in such domains.

Developmental aspects. Skill acquisition has, for the most part, been studied in college students, without taking into account developmental aspects. With a decade or more of regular practice, it is necessary to consider developmental issues within a life-span perspective.

If ultimate level of performance is a monotonic function of prior practice, one would expect that the highest level of performance would be attained late in life. However, research on outstanding artistic and scientific contributions or world records in sports does not support that view. Instead, peak sports performance is most frequently observed between the age of 18 and 25, and major scientific discoveries and outstanding artistic creations are most frequently accomplished before the age of 40 (Ericsson and Crutcher, 1990). In accordance with earlier findings that an exceptional level of performance requires a decade or more of practice, it is essential to get an early start in the chosen domain of expertise. Thus, the developmental period prior to adulthood is critical, especially in the preparation for performance in sports.

Instruction and material resources. The developmental perspective is also very important in considering the necessary resources for optimal acquisition of skill, namely the availability of excellent instruction, time for practice, quality of practice equipment, and access to practice facilities. With respect to available time, society imposes different obligations varying with age. For example, when individuals reach adulthood, they are expected to be able to support themselves and make a living. Hence, the most practical way for adults to continue their full-time commitment to their target activity is to derive their living from that activity – to become professionals.

At high levels of performance, the quality of the teacher is increasingly important, and performers at an international level have almost invariably been instructed by master teachers, who themselves had once achieved that level or have instructed other international level performers (Bloom, 1985). In addition, a number of essential aspects of optimal practice and instruction depend on financial resources. High quality practice equipment is often expensive, the cost of instruction is high, and access to practice facilities is often limited. Children, in particular, often need transportation to and from training facilities.

Distribution of resources. In domains like music and sports, millions of motivated individuals aspire to reach exceptional levels of performance and engage in regular practice. However, society cannot support all these individuals' lifelong efforts to reach their highest level, and access to the best educational institutions with master teachers is necessarily limited. Hence, parents, teachers and educational institutions constantly evaluate the future potential of students, based on their current level of performance, usually in comparison with the performance of their peers. Although differences in performance are a function of both accumulated skill and unique inherited characteristics (talent), there has been a tendency to attribute superior performance, especially at an early age, primarily to inherent talent.

Without judging the relative importance of practice or talent, it seems that the very attribution of talent and the labelling of a person as talented plays an important role in the process of acquiring expertise. For example, parents are more willing (motivated) to make special efforts if their child is perceived to demonstrate unique characteristics or a special talent. Bloom (1985) notes that usually only one child per family receives special attention.

If children and adolescents invest a great deal in an activity, often at the expense of other options and interests, they must be confident that the sacrifice is worthwhile. The best protection against self-doubt is the conviction that they are especially talented and therefore uniquely destined for success.

Summary. It is possible to account for individual differences in performance within the skill acquisition framework. In many domains of real-life expertise, certain types of practice activities have been identified which decidedly improve performance. As a first approximation, we assume that the current level of performance is a monotonic function of the amount of practice time. Before specifying the model in more detail, we should like to point out that accumulated skill has many of the properties often attributed to inherent characteristics such as talent. If, for example, two individuals of the same age differ dramatically in accumulated practice time, for example 1,000 vs. 2,000 hours, there is no way for the less trained individual to catch up with the more experienced person, if both maintain the same weekly practice schedule.

Within our theoretical framework of the acquisition of exceptional performance, it is important to maximize the amount of practice accumulated for one's age. At those ages where external selection through awards and scholarships often means access to master teachers or admittance to musical academies and training camps, differences in accumulated practice are decisive in determining the prospects of one's career. We will first consider the empirical evidence regarding the benefits of an early start by reviewing the data on different starting ages. We will then review estimates of the amount and intensity of practice over long periods of preparation and their relation to the ultimate levels of performance.

In our review, we focus on three rather different domains, namely, chess, sports, and music, and make a cross-comparison. A common characteristic of these domains is that general schooling is not required as a prerequisite, and hence the respective skills could, at least theoretically, be acquired parallel to traditional education.

Ages of First Active Participation and Systematic Practice

Following our framework shown in Figure 1, we can identify different types of contact with a domain which reflect increasing degrees of involvement. First the individual has to be exposed to the domain before any learning is possible. Secondly, the individual engages in *active participation* in the domain, which requires access to equipment and some instruction about rules and what to do. Finally, the individual will engage in *systematic practice* and training. Table 1 lists results from different studies and, whenever possible, indicates the specific question asked to assess the corresponding type of events.

Table 1.   Mean ages at the beginning of active participation and of systematic practice for regional, national, and international performance at chess, sport and music

Domain	Source	Number of subjects/performance level of subjects	Mean age at the beginning of active participation	Mean age at the beginning of systematic practice
Chess	Krogius (1976)	40 world class	9.75 (learning the rules)	
	Mayr (1989)	25 national level	10.3 (playing chess)	13.8 (joining a club)
	Mayr (1989)	4 international level	7.25 (playing chess)	10.5 (joining a club)
Sport				
Tennis	Monsaas (1985)	26 international	6.5	8 (receiving tennis lessons)
Swimming	Kalinowski (1985)	21 international	4.5 (swimming lessons)	about 7 (joining a swimming team)
Ice skating	Kaminski *et al.* (1984)	8 national	6.3 (first contact)	8.0 (systematic training)
Swimming	Kaminski *et al.* (1984)	11 national	6.6 (first contact)	9.6 (systematic training)
Gymnastics	Kaminski *et al.* (1984)	16 national	6.4 (first contact)	8.2 (systematic training)
		17 adolescents, regional	6.9 (first contact)	9.7 (systematic training)
Runners	Sack (1980)	35 national		10.5 (joining a runners' club)
(improvers)		20 regional & district		12 (joining a runners' club)
(decliners)		19 regional & district		13.5 (joining a runners' club)
Music				
piano	Sosniak (1985)	21 international		5.7 (first piano lesson)
violin	Ericsson, Krampe, & Tesch-Römer (in preparation)	10 (best group)		7.0 (first violin lesson)
		10 (good violinists)		8.6 (first violin lesson)
		10 (music teachers)		7.7 (first violin lesson)

We shall briefly comment on the findings in the three different domains before turning to a general discussion of findings across domains and their implications for motivational factors in the acquisition of exceptional levels of performance.

Chess. The average starting age for excellent chess players is about 9 years and is remarkably consistent across the three samples reported in Table 1. Evidence for the importance of the starting age for the acquisition of international level performance is provided by Krogius (1976), who identified the age at which the players first attained an international level performance in a chess tournament. Using the data provided by Krogius (1976), we found that the starting age is closely correlated ($r = 0.48$, df $= 38$, p. < 0.001) with the age of the first achievement of international level performance.

The necessity of preparation could also be reflected in the relatively restricted ranges of starting ages of those individuals who eventually reach a world-class level. Krogius (1976) presents biographical data on world-famous chess masters born in the nineteenth and twentieth centuries. The oldest starting age among Krogius' grandmasters was 17. If we restrict the analysis to chess players born in this century, the oldest starting age is 14 and the mean starting age is 9 years. According to Mayr (1989), contemporary grandmasters start at about 7 years of age, which suggests a historical trend toward a younger starting age. Since the age of systematic practice in chess is difficult to assess, it is important to note that the age of joining a chess club is younger for the contemporary grandmasters than for contemporary national level chess masters in Mayr's sample ($t = 2.59$, df $= 27$, p < 0.05). In general, high-level chess players start quite young and those who start with systematic practice early are more likely to reach international levels.

Sports. Table 1 lists the starting ages of high-level performers in four different types of sports. The average starting age is uniformly young across the different types of sport and ranges from 4.5 to 7 years of age. Systematic training usually begins two years later, on average between the ages of 7 and 10. The importance of the starting age is suggested by the finding that gymnasts performing at national level start systematic training almost two years earlier than those performing at regional level (Kaminski *et al.*, 1984). Similarly, we find that the international-level swimmers studied by Kalinowski (1985) tend to start systematic training three years earlier than the national-level swimmers studied by Kaminski *et al.* (1984). Sack (1975) examined a large sample of 17 year old runners performing at the national, regional, and district level. When Sack (1980) re-examined the runners five years later, he found that the mean age of joining a runners' club for both successful and unsuccessful runners at the national level was 10.5 years, whereas the mean ages for successful and unsuccessful runners at the combined regional and district level was 12 and 13.5 years, respectively. In summary, ages for starting systematic practice are uniformly young and appear to be considerably younger for the best performers.

Music. Table 1 shows the average starting age for playing violin and piano, taken from four different samples. The average age of starting to take lessons is uniformly young. Evidence for the importance of the starting age is suggested by the much younger ages of the international-level performers studied by Sosniak (1985; see also Chapter 8 in this volume) compared to the other groups of musicians. One needs to be cautious, however, in comparing starting ages across instruments because the violin, for example, is a more difficult instrument for a child to handle. Ericsson *et al.* (in preparation) found that their best group started almost two years before their middle group. The violinists of the least accomplished group had starting ages comparable to the best group, but they had more interruptions and lower weekly practice times during adolescence than the other two groups. In summary, musicians tend to begin with systematic practice at an early age and early starting ages seem to facilitate attaining high levels of performance later on.

Summary and discussion of starting ages. Consistent with the hypothesis derived from the skill-acquisition framework, the starting ages for the three domains are uniformly young. Comparisons of groups of individuals differing in their level of ultimate performance show that the best performers on average have the youngest starting ages, although some of the differences are not statistically reliable due to a large variability in the starting ages. Within our theoretical framework, we do not expect a strong relationship between starting ages and ultimate performance, since a young starting age only provides a head start which must be followed by increasing amounts of continued practice in order to maintain a high level of performance into adulthood. Furthermore, it is likely that similar early preparation effects can be attained by engaging in other related activities, such as general involvement in physical activities in preparation for specific sports (Monsaas, 1985).

The average age for starting systematic practice amongst the élite performers in each of the domains is around 7 years of age, which is close to the age of starting school in most countries around the world. One could argue that the starting ages of élite performers have approached the lower bound for the earliest possible age of useful systematic practice.

It seems unreasonable to attribute the early exposure and the early beginning of systematic practice of young children to the children themselves, as their environment and activities are primarily controlled by their parents. Parents with an active interest in music and various sports will naturally expose their children to these activities at earlier ages as part of the family's leisure time. Consequently, at least one of the parents of élite performers has often been found to be interested and active in the same or a similar domain (Bloom, 1985; Fowler, 1969; Scheinfeld, 1956). At some point the child starts enjoying the activity and shows sufficient signs of promise to be encouraged to start systematic practice. It is commonly believed that early signs of promise reflect inherent talent, but this belief is questionable. First, the early performance is only outstanding with reference to other children in the immediate environment. Furthermore, even the performance of very young children may reflect acquired characteristics, as more recent research has shown that many relevant functions can be improved by externally guided activities (Leithwood and Fowler, 1971; Shuter-Dyson and Gabriel, 1981).

According to our framework, systematic practice is not inherently motivating and we must therefore carefully consider how it is initiated and maintained. During the initial playful exposure, the child develops an interest in the domain and is rewarded by the appreciation of peers and adults. The start of systematic practice appears to be initiated by one of the parents and viewed as instrumental to further improvements (Bloom, 1985: Schindler *et al.*, 1988). In the beginning, supervised practice and practice alone are short in duration and children receive a lot of encouragement from teachers and parents. The parents closely monitor their children's progress, often encourage them by stressing their attained improvement compared to earlier levels of performance (Bloom, 1985). They also help their children to acquire good practice habits. All these findings are consistent with the view that practice is not inherently motivating and is maintained, at least initially, through the active support of teachers and parents.

Sustaining and Increasing the Level of Practice through Adolescence and Early Adulthood

In this section, we review empirical evidence on the amount of training and practice as a function of age, and on the relation between levels of practice and performance. Whenever available, we also report relevant information regarding the motivational issues given in Figure 1. The results are reported separately for the three types of domain.

Chess. Unfortunately, we did not find any evidence on the amount of time élite chess players spend playing and studying chess. There are, however, some unique data available about improved competence in chess as a function of age (Elo, 1978). With the Elo Rating System, it is possible to assess the chess skills of young chess players with the same interval scale used for adults. By analysing the development of chess skills of many individuals who reached world class, international level, and national level, Elo (1978) found that at the ages of 11–12 years, differences in chess ability were relatively small between the three groups of subjects, who all played at the level of average adult chess players. Large improvements in chess ability were observed for the players during adolescence (12–18 years of age). From the ages of 18 to 22, improvements start levelling off and differences in chess ability between the three groups remain relatively unchanged. These results are unique within the three domains in that music performance is not rated on an age-independent scale and physical growth during adolescence seriously confounds available measures of sports performance.

Sports. Several studies describing various aspects of the daily lives of athletes permit an estimation of the weekly amount of time spent on their sport as a function of age. These estimates are presented in Table 2, along with information on the definition of the time estimated and the method of estimation.

In interviews of adult international-level swimmers (Kalinowski, 1985) and tennis players (Monsaas, 1985), the subjects were asked questions about their 20 year long period of preparation, and were also asked to estimate retrospectively the weekly involvement in the sport for the age periods corresponding to Bloom's (1985) stages of career development. Both studies show comparable increases in weekly involvement as a function of increased age.

National-level athletes of 12–13 years of age were interviewed about their current level of training by Ruoff (1981). They were asked to estimate how long they actually trained – excluding travel time and subsequent shower – for the hardest and the easiest day of a typical week and also for a Sunday. The same subjects were contacted three years later by Kaminski *et al.* (1984) using the same methods. From the time estimates, one can calculate time spent practising, which at the earlier age comes to about 14 hours per week. Those individuals who had remained at the national level three years later practised more (16 hours per week) than the other active athletes (13 hours per week). The better athletes practised virtually every day of the week, whereas the other athletes took a day off during the weekend. When athletes' time estimates for daily activities were compared to those of a control group, Kaminski *et al.* (1984) found that athletes' training occurred primarily at the expense of leisure time. Kaminski *et al.* (1984) also identified athletes who had stopped competing during the

Table 2. Estimated amount of weekly training and practice as a function of age for regional, national, and international level athletes

Type of sport and performance level of athletes	Swimming (international)	Tennis (international)	Swimming, ice-skating, gymnastics (national)	Swimming, ice-skating, gymnastics
Source:	Kalinowski (1985)	Monsaas (1985)	Ruoff (1981)	Kaminski, Mayer, and Ruoff (1984)
Estimation procedure:	Retrospective estimates of typical duration during the early and middle stages made over 10 years later	Hours a week playing tennis	Concurrent estimates of the hardest and easiest day of a typical week	
Definition of estimated time	Total practice time including warm-up and strength training		Total training time excluding travel time, showering and subsequent relaxation	

AGE	HOURS PER WEEK		
	International level	National level	Below national level (regional)
7			
8			13.4
9	12–16	16.8	
10			
11			
12		14.2	
13	24–30	21.4	
14			
15			16.2
16			

preceding three years. These individuals spent 4.5 hours a week on sports, which was indistinguishable from the estimate for the control group of non-athletes.

Based on the questionnaire responses of a large sample of 17 to 18 year old male runners, Sack (1975) estimated the frequency of training during a week for runners at different levels of performance. Runners at the national level trained 4.9 times per week and runners at regional and local levels 4.2 and 3.2 times per week, respectively. Apart from the number of appearances at national championships, the most adequate predictor of the subjects' best running performance was the frequency of training (r = 0.56). Questionnaire items referring to motivation (like 'regular training' and 'training during holidays') were reliably correlated both with frequency of practice and performance. Four years later, Sack (1980) contacted the runners again and divided his sample into runners with improved running performance and those with declined running performance. The running performance of improvers and decliners did not differ at the initial contact. Sack found no differences in the age of joining the sports club and of starting specialized long-distance training, and only small differences in reported training frequency at initial contact (4.8 and 4.5 times a week for improvers and decliners, respectively). However, more improvers than decliners reported that their parents were active in sports in their own youth and were supportive of their children's sports activity. The improvers' questionnaire responses revealed a higher motivation for pursuing a sports career than those of the losers: for more improvers than decliners sport was the most important area of their life, and improvers thought more about training and competition, and practised more often without training partners, during holidays or in bad weather.

Even among high-level adult runners, amount and intensity of practice emerge as the best predictor of running performance. Hagan *et al.* (1981) found that the regularity and amount of practice during the nine weeks prior to a marathon race were strongly related to running times. The length of training runs and the total distance covered per week accounted for nearly half of the variance in actual running times in the marathon (Hagan *et al.*, 1981).

Music. Most of the studies providing information on the amount of practice of high level musicians have already been described in the previous section, as Ruoff (1981) and Kaminski *et al.* (1984) included a group of musicians in their study of athletes, and Sosniak's (1985) study of international-level pianists closely parallels the studies of athletes by Kalinowski (1985) and Monsaas (1985). These studies show a remarkable agreement between athletes and musicians on amount of practice as a function of age.

In addition, Ericsson *et al.* (in preparation) have conducted a study explicitly designed to assess the role and amount of practice in high-level musicians. Among the students at the Music Academy of Berlin they identified the *best* violinists, who were judged by their music professors to have the potential for a career as an international-level soloist. Two comparison groups of violinists were recruited from the same Music Academy. One of these groups consisted of *good* music students of the same department. The other comparison group consisted of students in the department for *music teachers*, which has lower admission criteria.

As part of a larger biographical interview, each violinist estimated his or her weekly amount of practice alone for each year of their lives. The average number of hours of practising alone per week for each of the three groups is shown in Figure 2 as a function of the violinist's age. For comparison, the estimates of practice times from Sosniak (1985; international level pianists), Ruoff (1981) and Kaminski *et al.* (1984; national level musicians) and Schindler *et al.* (1988; graduates from music academies in southern West Germany) are also included in the graph.

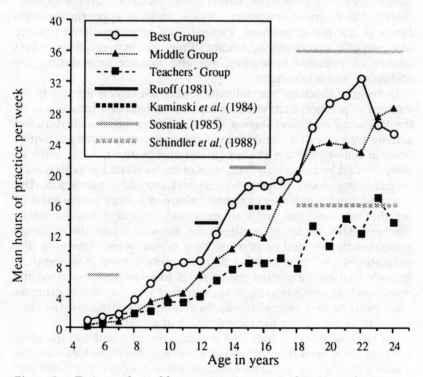

Figure 2. Estimated weekly practice times as a function of age

The two best groups of the Ericsson *et al.* study practised reliably more than the music teachers during adolescence, and the best students tended to practise more than the good students in late childhood and adolescence. At age 18 and older, there is no evidence of differences in the amount of practice between the two best groups of violinists, while the music teachers spend only half as much time on practising alone. The estimates of times for practice alone found by Ericsson *et al.* are reasonably consistent with estimates of musical activity and practice in other studies shown in Figure 2, when we consider the previously discussed differences in starting ages across studies and the restrictive definition of practising alone.

According to our theoretical framework, the most important variable determining acquired skill is the cumulated amount of practice. Based on the weekly practice times per year, one can easily calculate the number of hours a given violinist has practised for a given age. To avoid any biased assessments resulting from changes in practice behaviour due to the influence of the Music Academy, the cumulated practice time at age 18 (prior to entering the academy) was submitted to a statistical analysis. The best subjects had practised about 7,400 hours on average at that age, which is reliably more than the approximate 5,300 hours of the good subjects and the approximate 3,400 hours of the music teachers. The measure of accumulated practice integrates the marginally significant differences between the two best groups of violinists in starting age and practice time during late childhood and adolescence.

In order to check on our violinists' ability to estimate accurately the amount of practice, each violinist kept a detailed diary for a week. At the following interview session, the violinist encoded each recorded activity into one of several defined categories of everyday activities used in time-budgeting studies (Juster and Stafford, 1985), such as sleeping and body-care, or categories of music related activities, such as practising alone, playing for fun and receiving instruction. The average number of hours of practice alone in a week was around 24 for the best and the good subjects and around 9 for the music teachers. The pattern of results is the same as when the violinists estimated the amount of practice for a typical week. However, the estimates are 4–7 hours higher than amounts derived from the diaries, even when we restrict the analysis to violinists who rated the diary week as being typical. It appears that when violinists estimate their practice in a typical week, they report the amount that they aspire to attain, rather than the amount of actual practice.

An analysis of the diaries also revealed that the best and the good subjects slept, including afternoon naps, significantly more than the music teachers – by almost a full hour more per day. It appears that the best violinists practice more often in the morning just after waking up and more often sleep for brief periods during the afternoon (napping).

Summary and Discussion of Time of Practice as a Function of Age

In this summary, we shall focus on comparisons of results across studies from different types of domain.

Considering that many studies relied on retrospective estimates made years later and on informal definitions of activities, the results reviewed above are remarkably consistent. Practice activities occur on a fairly fixed schedule and vary little from week to week, and therefore can be recalled many years later with reasonable accuracy. All the studies on sports and music involving more than one measuring point show that the amount of practice of high-level subjects increases steadily as a function of age. Increases in practice time are observed even during adolescence, when school activities are very time-consuming, and high-level performers sacrifice primarily leisure time for their practice. When adolescent athletes no longer participate in competitions, their levels of practice fall off to levels comparable to those of control subjects, even though they often maintain interest and keep on participating in other sports club activities (Kaminski *et al.*, 1984). It appears that high-level musicians and athletes reach their maximal training level around the age of 20. Athletes dropping out of sports at around 20 years of age most frequently stop because of conflicts with school/professional career, time constraints and injuries (Sack, 1980).

Most interestingly, high-level subjects in different domains, such as sports and music, appear to spend similar amounts of time training, when subjects of the same level are studied with a similar interview method. Furthermore, the reported amount of practice is often highly correlated with the performance level of the subjects. Even when subjects with different levels of performance report similar current amounts of practice, there is usually a difference in the amount of practice accumulated during their careers (Ericsson *et al.*, in preparation).

Most of the reviewed results concern duration of practice, because this can easily be recalled by the subjects and verified by the experimenters. However, our theoretical framework stresses the importance of intensity of training, which is much more difficult to assess. Some of the best evidence on the critical role of intensity of training comes from the findings reviewed by Ericsson (1990) on favorable anatomical changes resulting from physiological adaptation to intense practice of élite long-distance runners. However, intense practice also leads to injuries due to systematic wearing out of critical functions, such as 'runner's knee', shin splints, and Achilles tendonitis (Subotnick, 1977). The evidence for instrument specific physiological problems is well documented in élite musicians (Fry, 1986) where blisters, sores, tendonitis and muscle spasms are the most frequently reported problems (Caldron et al., 1986). The intensity of practice can also be inferred from the limited duration of practice sessions of musicians and athletes and the regular use of periods of rest between consecutive practice sessions. Along the same line, Ericsson et al. (in preparation) found that the violinists in the two best groups slept reliably longer than the music teachers, which suggests the need of the best violinists to recover from having spent almost three times as long practising. This hypothesis is strengthened by the fact that all three groups of violinists rated sleep to be more relevant for improving one's skill as a violinist than any other daily activity and most of the music related activities.

General Discussion

In our review we have shown that the acquisition of high and exceptional levels of performance is closely related to current levels of practice and the accumulated practice time during the entire career of high-level performers in sports, music, and chess. Across these three domains, we find that the best performers appear to have a relative advantage over other subjects of the same age in their level of acquired skill due to earlier starting ages and higher levels of sustained practice for their age. Interest in the domain is generally established well before systematic practice is begun. Systematic practice is mostly initiated by parents, who very actively support and reward the acquisition of practice habits. Increases in the weekly amount of practice occur throughout adolescence, often in response to the increased demands of a more advanced teacher and coach. At the age of about 20, the level of practice has reached its maximal or optimal level. Our results extend the findings of Bloom (1985) and his collaborators, in so far as we have shown that performers at levels below international level tend to engage in less practice.

The lack of inherent motivation arising from practice is best illustrated by the fact that once individuals stop participating in public competition, their activity in that particular domain falls to the level of recreation found for control subjects (Kaminski et al., 1984). During adolescence, leisure time is primarily decreased to allow sufficient time for practice, giving rise to motivational conflicts which might account for comparatively large differences in violinists' practice times before they finally reach their different peak levels of performance (Ericsson et al., in preparation).

The factors that increase or sustain the level of practice we call motivational. Just as the current level of performance .reflects the accumulated effects of long-term practice, we argue that in the same way the factors sustaining a given level of practice over an extended time period reflect both a life style and a physiological preparedness which have been gradually acquired. By making practice activities an integrated part of one's daily life with only gradual increments in duration and intensity over time, physiological adaptations can take place easily and practice becomes habitual without the need for deliberate control and explicit incentives. Similarly, the social interactions of the élite performers primarily include other performers and coaches or teachers in the domain (Bloom, 1985), thus insulating performers from different systems of values and motivational conflicts.

The need to slowly increase one's intensity of practice is well known in sports. In spite of this, the phenomenon of 'over-use' due to rapid increase in practice occurs often in sports and interestingly enough even in music (Newmark and Lederman, 1987). In direct contrast to such abrupt changes and harmful stresses, Ericsson *et al.* (in preparation) found considerable evidence in top-level violinists for mechanisms that maintain an equilibrium of high levels of practice. The active preservation of an equilibrium is best illustrated by the increased amount of sleep associated with the much higher levels of practice of the two best groups of violinists. It seems likely that many forms of 'burn out' can be accounted for by continued depletion of the individual's resources. Such violations of maintained equilibrium are most likely due to disregard of or even inability to monitor one's own current state.

In this chapter we restricted our review to three domains with relevant empirical evidence. Sports and music are particularly suited to our theoretical framework, as teachers and coaches guide the individual's practice activity with explicit instruction. The practice activities can also be clearly distinguished and thus can be readily recalled and estimated by the individuals themselves. For chess, on the other hand, there is no available taxonomy of chess related activities and no clear consensus on which activities are most beneficial to the improvement of chess skill. The domains of scientific activities similarly lack an analysis of the corresponding activities of accomplished scientists and graduate students. Even in science, however, attempts to quantify the higher commitment of outstanding scientists have been made. Two of the most influential psychologists, Simon (Hayes, 1981) and Boring (Bruner, 1983), have independently claimed that it is necessary to work 80 hours per week for an extended period to have a chance of reaching an international level in science. In comparison, musicians at music academies estimate that they spend on the average 59 to 69 hours in a typical week on music related activities (Ericsson *et al.*, in preparation; Schindler *et al.*, 1988). When Ericsson *et al.* (in preparation) compared these estimates to the actual amount of time spent on musical activities during the diary week, they found the same pattern of results for the three groups, although the estimates for the typical week were about ten hours higher showing a bias towards overestimation. Only when Ericsson *et al.* instructed their violinists to infer their time allocation for an imagined ideal situation with a handsome fellowship, did the best violinists and the music teachers intend to spend 80 and 76 hours respectively, whereas the good students estimated 64 hours per week. In summary, the available empirical data suggest that even very successful individuals spend only 50 to 70 hours a week thus falling short of the recommended 80 hours. Based on our model and the reviewed data, the 80-hour week should most likely be viewed as a goal which cannot be sustained under normal conditions for a long time.

We conclude that it is possible to study and quantify aspects of the long developmental history and the daily lives of high-level performers in different domains. The empirical evidence shows that the development of élite performance is closely related to the amount of practice during this period. However, to engage in practice is not a natural and inevitable consequence of early exposure and interest in the domain, because the practice activity is not inherently motivating. Parents of élite performers therefore appear to play an essential role in providing social rewards and support to start and sustain regular practice of their children. Later in development, the future élite performer will be viewed as an individual who successfully negotiates a number of constraints in order to maximize and optimize his or her accumulation of practice. Our framework based on skill acquisition offers a new perspective on individual differences in high-level performance and a first step towards an understanding of the complex motivational factors which sustain the efforts to attain exceptional levels of performance.

Acknowledgement: The thoughtful comments and suggestions on earlier drafts of this chapter by Irmgard Pahl and Natalie Sachs-Ericsson are gratefully acknowledged.

REFERENCES

ANDERSON, J.R. (1982) Acquisition of cognitive skill. *Psychological Review*, *89*, 369–406.

BLOOM, B.S. (1985) Generalizations about talent development. In B.S. Bloom (Ed.) *Developing Talent in Young People*, (pp.507–549). New York: Ballantine Books.
BRUNER, J. (1983) *In Search of Mind*. New York: Harper & Row.
CALDRON, P.H., CALABRESE, L.H., CLOUGH, J.D., LEDERMAN, R.J., WILLIAMS, G. and LEDERMAN, J. (1986) A survey of musculoskeletal problems encountered in high-level musicians. *Medical Problems of Performing Artists*, 1, 136–139.
CHASE, W.G. and SIMON, H.A. (1973) The mind's eye in chess. In W.G. Chase (Ed.) *Visual Information Processing*, (pp.215–281). New York: Academic Press.
CHI, M.T.H., GLASER, R. and REES, E. (1982) Expertise in problem solving. In R.S. Sternberg (Ed.) *Advances in the Psychology of Human Intelligence, Vol.1, pp.1–75. Hillsdale, NJ: Erlbaum.*
CSIKSZENTMIHALYI, M. (1975) *Beyond Boredom and Anxiety*. San Francisco: Jossey-Bass.
ELO, A.E. (1978) *The Rating of Chessplayers, Past and Present*. London: Batsford.
ERICSSON, K.A. (1990) Peak performance and age: An examination of peak performance in sports. In P.B. Baltes and M.M. Baltes (Eds), *Successful Aging: Perspectives from the Behavioral Sciences*, (pp. 164–195). Cambridge: Cambridge University Press.
ERICSSON, K.A. and CRUTCHER, R.J. (1990) The nature of exceptional performance. In P.B. Baltes, D.L. Featherman and R.M. Lerner (Eds) *Life-span Development and Behavior, Vol.10*, (pp. 187–217). Hillsdale, NJ: Erlbaum.
ERICSSON, K.A., KRAMPE, R.Th. and TESCH-RÖMER, C. (in preparation) *Prudent practice makes perfect: An examination of the daily lives of three groups of violinists at different levels of performance.* Berlin: Max Planck Institute for Human Development and Education.
FOWLER, W. (1969) The effect of early stimulation: The problem of focus in developmental stimulation. *Merrill-Palmer Quarterly*, 15, 157–170.
FRY, H.J.H. (1986) Incidence of overuse syndrome in symphony orchestra. *Medical Problems of Performing Artists*, 1, 51–55.
HAGAN, R.D., SMITH, M.G. and GETTMAN, L.R. (1981) Marathon performance in relation to maximal aerobic power and training indices. *Medicine and Science in Sports Exercise*, 13, 185–189.
HAYES, J.R. (1981) *The Complete Problem Solver*. Philadelphia, PA: The Franklin Institute Press.
HUNTER, I.M.L. (1990) Exceptional memory performers: The motivational background, (this volume).
JUSTER, F.T., and STAFFORD, F.P. (Eds) (1985) *Time, Goods and Well-being*. Ann Arbor, Michigan: Institute for Social Research, The University of Michigan.
KALINOWSKI, A.G. (1985) The development of Olympic swimmers. In B.S. Bloom (Ed.) *Developing Talent in Young People*, (pp.139–192). New York: Ballantine Books.
KAMINSKI, G., MAYER, R. and RUOFF, B.A. (1984) *Kinder und Jugendliche im Leistungssport*. [Children and adolescents in high-performance sports]. Schorndorf: Hofmann.
KROGIUS, N. (1976) *Psychology in Chess*. New York: RHM Press.

LEITHWOOD, K.A. and FOWLER, W. (1971) Complex motor learning in four year olds. Child Development, 42, 781–792.

LESGOLD, A.M. (1984) Acquiring expertise. In J.R. Anderson and S.M. Kosslyn (Eds) Tutorials in Learning and Memory: Essays in honor of Gordon Bower, (pp.31–60). San Francisco: W.H. Freeman.

MAYR, U. (1989) Personal communication of unpublished data from a study by J. Doll and U. Mayr (1987) Intelligenz and Schachleistung – eine Untersuchung an Schachexperten. [Intelligence and achievement – a study of chess masters]. Psychologische Beiträge, 29, 270–289.

MONSAAS, J.A. (1985) Learning to be a world-class tennis player. In B.S. Bloom (Ed.) Developing Talent in Young People, (pp.211–269). New York: Ballantine Books.

NEWELL, A. and ROSENBLOOM, P.S. (1981) Mechanisms of skill acquisition and the law of practice. In J.R. Anderson (Ed.) Cognitive Skills and their Acquisition, (pp.1–55). Hillsdale, NJ: Erlbaum.

NEWMARK, J. and LEDERMAN, R.J. (1987) Practice doesn't necessarily make perfect: Incidence of overuse syndromes in amateur instrumentalists. Medical Problems of Performing Artists, 2, 142–144.

RUOFF, B.A. (1981) Psychologische Analysen zum Alltag jugendlicher Leistungssportler. Eine empirische Untersuchung (kognitiver Repräsentationen) von Tagesabläufen. [Psychological analyses of everyday life in adolescent élite-performance athletes. Empirical studies of cognitive representations of daily routines]. München: Minerva.

SACK, H.-G. (1975) Sportliche Betätigung und Persönlichkeit. [Sports activity and personality]. Ahrensburg: Verlag Ingrid Czwalina.

SACK, H.-G. (1980) Zur Psychologie des jugendlichen Leistungssportlers. Eine exemplarische Längsschnitt-Untersuchung an männlichen und weiblichen Langstreckenläufern über einen Zeitraum von vier Jahren am Ende der Adoleszenz. [The psychology of élite adolescent athletes. A longitudinal study of male and female long-distance runners over a period of four years towards the end of adolescence]. Schorndorf: Hofmann.

SCHEINFELD, A. (1956) The New Heredity and You. London: Chatto & Windus.

SCHINDLER, G., LULLIES, S. and SOPPA, R. (1988) Der lange Weg des Musikers: Vorbildung – Studium – Beruf. [The long road towards becoming a musician: preparatory training – studies – employment]. München: Bayerisches Staatsinstitut für Hochschulforschung und Hochschulplanung.

SHUTER-DYSON, R. and GABRIEL, C. (1981) The Psychology of Musical Ability (2nd edn). London: Methuen.

SIMON, H.A. and CHASE, W.G. (1973) Skill in chess. American Scientist, 61, 394–403.

SOSNIAK, L.A. (1985) Learning to be a concert pianist. In B.S. Bloom (Ed.) Developing Talent in Young People, (pp.19–67) New York: Ballantine Books.

SUBOTNICK, S.I. (1977) A biomechanical approach to running injuries. Annals of the New York Academy of Sciences, 301, 888–899.

EXCEPTIONAL MEMORY PERFORMERS: THE MOTIVATIONAL BACKGROUND

Ian M.L. Hunter

Throughout recorded history it has been noted that some people show exceptional accomplishments of memory. Their feats are dazzling. Their performances are mysterious. Their abilities are enviable. How are we to understand such people?

In order to pursue this question, I have taken the approach of a field naturalist and collected a corpus of case studies, casting a wide net over different cultures and historical periods. Each case concerns an outstanding memory performer, a star. And each gives information about three things, namely, the nature of the performance, the person's biographical background, and his or her social-cultural milieu.

The resulting corpus is not, in any sense, exhaustive. Nor is every case as detailed as might be wished. Nevertheless, the findings supply the kind of evidence needed if we earnestly seek to understand people with exceptional abilities. In particular, the body of research findings compels us to recognize that accomplishments cannot be explained by some single, simple cause. They develop over time, and in a social context, and through the interactions of many factors. Accomplishments are, for example, sometimes attributed merely to some supposed 'special gift of nature'. Special constitutional gifts may be involved but, even so, many other factors operate to bring the gifts to fruition. Appeals to special gifts are, at best, too simple and, at worst, misleading.

While mulling over the corpus as a whole, I have found that three themes emerge again and again. One is the organization or architecture of the memory feat viewed as a knowledge-based skilled performance. One is the performer's background of motivation and experience. And one concerns outside observers and how they attempt to explain the performances. These three themes intertwine and, in this chapter, I shall dwell most on the theme of motivational background.

Motivational background. When we encounter an exceptional memory performer, it is valuable to look at the biography. What are the person's main interests, values, attitudes, and pursuits? In most cases, and perhaps in all, we find a life style marked by involvement in selected orientations. The involvement is usually intense and persistant, extending over years. Two consequences flow from this.

First, the involvement has provided special experiences, special attitudes, and special bodies of knowledge and skill. These turn out to underlie the exceptional memory performance. In other words, the performance is mediated by knowledge, attitudes and skills that are, for the performer, already highly familiar and well practised.

Second, the observer is usually unfamiliar with, or even unaware of, the biographical backdrop that lies behind the performance. It is the unusualness of the performance that is striking and, by considering this in isolation, the observer tends to assume some memory faculty that is either a rare gift, or defies understanding, or is supernatural.

The role of motivational background is all too easy to ignore, even although its effects have long been recognized. Listen, for example, to William James.

> Most men have a good memory for facts connected with their own pursuits. The college athlete who remains a dunce at his books will astonish you by his knowledge of men's 'records' in various feats and games, and will be a walking dictionary of sporting statistics. The reason is that he is constantly going over these things in his mind, and comparing and making series of them. They form for him not so many odd facts, but a concept-system – so they stick. So the merchant remembers prices, the politician other politicians' speeches and votes, with a copiousness which amazes outsiders, but which the amount of thinking they bestow on these subjects easily explains. (James, 1890, vol.1, p.662)

Plan of the chapter. The plan is to review a corpus of case studies about exceptional memory performers, and to use the theme of motivational background as a guide. I shall divide the chapter into four sections. The first takes, as its starting point, a young man named Steve Faloon. The second considers the observer's frame of reference. It asks how this influences the ways in which human accomplishments are viewed. The third begins with a memory artist called K. And the fourth starts with Thomas Macaulay. Finally, a short postscript emphasizes the crucial role of a person's long-term motivational background and the importance of the enduring ethos of values to which individuals are exposed throughout their lives.

Steve Faloon

The striking accomplishments of this American university student were his dealings with the digit-span memory task. In this task, you hear a random sequence of digits spoken only once and at a rate of one digit per second: you then try to repeat back the sequence. Few people can be relied upon to repeat correctly a sequence of more than seven digits. Steve repeated any sequence up to 80 digits.

He acquired this feat by involving himself, as subject, in a psychological experiment conducted by W.G. Chase and K.A. Ericsson at Carnegie-Melon University. The aim was to discover what happens when someone has large amounts of practice with the digit-span task. For an outline of this mammoth and meticulous experiment see Hunter (1986) and also Ericsson (1985). Involvement in the experiment gave Steve the impetus, and the opportunities and encouragements that sustained, over a period of two years, more than 200 hours of concentrated practice directed at dealing better with the task. At the outset, his span was the normal seven digits. But with practice, the knowledge and skills he gained enabled him to deal with longer and longer sequences. When the experiment ended, his span was 81, and still improving.

The ways in which Steve developed his dealings with the task were akin to those that occur in athletic training. Athletes who win Olympic medals have background training that is prolonged and finely adjusted to each phase of progress. In the careers of athletes, an essential ingredient is the motivation to sustain extended training. So too in the careers of what might be called memory athletes.

Motivation on its own is not enough. An untrained person cannot gain an Olympic medal simply by an act of will. Nor is sustained training sufficient. It can be inappropriate in various ways, and can even establish habits and techniques that actually hinder progress. Nonetheless, the motivation to sustain training, although not sufficient, is essential for athletic prowess. It is noteworthy that Steve was a keen competitor in athletic running events: he had already shown a disposition to take on long-haul challenges. His athletic background would also have made him familiar with the need to manage personal resources during extended training.

As an aside, it may noted that the digit-span memory task has been used by experimental psychologists for a century. It was in the early 1980s that Steve attained his record score of 81. Since then, a second student has raised the record to 100. He, like Steve Faloon, was a keen athlete and he benefitted from learning about Steve's experiences. Why, prior to the 1980s, was it commonly assumed that such scores lay beyond human reach? Because no one had been motivated to make the demanding efforts needed to reach these high levels of performance. Steve's case raises three issues that recur throughout the corpus as a whole: values, the amount of practice, and the effects of practice.

Values. Are scores of 81 or 100 worth the effort, the dedication, and the facilities needed for training? In terms of what most of us value, we would not readily engage in the long-haul training that is needed. We live in a culture where large digit-span scores do not have the value that is placed on, say, athletics, or chess, or music. Yet, if digit-spans were so valued, many people would be motivated to acquire long spans.

Values are important for motivation. They influence which of our many human possibilities are encouraged. And it turns out that people with exceptional memory abilities often do place great value on, and have motivational investment in, pursuits that other people regard as pointless. To illustrate, consider in conjunction the cases of S (Luria, 1969), of VP (Hunt and Love, 1972) and of A.C. Aitken (Hunter, 1977). Each case shows a unique configuration but also shows that unusual accomplishments are encouraged by unusual, long-standing enthusiasms. Excerpts from these three case reports are included in Neisser (1982).

Amount of practice. Why does Steve Faloon's record score require so much training? A lot is known about the architecture of his feat: what he is actually doing while listening to a string of digits and, later, while recalling the string. To summarize briefly, he takes incoming digits in groups of three or four, encodes each group into a memorable unit, locates the unit in a predetermined structure, and then deals likewise with the next group of digits. When he comes to recall, he works through the overall structure he has imposed, regenerates the memorable units at each distinctive location and, thence, produces the digits in their correct sequence.

All of this involves the deft use of a large repertoire of knowledge-based skills. The components of this repertoire had to be evolved, and Steve had to become fluent in their use. Only then did he come into possession of the resources that underlay his digit-span score. The size and intricacy of the underlying repertoire of knowledge and skill make large amounts of practice essential. Steve's feat is not based on some simple trick or 'memory secret' that can be imparted to other people so as to enable them, without effort and practice, to emulate his performance.

Effects of practice. The end result of Steve's practice was that he acquired what can be described correctly as a domain specific mnemonic system. This system was tailored superbly well to the requirements of a specific type of memory task, namely, the digit-span task. But the applications of the system were fairly narrowly confined to this type of task. He did not strengthen general purpose memory or retentiveness. The effects of Steve's practice were to change his repertoire of knowledge, skill and attitude, but not to increase some supposedly general power of memory. This is also true of other people who have acquired exceptional memory through practice.

There are, for example, artists who become expert in examining paintings in such a way as to be able to reproduce close copies from memory (Boisbaudran, 1911). There are people who acquire mnemonic systems that enable them to deal with specific types of memory task involving the memorization of lists of material that are normally regarded as meaningless. Thus, one individual used a system to memorize lists of words that were presented under timed, rapid-fire conditions (Gordon *et al.*, 1984). Another person made use of a system in order to memorize, in his own time, the number pi to more than eleven thousand places (Smith, 1983, pp.64–7). There is the case of John Conrad, a restaurant waiter, who successfully set out to train himself to take and deliver the orders given by a large group of diners, without any written notes (Singular, 1982; Ericsson and Polson, 1988). In these cases, the people concerned are typically no better than average at memory tasks that fall outside their specialism. Clear cases of this are cited by Smith (1983, p.48ff) who discusses the memory skills of various mental calculators.

These findings about the more or less specific effects of practice cast doubt on the popular notion of a content-free power of memory that is improvable through practice regardless of the domain of memory task involved. It is true that, with practice, almost anyone can improve performance on any particular class of memory task. It is true that, with extended and felicitous practice, people can acquire memory abilities of Olympic stature. It is also true that practice can encourage people to value, or to de-value, memorization as an end in itself. But the notion that practice can improve general purpose memory is probably a fiction.

To conclude this section, Steve Faloon's case demonstrates vividly that an unusual background of motivation and experience can have extremely powerful effects on memory accomplishments. Steve corroborates the remark made in 1769 by Joshua Reynolds, the portrait painter, in relation to artistic abilities.

> Not to enter into metaphysical discussions on the nature or essence of genius, I will venture to assert, that assiduity unabated by difficulty, and a disposition eagerly directed to the object of its pursuit, will produce effects similar to those which some call the result of *natural powers*. (Reynolds, 1975, p.35)

Finally, notice that Steve's mnemonic system works unobtrusively and, so to say, behind the scenes. Because of this, observers who are unaware of Steve's system might easily interpret his performance within a frame of reference that leaves out what is crucial. The next section considers this issue of the frame of reference within which observers notice and interpret exceptional memory performers.

The Observer's Frame of Reference

From the sixteenth century onwards, Westerners became increasingly aware of people who lived in what were regarded as primitive cultures. It was often reported that primitive people had exceptional powers of memory. Nowadays, we can see that many of these reports were misinterpretations due to ethnocentric frames of reference. Reporters failed to appreciate that other cultures have other life styles and interests. To illustrate, consider Lévy-Bruhl (1925) who held a theory that primitive people have a different mentality which he called 'pre-logical'.

> The preconnections, preperceptions, and preconclusions which play so great a part in the mentality of uncivilized peoples do not involve any logical activity: they are simply committed to memory. We must therefore expect to find the memory extremely well developed in primitives, and this is, in fact, reported by observers. (p.110)

In support, he cites the following kinds of observation.

> 'In many respects,' say Spencer and Gillen of the Australian aborigines, 'their memory is phenomenal.' 'Not only does a native know the track of every beast and bird, but after examining any burrow, he will at once, from the direction in which the last track runs, tell you whether the animal is at home or not. . . . Strange as it may sound . . . the native will recognize the footprint of every individual of his acquaintance.' The earliest explorers of Australia had already referred to this marvellous power of memory. Thus Grey tells us that three thieves were discovered by their footprints. 'I got hold of an intelligent native of the name of Moyee-e-nan, and accompanied by him, visited the garden whence the potatoes had been stolen; he found the tracks of three natives, and availing himself of the faculty which they possess of telling who has passed from their footmarks, he informed me that the three thieves had been the two wives of a native . . . and a little boy named Dal-be-an.' Eyre is astonished at 'the intimate knowledge they have of every nook and corner of the country they inhabit.' (pp.110–1)

Now, these performances are unusual from a Western standpoint. But in another culture the way of life may motivate people to notice, remember and know about things that have no salience in the culture from whence the observer comes. With fuller appreciation of cultural differences, we may change our view about exceptional memory in other cultures.

Cultural differences. People in other cultures do sometimes show memory performances that are strikingly superior by Western standards. Take the Australian Aborigines who live in desert regions (see Hunter, 1979, and Kearins, 1981). Whether their accomplishments are influenced by genetic selection is open to conjecture. What is certain is that their memory performances are of a kind that is adaptive to daily life in the traditional Aboriginal terrain and culture. The pervasive requirements of their everyday life could well exert far-reaching effects on the mental development of anyone constantly exposed to them.

In contrast to the constitutional interpretations of Lévy-Bruhl, consider Bartlett's account of the Swazis of South Africa (Bartlett, 1932). He reports the striking episode of the Swazi herdsman who recalled details of the cattle purchased by his employer a year earlier. Bartlett interprets this in a cultural frame of reference: he stresses that, in Swazi culture, cattle and all dealings with them attract tremendous day to day interest and are highly salient in people's daily preoccupations. Consider also the sensitive account which Gladwin (1970) gives of navigational knowledge and skill in Micronesia.

With fuller appreciation of cross-cultural differences, we even come to recognize that some of the memory accomplishments we take for granted in our own culture do not occur in other cultures. Take the 'free recall task' in which you hear a list of words and then try to recall as many of the words as you can. You hear the words in random sequence but they are taken from several categories such as names of foods and names of utensils. You are likely to recall the words, not in the sequence in which you heard them, but in clusters according to category, for example, the food words are recalled together and the utensil words together. When this type of task is given in Western cultures, it is found that almost all normal children develop, between the ages of six and ten years, an increasing use of clustered recall. But this development does not occur in normal children who live in the Kpelle culture, an African culture that does not involve literacy and formal schooling (see Hunter, 1985a). In short, the development of clustered recall is not inevitable. It is an adaptation to knowledge-handling practices that are so commonplace in our culture that we, who are immersed in the culture, fail to be aware of the effects they exert on mental development.

Differences within a culture. Even when we confine attention to our own culture, we find people who become expert in special skills, such as chess or telegraphy and, as a by-product, perform what can rightly be described as exceptional feats of memory. Take the 'chessboard reconstruction task' in which you are briefly shown a display of chess pieces on a chess board and, after the display has been removed, you try to recall it in detail. Chess experts do well in this task, and to an extent that baffles those of us who are unskilled in chess (see Chase and Simon, 1973; Binet, 1966). For us, the task seems to call for brute memory. But for chess experts, the task enables them to deploy their intimate knowledge of chess and to grasp the display in terms of familiar patterns of pieces. Likewise, in the field of telegraphy, an expert can listen to and reproduce a lengthy sequence of dots and dashes with which a novice cannot cope. The feat of memory is, again, a by-product of special expertise which the novice has not acquired.

Clearly, then, performers who strike observers as having some mysterious memory faculty can turn out to be deploying familiar knowledge and well-practised skills. This point may seem obvious, but it has often been disregarded in the history of psychology. Investigators have repeatedly tended to explain exceptional performances by postulating corresponding constitutional faculties. This tendency is seen, at its height, in the nineteenth century doctrine of phrenology. I shall illustrate the tendency by referring to the frames of reference that were brought to two phenomena, namely, oral traditions in non-literate cultures, and *idiots savants*.

Oral traditions. How can non-literate cultures, without benefit of written records, transmit knowledge of family histories, legends, epics and ballads? In the eighteenth and nineteenth centuries, Westerners approached this question by assuming what was, to them, a familiar frame of reference – written literature. They even referred to oral traditions as 'oral literatures'. This frame implied that, in non-literate cultures, there must be people with a memory gift for listening to long sequences of spoken material and remembering them word for word with, as it were, tape-recorder memory. But it turns out that people do not have tape-recorder memory and that the literature based frame of reference is entirely mistaken when applied to non-literate cultures (Hunter, 1985).

To be specific, take the Yugoslav singers of epic songs who were thoroughly studied in the 1930s (Lord, 1960). These singers lived in a culture that was mainly non-literate. Most could neither read nor write. Yet they sang long epic tales. It turned out that they were expert in a kind of accomplishment that involved highly skilled improvization. They used an intricate repertoire of compositional constraints which they had acquired through extensive experience and practice. They used these constraints to compose the epic afresh each time it was sung. Their performances in rendering an epic were not at all comparable to the verbally fixed ɪecall of a memorized piece of literature. In modern literate cultures, the Yugoslav's kind of compositional accomplishment is unfamiliar, although not entirely so. (See the study of ballad singers in North Carolina by Wallace and Rubin, 1988 and 1988a.)

Idiots savants. This French term dates from the early nineteenth century and refers to people who show an island of special ability amid general mental handicap. The island is not usually excep-tional by normal standards, but occasionally it is. For example, Noel Paterson, at the age of 23 and with an IQ of 60, is remarkably able, by any standard, to memorize melodies that are played to him on the piano. His case is reported by Sloboda *et al.* (1985) and by Sloboda (1986, pp.35–7). These reports establish two things. First, Noel's ability is not of a tape-recorder kind but involves knowledge of conventional musical structures. Second, he has been preoccupied for 15 years or more with music. His preoccupation, day in and day out, has excluded almost all other activities and has certainly provided opportunity for extensive amounts of special experience and practice.

So also with David Kidd whose compulsive preoccupation is with calendar calculations. Give him any date and he will, after two or three seconds, tell you the day of the week on which the date fell (or will fall). At the age of 28, David has spent more than 15 years preoccupied almost exclusively with calendars and calendar calcula-tions, and his performances show some use of rule based procedures. He is one of several idiot savant calendar calculators studied by O'Connor and Hermelin (1984) and Hermelin and O'Connor (1986). See also the case studied by Howe and Smith (1988).

There is still much to be learned about idiots savants with ge-nuinely exceptional intellectual accomplishments, but there is general appreciation that their abilities arise largely from the effects of emo-tional and motivational dispositions. However, early investigators tended to view idiots savants as being endowed with special intellec-tual aptitudes. In 1908, for example, the first edition of a standard textbook on mental deficiency had a chapter entitled 'Idiots savants' (Tredgold, 1908). The frame of reference assumed a special intellec-tual gift. Just as normal adults can suffer brain injuries that debilitate but spare certain abilities, so were idiots savants assumed to have constitutionally impaired brains in which certain aptitudes were spared. In the ninth edition of the textbook (Tredgold and Soddy, 1956), the chapter is still included but the frame of reference has now shifted from spared aptitudes towards motivational and emotional factors. The authors remark that the original author:

was inclined to postulate an increased development of certain groups of neurones. However, today, it seems more probable that the condition is more of emotional origin and may be allied to the group of 'damaged' children described earlier in this volume, in which intellectual development has become cut off from the main stream of development and has become obsessionally canalized. The two boys, Mischa and Arthur represent a condition allied to that of the idiot savant. (See chapter xi). (p.448)

The star memory performer to whom I now turn illustrates some of the characteristics of the idiot savant.

The Memory Artist called K

This American did a vaudeville act that rested on his answering factual questions about, for example, the populations of American cities, the number of rooms in leading American hotels, distances between cities, lengths of rivers, and heights of mountains. He had thousands of such factual morsels at his fingertips. He was billed as 'memory artist' and 'genius', and he believed his own publicity that he had unusual powers to learn, retain, and recall facts.

When he was 38 and had been working with his act for more than ten years, he was studied by Jones (1926). K cooperated willingly in the study, gave information about his past history, and took various tests.

As regards biography, K had a history of poor school work, difficulty in social relations, and a marked compulsion to measure and count.

One month I counted the number of bites of food I took, and it was 9,510 bites. I counted the number of steps doing chores around the house, and the number of steps from our door-step to the post-office four miles away. I bought a yardstick and measured how far it was to a spring in the woods, and it was 223 yards. (p.375)

K left school at 17 and, a few years later, began his career as a memory artist. As a result of newspaper reports about his special interests, he was promised an engagement in a vaudeville circuit if he would memorize the 1910 census for towns of over 2,000 in population. He claimed that he did this in about three weeks, working from six to eight hours a day. Once started on his career, he kept adding new quantities of data to his equipment. At the time of the study, he had compiled a handbook containing 130 pages of data, and was at work on a larger compendium. 'Dripping with facts, he is under a compulsion to talk shop at every opportunity. When on tour, his letters read like an abstract from the World Almanac; no statistical morsel is too slight to be mentioned.' (p.376)

K took an IQ test (the Stanford Revision) and gained an IQ score in the upper 70s. With the auditory digit-span task, he correctly repeated sequences of six digits, but three trials with seven digits resulted in uniform failure. He took several tests where he was given material to memorize and recall under timed conditions, for example, pairs of words. His scores fell far below the norms for average college students. Jones summarizes as follows.

> We are not then confronted with the task of explaining a high memory ability coupled with a dull intelligence, but rather with the analysis of the *drive* which has led a person with inferior general capacities (as inferior in his special field of memorizing as in other functions) to devote his life to pseudo-intellectual activity. (p.374)

It turns out, then, that K owed his repertoire of unusual factual knowledge, not to superior intellectual gifts, nor to a mnemonic system, but to strong, narrowly channelled motivation. Was his doggedness misguided? Many people might say so. But notice that it had value so far as K was concerned. It gave him a livelihood, public recognition, self-respect, a purpose in life, a role in society. And it gave all this while allowing him to engage in pursuits of the kind he relished above all others. He attributed his accomplishments to 'genius', but it would be uncharitable to insist that he recognize his error. The fact is that he did have exceptional memory accomplishments, even though they arose through obsession rather than exceptional, or even average, intellectual abilities. It could be said that he was a socially successful idiot savant.

Methods of investigation. The case of K raises a general issue about psychological investigation. Jones gave K some standardized tests. Now, suppose the results of these tests were the only information we had about K. They give no inkling that he could earn his livelihood as a memory artist. In the context of Jones's study, the results were illuminating but, taken in isolation, the results fail to capture any of the characteristics that brought K to notice in the first place. This alerts us to be circumspect about how we study people with unusual accomplishments. We need to consider their background and to include tests that allow them to work in their own preferred ways.

As it happens, Jones did ask K about his customary habits of memorizing, and got the following comment.

> I can memorize things best when I see them on paper, and best of all when I write them down. Anything new I usually like to write three or four times so as to be sure not to forget it. About once a year I try to brush up everything I know, and go over all the facts in my notebooks. (p.372)

Jones also gave K some memorizing tasks that K was free to tackle as he wished. He was, for example, shown a ten digit number and asked to memorize it. He studied it for 35 seconds, and gave a perfect recall after a four hour interval. He described his procedure as follows:

> When I saw this number I read it as 4,836,179,621. I remembered 4 because of the 4th of July. 836 I just had to memorize, without any help, but if I were doing it again it would probably occur to me that 836 was the Chinese population of the state of Texas in 1910, and then I couldn't forget it. 179 is easy to remember because that is the number of miles from New York to Harrisburg, and 621 is the number of a house I know in Denver, Colorado. (p.372)

In this test, we see something of K's distinctiveness. He shows his acquaintance with lots of numerical facts; and he uses these to form groups that he can encode in terms of familiar knowledge.

How was his knowledge organized? By their nature, the factual morsels did not lend themselves to much in the way of organization. For the most part, he must have known them merely as isolated pairs of items, for example, a town and its population. But some organization may have come from the written handbooks on which he laboured. Jones gives no details about these written records and we can only speculate as to whether or not they were constructed according to some system.

Leslie Welch. This Englishman did an act, on radio and stage, which involved him answering questions about sporting statistics. He was billed as 'The Memory Man'. In the early 1960s, I interviewed him at the height of his successful career (he was born in 1907), and the following points emerged. He was a man of good general intelligence who had been a sports journalist and eventually edited a weekly newspaper devoted to sports. Needless to say, he was enthusiastic about sports and knew a lot about the world of sport. On the basis of this knowledge, he developed his secondary career as a memory entertainer (see Barlow, 1951, pp.164–5).

The requirements of his secondary career motivated him to adopt a more systematic policy about assembling written records and brushing up on them from time to time. He was selective about the information he kept in mind, and regularly discarded factual items that did not serve the purposes of his act. He also developed techniques of audience interaction. During a performance, he invited questions from the audience and could, to some extent, guide the lines along which the questions came. Also, he could often ignore a question to which he did not know the answer. When he did take such a question, his routine was to admit ignorance, ask for the answer, and promise truthfully that he would know the answer if the question came up again.

He did not regard himself as having any unusual gifts of memory. As he saw himself, he just knew a lot about a domain in which he had been keenly interested for many years, and had added a few theatrical techniques. His knowledge of sporting statistics was organized in terms of a variety of intersecting themes which he could use in order to discuss and comment upon the world of sport. In this regard, he differed from K. K piled up self-contained morsels while Welch was something of a scholar. Our next star performer was a scholar on a grand scale.

Thomas Macaulay

This Englishman (1800–1859) was a scholar in many fields and is legendary for his memory. He commanded immense ready knowledge about history, the law, politics, languages, and literature. Charles Darwin met him at the house of Lord Stanhope, the historian, and recorded the following.

> Lord Stanhope once gave me a curious little proof of the accuracy and fullness of Macaulay's memory. Many historians used often to meet at Lord Stanhope's house; and, in discussing various subjects, they would sometimes differ from Macaulay, and formerly they often referred to some book to see who was right; but latterly, as Lord Stanhope noticed, no historians even took this trouble, and whatever Macaulay said was final. (Darwin, 1958, p.38)

Macaulay can be taken as a prototype for the scholar whose knowledge is organized in a dense web of intersecting themes. New material is grasped in terms of more than one theme, and is recalled for its relevance to more than one theme. Thus, the new material, if it interests the scholar, is richly encoded and can be recalled for a variety of purposes. If Macaulay's purpose was to recall the material with full exactness, this he could often do. If his purpose was to recall features of the material that were relevant to one or another theme, this he could also often do.

Macaulay's biography by Trevelyan (1978) shows that Macaulay's memory accomplishments were formidable and an integral part of his scholarly life style (see Hunter, 1985). He had a passion for language related materials, knew a lot about them and kept his knowledge alive by constantly using it and relating it to new knowledge. In the field of history, he habitually imagined himself participating in the concrete circumstances of historical episodes (what he called castle building) and was always alert to pick up further circumstantial details.

Long-haul scholarship. Take the work for which he is best known, his multi-volume *History of England*. He conceived this work as a long-term undertaking. He gave up a prosperous public career and most of his social life in order to clear his time and energy. He searched out, read, and devoured quantities of documentation. He pieced his material together to construct a story that was not merely coherent but expressed a political philosophy. This story became what is now called the Whig view of history. On top of this, he put immense efforts into making his *History* attractive to read: he deliberately worked into it human interest, picturesque detail, and narrative thrust. This mammoth undertaking occupied years. It required sustained motivation. It demanded acquiring, managing, and synthesizing huge ranges of knowledge.

Now, other scholars have completed similarly dedicated, long-haul courses, for example, Charles Darwin on evolution, Edward Gibbon on the history of the Roman Empire, Samuel Johnson on his *Dictionary*, and James Boswell on his biography of Johnson. When we look into the daily lives of such people, as we often can through written records, what is most striking is that they pursued their chosen fields with a dedication and industry that precluded what many people would regard as a normal life.

These long-haul scholars knew a great deal about their fields and, on this ground, they are often described by outsiders as having exceptional memory. But interestingly, they themselves seem typically to take a different view and regard themselves as having only ordinary memory abilities. It is my general impression that it is the outsider who tends to talk about remarkable memory while the insider talks more about the cumulative effects of industry. There are two notable exceptions to this general impression. One is James Boswell who publicly claimed a special facility for remembering the conversations of Dr Johnson. We now know a lot about how Boswell assiduously gathered and recorded these conversations, and it turns out that the claim was made mainly for publicity purposes, to assure readers of the authenticity of the conversations in *The Life of Johnson* (see Hunter, 1984). The other notable exception is Macaulay.

Macaulay stressed his mastery of memory. This was important to his self-esteem and to the public image that he actively fostered. It motivated him to learn written materials by heart, and to show off to others, as well as to himself, that he had done so. It led him to scorn people who boasted poor memory: 'They reason thus, the less memory the more invention' (Trevelyan, 1978, vol.2, p.413). He was, of course, not unique in being influenced by a strong self-image. Many people have been motivated by a sense of destiny or of possessing a special talent that needed expression. But he was certainly unusual in placing memory at the very centre of his self-image.

Selectivity. Nevertheless, he was selective about what he noticed and remembered. He had, for example, no interest in music. For him, music had no value. It was noise that got in the way of conversation. Thus, at a social gathering in Windsor Castle: 'I got on as well as I could. The band covered the talk with a succession of sonorous tunes. "The Campbells are coming" was one.' Trevelyan notes that 'this is the only authentic instance on record of Macaulay's having known one tune from another' (vol.2, pp.223–4).

When we view Macaulay's legendary memory in the detailed setting of his life and values, the following comment by William James applies.

> Let a man early in life set himself the task of verifying such a theory as that of evolution, and facts will soon cluster and cling to him like grapes to their stem. Their relations to the theory will hold them fast; and the more of these the mind is able to discerne, the greater the erudition will become. Meanwhile, the theorist may have little, if any, desoltory memory. Unutilizable facts may be unnoted by him and forgotten as soon as heard. An ignorance almost as encyclo-paedic as his erudition may coexist with the latter, and hide, as it were, in the interstices of its web. (James, 1890, vol.1, pp.662–3)

Macaulay's love of language and its uses was strongly shaped by his admiration for the classical art of oratory. This art takes us to the earliest recorded collection of cases of exceptional memory and, so, is a theme on which the present chapter may suitably end.

Classical oratory. Oratory or rhetoric or public speaking was especially valued in Classical Greece and Rome. Its techniques were examined and written about at length, but not with the aim of mere theorizing. The aim was practical, to help speakers master the skills of legal and political public discourse. A speaker had to inform, persuade, and hold the attention of his audience. To achieve this, he had to do several things by way of preparation, and these were considered under the headings of the so-called parts of rhetoric. There were usually five parts. Gather your information (called 'invention'). Arrange your information in some order ('disposition'). Select words to express your information ('elocution'). Make sure you will be able to remember what you plan to say ('memory'). Finally, deliver your speech effectively in public ('action').

Each part of rhetoric had detailed aspects, and it was the memory part that brought mention of named people with remarkable memory. The aim was to review the full repertoire of knowledge-handling skills that an orator might use to ensure he remembers what he hears in public debate and what he wants to say. People with exceptional memory were of interest for the techniques they could offer. These techniques were examined, not as procedures to be followed slavishly, but as resources to be understood and drawn upon according to taste and the demands of the situation. They included such things as mastering a brief, writing out a speech verbatim beforehand, improvising from a mental précis, rehearsal, and mnemonics. Orators discussed these techniques and the contexts in which they applied; and the cultivation of these techniques led orators to become star memory performers. See Quintilian's marvellously perceptive books about the art and education of orators (Butler, 1922): the memory part is mainly in Book X and Book XI.

Postscript

I have tried to review a corpus of case studies about people with exceptional memory accomplishments. I shall now sketch the landscape that seems, to me, to emerge.

The bedrock is motivation and experience. The star performers have a background of special interests, experiences, and bodies of knowledge and skill. This background is easily overlooked by outside observers who view the memory performances in isolation.

Regarding the ways in which memory stars organize their knowledge, the three cases I have taken as starting points mark three distinguishable modes: the mnemonic, the piling up, and the scholarly. These modes are not, however, exclusive. Cases can be found that blend these modes in various ways.

Regarding memory improvement, three points emerge:

1. There are techniques to be learned from star memory performers. But they are not simple 'memory secrets' to be detached from context and taken over without effort. They have to be approached, as they were by classical orators, as techniques with properties to be understood and with effects that require appropriate practice.

2. It would be excessive to claim that everyone could come to emulate any of the star performers. Could K become a Macaulay?

3. It is likely that a large proportion of people could become memory stars, but only at the cost of changing to another life style that gives priority to different interests and pursuits. The memory accomplishments of, say, James Boswell are not gained without adopting much of his life style and values.

Regarding the general issue of encouraging accomplishments of whatever selected kind, the central message from the corpus is, in a word, *values*. In relation to any individual, it is informative to ask the following question. What are the dominant values, explicit and implicit, in the world in which they live? What are the valued life styles, activities, role models, assumptions, beliefs, and aspirations? What, in brief, is the motivational background to the person's life, day by day, year by year? The answer to this question predicts much about the activities the person will undertake and sustain, and these predict much about the accomplishments that will come to fruition. Particular accomplishments are, so to say, the fruits of a person's line of sustained and habitual involvements, and these particular fruits do not fall to people who undertake a different line of involvements.

REFERENCES

BARLOW, F. (1951) *Mental Prodigies*. London: Hutchinson.
BARTLETT, F.C. (1932) *Remembering*. Cambridge: Cambridge University Press.
BINET, A. (1966) Mnemonic virtuosity: a study of chess players. *Genetic Psychology Monographs*, 74, 127–162. (First published in French, 1893)
BOISBAUDRAN, H.L. (1911) *The Training of the Memory in Art*. London: Macmillan.
BUTLER, H.E. (1922) *The Institutio Oratoria of Quintilian, vol.IV*. London: Heinemann.
CHASE, W.G. and SIMON, H.A. (1973) The mind's eye in chess. In W.G. Chase (Ed.) *Visual Information Processing*, (pp.215–281). New York: Academic Press.
DARWIN, F. (1958) *The Autobiography of Charles Darwin and Selected Letters*. New York: Dover Publications. (First published 1892)
ERICSSON, K.A. (1985) Memory skill. *Canadian Journal of Psychology*, 39, 188–231.
ERICSSON, K.A. and POLSON, P.G. (1988) An experimental analysis of the mechanisms of a memory skill. *Journal of Experimental Psychology: Learning, Memory, and Cognition*, 14, 305–316.
GLADWIN, T. (1970) *East is a Big Bird: Navigation and Logic on Puluwat Atoll*. Cambridge, Mass.: Harvard University Press.
GORDON, P., VALENTINE, E. and WILDING, J. (1984) One man's memory: a study of a mnemonist. *British Journal of Psychology*, 75, 1–14.
HERMELIN, B. and O'CONNOR, N. (1986) Idiot savant calendrical calculators: rules and regularities. *Psychological Medicine*, 16, 885–893.
HOWE, M.J.A. and SMITH, J. (1988) Calendar calculations in 'idiot savants': how do they do it? *British Journal of Psychology*, 79, 371–386.
HUNT, E. and LOVE, T. (1972) How good can memory be? In A.W. Melton and E. Martin (Eds) *Coding Processes in Human Memory*, (pp.237–260). Washington, D.C.: Winston.
HUNTER, I.M.L. (1977) An exceptional memory. *British Journal of Psychology*, 68, 155–164.
HUNTER, I.M.L. (1979) Memory in everyday life. In M.M. Gruneberg and P.E. Morris (Eds) *Applied Problems in Memory*, (pp.1–24). London: Academic Press.
HUNTER, I.M.L. (1984) Lengthy verbatim recall (LVR) and the mythical gift

of tape-recorder memory. In K. Lagerspetz and P. Niemi (Eds) *Psychology in the 1990s*, (pp.425–440). Amsterdam: North-Holland.

HUNTER, I.M.L. (1985) Lengthy verbatim recall: The role of text. In A.W. Ellis (Ed.) *Progress in the Psychology of Language, vol.1.*, (pp.207–235). London: Lawrence Erlbaum.

HUNTER, I.M.L. (1985a) Memory development: The cultural background. In A. Branthwaite and D. Rogers (Eds) *Children Growing Up*, (pp.104–111). Milton Keynes: Open University Press.

HUNTER, I.M.L. (1986) Exceptional memory skill. In A. Gellatly (Ed.) *The Skilful Mind*, (pp.76–86). Milton Keynes: Open University Press.

JAMES, W. (1890) *The Principles of Psychology*. New York: Henry Holt.

JONES, H.E. (1926) Phenomenal memorizing as a 'special ability'. *Journal of Applied Psychology*, 10, 367–377.

KEARINS, J. (1981) Visual spatial memory in Australian Aboriginal children of desert regions. *Cognitive Psychology*, 13, 435–460.

LÉVY-BRUHL, L. (1925) *How Natives Think*. London: Allen & Unwin.

LORD, A.B. (1960) *The Singer of Tales*. Cambridge, Mass.: Harvard University Press.

LURIA, A.R. (1969) *The Mind of a Mnemonist*. London: Cape.

NEISSER, U. (1982) *Memory Observed*. San Francisco: Freeman.

O'CONNOR, N. and HERMELIN, B. (1984) Idiot savant calendrical calculators: maths or memory? *Psychological Medicine*, 14, 801–806.

REYNOLDS, J. (1975) In R.R. Wark (Ed.) *Discourses on Art*. New Haven: Yale University Press. (First published 1797)

SINGULAR, S. (1982) A memory for all seasonings. *Psychology Today*, 16, no.10, 54–63.

SLOBODA, J.A. (1986) Acquiring skill. In A. Gellatly (Ed.) *The Skilful Mind*, (pp.26–38). Milton Keynes: Open University Press.

SLOBODA, J.A., HERMELIN, B. and O'CONNOR, N. (1985) An exceptional musical memory. *Music Perception*, 3, 155–170.

SMITH, S.B. (1983) *The Great Mental Calculators*. New York: Columbia University Press.

TREDGOLD, A.F. (1908) *Mental Deficiency*. London: Baillière, Tindall & Cox.

TREDGOLD, R.F. and SODDY, K. (1956) *A Text-book of Mental Deficiency* 9th ed. London: Baillière, Tindall & Cox.

TREVELYAN, G.O. (1978) *The Life and Letters of Lord Macaulay*. Oxford: Oxford University Press. (First published 1876)

WALLACE, W.T. and RUBIN, D.C. (1988) Memory of a ballad singer. In M.M. Gruneberg, P.E. Morris and R.N. Sykes (Eds) *Practical Aspects of Memory, Vol.1*, (pp.257–262). London: Wiley.

WALLACE, W.T. and RUBIN, D.C. (1988a) 'The Wreck of the Old 97': a real event remembered in song. In U. Neisser and E. Winograd (Eds) *Remembering Reconsidered*, (pp.283–310). Cambridge: Cambridge University Press.

THE TORTOISE, THE HARE, AND THE DEVELOPMENT OF TALENT

Lauren A. Sosniak

> The hare was once boasting of his speed before the other animals . . . 'I shall challenge any one here to race with me.'
>
> 'The tortoise will not have a chance!' cried the fox.
> 'Wait and see,' said the owl.
>
> The Hare and the Tortoise
An Aesop Fable

The moral to *The Hare and the Tortoise* concerns the power of perseverance and determination over more obvious (and frequently physical) attributes. The fable has been constructed carefully to favour purposefulness over natural ability and early advantage: the race was sufficiently long and the hare sufficiently distracted (and distractible) for the 'unexpected' result to occur. If the course had been a short one, or the hare had been single-minded, there is no doubt that the outcome would have been different.

It is my contention that the development of talent needs to be understood as a variant of this well-known Aesop fable. I will argue in this chapter that the development of talent is a long-term process, and the time it takes for such development has important consequences for the ways we need to think about supportive educational theory and practice. I will also argue that because the development of talent is a lived experience, it needs to be considered in light of the attractions and distractions associated with motivation to pursue a particular course of study over an extended period of time.

AN EMPIRICAL FOUNDATION

The data that provide the foundation for description and argument in this chapter are drawn from the Development of Talent Research

Project, a five-year study conducted by a team of researchers, under the direction of Benjamin Bloom, at the University of Chicago (Bloom, 1985). The subjects for that study were groups of individuals who, though relatively young, had realized exceptional levels of accomplishment in one of six fields: concert piano, sculpture, swimming, tennis, mathematics, and research neurology (two artistic disciplines, two psychomotor activities, and two academic/intellectual fields). The focus of the investigation was on the roles of the home, teachers, schools and other educational and experiential factors in discovering, developing and encouraging unusually high levels of competence.

More specifically, the study was concerned with questions like: How did an individual's involvement with the chosen field begin? How did he or she work at the activity – how were time, materials and other resources used? What roles did family and teachers play in the learning process? How were interest and involvement maintained? The plan was to search for regularities and recurrent patterns in the educational histories of groups of clearly accomplished individuals, hoping that such consistencies might shed light on how the development of talent is achieved.

The project explored the lives of 120 talented individuals in all, approximately 20 in each field. Restrospective, semi-structured, face-to-face interviews were conducted with the individuals who met criteria of exceptional achievement set by experts in their respective fields. Parents were interviewed as well, by telephone, for corroborative and supplementary information. All interviews were tape-recorded. Data analysis was a process analogous to superimposing the unique histories one on the other, and identifying the patterns that were common across most cases – first within each field and later across the fields (see, for example, Glaser, 1965).

THE LONG-TERM NATURE OF THE DEVELOPMENT OF TALENT

The educational histories of the individuals we studied indicate, without exception, that the development of talent takes a considerable amount of time. None of the individuals in our sample demonstrated remarkable talent in short order. All spent many years developing the understandings, the skills and the attitudes that would eventually allow them to be recognized as experts in their respective fields.

How long does it take to develop talent? The question is not easy to answer with any precision. In fields such as playing concert piano or swimming, there are markers one can use to estimate the length of the process. In our study we found that pianists worked for an average of 17 years from their first formal lessons to their first international recognition. The fastest 'made it' in 12 years; the slowest took 25. For the swimmers, 15 years elapsed, on average, between the time individuals began swimming just for fun and the time they earned a place on an Olympic team.

The scientists, mathematicians and sculptors were unlikely to be recognized for truly outstanding achievement much before their 30th birthday. Unfortunately, we have no clear markers in these fields to use as indications of initial involvement. We do have reason to believe, however, that the process of developing talent even in these areas began very early. For our sample as a whole, parents' values and interests, which were translated into family activity involving even the youngest children, typically helped us understand the direction, although certainly not the degree, of the talented individuals' subsequent development (Sloane, 1985).

Of course, the fact that it takes long time to develop talent is hardly surprising. Others have noted the same phenomenon (Gruber, 1986; Glaser and Chi, 1988). In fact, our interview schedule was constructed to reflect this possibility. We were quite surprised, however, by two findings related to the long-term development of talent. First, as far as we could tell, for much of the time the individuals spent learning to be as good as they are today, it would have been impossible to predict their eventual accomplishments. Second, the process of developing talent over the long term apparently divided itself into three distinct phases with qualitatively different concerns and consequences. Each of these findings will be discussed in turn.

The Unpredictability of the Development of Talent

Unlike the hare in Aesop's fable, the individuals in our study typically did *not* show unusual promise at the start of the long-term experience. They were not 'prodigies' in the way that the stereotype of talent development would have us expect – regardless of whether we define prodigiousness by demonstrated ability or by subjective recollections from parents or the individuals themselves. Early in their experiences with their fields they did not demonstrate abilities significantly beyond those appropriate for their age; they may well have had such abilities, of course, but these either were not noticed or not noticeable.

The pianists, for example, had begun taking lessons by the age of six, on average, and were playing in small recitals organized by their neigbourhood teachers within a year or so. Seven years later, by the time they were 13 or 14, most were playing in local competitions, or at annual adjudicated contests. Even after seven years of study and practice, the youngsters reportedly were as likely to fall short in these competitions as they were to outshine their peers. Similarly, the swimmers spent an average of eight years swimming in national competitions before they began to place (to come first, second or third) in those events.

Parents were somewhat more generous in their subjective recollections of early unusual promise than could be verified by objective evidence. ('He was always the hit of the [recital] because he was so far advanced than the other children who had been taking lessons.') Still, for every parent who had seen a talent just waiting to be developed, there was a counterpart who was taken quite by surprise, many years later, when his or her child began demonstrating considerable talent in a particular area. One pianist's father who was more knowledgeable about music than most recalled: 'I would have started [the child] with a better teacher – at a conservatory – if I had known he was going to become a concert pianist . . . At that time, I didn't think it was important.' A number of mothers told us they perceived another child in the family to have more 'talent', but were subsequently impressed by the tenacity of the sibling who was eventually to become part of our sample.

The individuals themselves were similarly divided in their assertions regarding early unusual promise. Some remembered being told at an early age 'I was going to be great and famous, and how unusual I was'. More were quite explicit that their 'talent' was not noticeable for a considerable number of years. 'I was not a wunderkind,' they told us in various ways. 'They didn't say I had talent until age 16. . . . By then I had worked my ass off!'

Although in large measure our sample did not show unusual promise at the start of the long-term process of developing talent, a small number of individuals could be identified objectively as unusually accomplished at an early age. We believe that these exceptions are as notable for what they reveal about the larger group, and about the nature of traditional means for marking unusual promise, as for the unusual potential they signal in a small portion of our sample. The most prodigious individuals in our study include: two of the 21 concert pianists who won children's competitions which gave them the opportunity to play with a symphony orchestra by the age of 10; one of the swimmers who was a national champion in his age group by the age of 11; and one of the mathematicians who was enrolled in college mathematics courses by the age of 13.

These achievements are considerable indeed. Still, they must be compared side by side with the early demonstrated ability of the much larger number of individuals in our study which was either inconsistent ('one of the top ten year olds in the country; at eleven years, she was at the bottom of the heap'), strong but certainly not outstanding, or even mediocre. Furthermore, at least in the case of the musicians and the swimmer referred to above, we must keep in mind that the extraordinary achievements reflect norm-referenced rather than criterion referenced standards. That is, the individuals had demonstrated they were better than their peers at activities that their age-mates were also undertaking.

We began our study with the question of how individuals were discovered and then, once identified, how they were helped to develop their talents; we found much the reverse. The youngsters spent several years acquiring knowledge and developing skills and dispositions appropriate for their fields before they were 'discovered' as the most talented in their family or in their neighbourhood and accorded the status of biggest fish in their small ponds. In turn, a discovery of this sort, by a parent or teacher, typically led to increased opportunities for development. Then, after several more years of work at increasingly more sophisticated levels, the youngsters were *re*discovered, and so on (Sosniak, 1985a). Gradually, the individuals we studied moved into increasingly more exclusive groups of potentially talented individuals. So slowly did the identification of extraordinary talent take place that the individuals were almost unaware of it happening. This pattern, unpredicted at the start, became more understandable in light of the systematic changes in the nature of teaching and learning over the long term which we found.

Phases of Learning and Teaching

The individuals we studied not only spent many years acquiring the knowledge and developing the skills and dispositions associated with exceptional talent, they did so for a considerable amount of time without any clear idea of where they were heading. There was no intention, at the start, to work towards a standard of excellence in a particular field of study; neither the individuals nor their parents had plans for a long-term commitment or dreams of eventual accomplishment. Exactly what was to be learned, and where it would lead, were decisions made and remade many times in the process of unusually successful learning. Without having to think about the enormity of all that was before them, the individuals and their parents did what seemed good or necessary for the moment.

The very long series of moments appear to have divided themselves into three distinct phases, periods reminiscent of Whitehead's (1929) writings on the rhythms of romance, precision, and generalization in education (Sosniak, 1985b; Sosniak, 1988). Each phase emphasized a particular view of what was being learned, and a particular attitude toward the processes of learning and teaching. Each phase presented different demands on the learner and those with whom he or she worked, and had qualitatively different consequences. The phases were not discrete, but they were dramatic in their particular emphases.

The earliest years of developing talent were filled with opportunities to explore field specific content without the need for behaving systematically or with demonstrated skill. Initiation to the field of talent most typically came early, and as a natural consequence of membership in a family that valued the activity. Although the parents of the individuals in our study seldom were professionally involved in the areas in which their child would later excel, more often than not they held an avocational interest in the field or closely related activity. As a consequence, the young children were exposed to activities associated with their subsequent talent fields, they were supported and rewarded for behaviours associated with the fields, and they learned a good deal in informal ways about knowledge and skills associated with the activity in which they would eventually excel.

The pianists, for example, listened to music almost from the time they were born, and learned to identify the names of well-known composers, musicians or musical pieces without anyone being conscious of the process of education. Mathematicians played with numbers and scientific ideas in similar ways. 'This is half, this is a quarter, this is an eighth,' a mathematician's father reportedly would say to his child as he fed him a breakfast omelette. Parents bought their children field-specific toys and showed genuine interest in the child's various field-specific activities. The talent field provided amusement for children and their parents, and an interest for them to share.

Early formal instruction in the fields for which special instruction was sought was similarly notable for the playfulness of the experiences. First teachers were remembered as having made lessons 'fun'. These teachers were said to be warm and enthusiastic and quick to provide a variety of rewards for any signs of interest or involvement. They threw coins to the bottom of a swimming pool to encourage children to learn to hold their breath and keep their eyes open under water. They put stars on the top of each page in a music book when the child had finished working on that page.

For the most part, during the early years of learning there was little attention to or concern about the 'correctness' of the work. The encouragement of interest and involvement took precedence over the assessment of progress in any formal way. Students, teachers and parents seemed unconcerned with objective measures of achievement. Virtually any effort was applauded by parents or teachers or both. The emphasis during this period was on engaging in lots of field-specific playful activity, and exploring the possibilities inherent in the activity. In the short run, this emphasis may have obscured or even inhibited early signs of unusual talent; in the long run, however, the extended period of early playful activity may have paid dividends of considerable consequence.

For relatively little effort, the learner got more than might be expected. The effect of the early years of playful, almost romantic involvement with a field seemed to be to get the learner involved, captivated, 'hooked' – motivated to pursue the matter further. Of course as would be true about playful situations of many sorts, the more time and attention the individuals paid to the matter, the more skilled they became. In the process of exploring, the students inevitably acquired knowledge and skill that would contribute to subsequent studies. Most importantly, perhaps, this knowledge and skill was gained in a manner that would encourage subsequent development. The individuals apparently had prepared themselves for the second phase of the development of talent.

During the second phase of the development of talent, teaching and learning became much more focused on the systematic acquisition of knowledge and development of skill. Playfulness gave way largely, but seldom entirely, to precision. The nature of the transition from the playful period to the period of precision is not clear, but the fact of the transition is obvious.

The second period of learning was marked by considerable attention to detail. The technical skills and vocabulary of the discipline, as well as its rules and logic, were addressed systematically by teacher and student alike. Youngsters who had toyed with the field earlier invested in the acquisition of specific pieces of knowledge and mastery of narrowly defined objectives. They were willing to engage in the same activity over and over, now consciously making slight variations each time, in the service of achieving some mark of excellence modelled by acknowledged experts in the field.

Instruction became more rational and less informal and personal than it had been earlier. Objective measures of achievement – the results of competitions and the like – provided both a personal sense of accomplishment and a means of planning subsequent instruction. Knowledgeable criticism from teachers and other experts in the field became as rewarding as applause had been earlier. The personal bond between teachers and students shifted from one of love to one of respect.

The student/teacher relationship was carried well beyond the regular lessons. Teachers encouraged, enticed and prodded students to take part in public activities – recitals, competitions, science fairs, mathematics clubs and so forth. Teachers arranged for the students to participate in activities with like-minded youngsters after school and during the summers, and they arranged meetings with professionals or expert teachers in the area. They introduced the students to important historical dimensions of the field through literature, recordings, collected works of art and the like. In various ways teachers provided a rich context for the more focused work that ruled this period.

In response to the students' involvement, parents began making significant sacrifices of time and money to arrange for better teachers, purchase necessary equipment, and travel to important events. Parents also began rearranging life in their homes to accommodate the demands of the children's developing talents. Someone was always available to chauffeur the children to classes or special events. Meals and weekend activities were planned around talent related concerns. Parents became more knowledgeable about the talent area along with their children.

The individuals themselves devoted increasing amounts of time to the talent area. This frequently required sacrificing other activities that previously had been a part of the youngsters' lives. They became strongly identified with the area by their age-mates and, often, by adults in their community. Over time, they began to identify themselves in terms of their area of interest and growing expertise.

During this second phase of learning the individuals developed skills, feelings of competence, and a modicum of awareness of the long-term possibilities of work in their respective talent fields. In the end, they were extraordinarily able, but still not sufficiently accomplished to be included among the best in their respective fields. Technical mastery still had to be integrated with a personal desire to pursue the field to its limits, and with a personal vision or style which could redefine the field in terms of the work of the individual rather than defining the individual in terms of the existing field.

The transition to the third phase of talent development was the most difficult, perhaps, and the most uncertain. It required a commitment of unprecedented proportion; virtually all of one's time, emotional energy and other resources had to be invested in field specific activity. In fact, it was typically towards the end of the second phase of learning, or the beginning of this third phase, that the individuals made their first conscious and visible commitments to the pursuit of excellence in their respective fields.[1] At last there was a clear end in sight for the work the individuals had been engaged in almost as matter of fact to this point.

During the third phase of learning the individuals typically studied with master teachers – teachers who were known either for their personal expertise in the field or for their work with students who had become acknowledged masters in the field. The opportunity to work with such individuals – a result of previous experiences which made the teachers known to the students and prepared the students to meet the teachers' prerequisite requirements – was viewed at first with considerable awe. The individuals reported being 'overwhelmed' by the idea of spending time with these role models, and feeling 'electricity in the air' when they were in the company of these teachers.

The nature of the teaching/learning relationship changed dramatically. A close personal bond between student and teacher was no longer an especially important part of instruction. Instead, the student had to share with the teacher a dedication to the field itself, and a devotion to advancing the work of the field in a personal way. An emphasis on specific details also fell by the wayside, in favour of a broader and more inclusive exploration of the activity of the field.

Instruction almost always took place in the context of the real world activity as it is engaged in by the most talented individuals in the field. Pianists 'performed' for their teachers, and analysed both their performance and the piece of music with their teachers as professional musicians might do in the course of their working lives. Mathematicians watched their teachers 'doing mathematics', and in turn were watched by their teachers while they tried their hand.

With the help of expert teachers, and like-minded peers who were similarly engaged in pursuit of excellence in the field, the individuals began to identify and develop personal concerns and ways of working. They began finding and solving their own problems, and working to satisfy themselves rather than their teachers. They immersed themselves completely and wholeheartedly in the worlds of their respective talent fields, and ultimately they became models of excellence in those fields.

In sum, the long-term process of developing talent was not simply a matter of becoming quantitatively more knowledgeable and skilled over time, or of working more intensely for longer hours. It was, predominantly, a matter of qualitative and evolutionary transformations (Sosniak, 1987). These were transformations of the individual, of the substance of what was being learned, and of the manner in which individuals engaged with teachers and field-specific content. Students progressively adopted different views of who they were, of what their field of expertise was about, and of how the field fitted into their lives.

Movement through the three phases was not always smooth, but it became quite predictable as we analysed the talented individuals' educational histories.[2] The individuals proceeded at different rates and in different ways. They did so with an enormous amount of prompting, guidance, structure, encouragement, and support from parents and teachers. The talented individuals demostrated in compelling fashion that the process of unusually successful learning is not all of one kind; rather, it must be understood in relation to the amount of experience the learner has with some subject matter, the meaning of the subject matter for the learner, and the purposes the learning might serve.

The three phases of learning identifiable in educational histories of extremely talented individuals make sense pedagogically. Together they seem to reflect the entirety of a learning experience – from getting involved; through mastery of skills and understanding; to finding the larger meaning and making the learning personal and worthwhile, and becoming educated about something. Furthermore, that which can be gained from each phase seems to be prerequisite for being able to make the most of the subsequent phases. If these phases of talent development are supported by further investigation, they will pose serious challenges to our historical concern for identifying talent early. They will also suggest new ways of thinking about teaching and the assessment of learning with the potential for developing talent more broadly than we can currently imagine. Given the long-term nature of developing talent, and qualitative shifts in teaching and learning over time, obvious early advantage may matter very little in our future efforts to promote success in various endeavours.

THE SOCIAL CONTEXT OF THE LIVED EXPERIENCE

The development of talent did not take place in a vacuum. It was not the experience of a single individual working alone to release the muse within. The development of talent was, quite clearly, a tribute to the support of many people and communities that valued the activities at which the individuals would eventually excel and valued the individuals' efforts in pursuit of excellence. Without considerable interpersonal support (from family, teachers, peers, and others), and without the less personal but no less social support of organized segments of society engaged in work in the different fields, it is unlikely that the individuals we studied would ever have been identified for their exceptional accomplishments.

As has been discussed earlier, initial interest in and value of the talent field was typically a consequence of membership in a family with adults who held those interests and values. Initial motivation to work at the activity, toward unspecified ends, was derived in no small measure from the very immediate and interpersonal rewards such work provided. There was no intention or indication that initial efforts might lead to a long-term investment in the pursuit of excellence in the field. Early interest and effort were sustained and nurtured by teachers and other adults who orchestrated activities which added to the amusement the youngsters could find in the talent field and gave them the opportunity to be rewarded by applause.

Later, teachers and other adults would help to maintain the students' interests and efforts by introducing the students to challenges which appealed to their developing competence and by making special opportunities available for summer study and for public demonstration of the students' skill. Parents supplied the resources and the encouragement that allowed the students to take advantage of the opportunities their teachers made available.

For much of the time that it took to develop talent, the individuals we studied were too young to find or create for themselves the host of activities and opportunities that teachers and parents made available. One of the more remarkable aspects of the educational histories of the individuals we studied surely must be the interdependent and self-sustaining system of mutual encouragement and support that was created with and for the individuals by parents, teachers, and other adults with whom the individuals had sustained, personal contact. Parents and teachers were willing and able to respond to a learner's development, and to change and grow with the learner in response to that development. Parents, teachers and the individuals appear to have alternately prodded one another, their changes being mutually dependent and enhancing. No one person was responsible for the long-term investment in the development of talent; together, however, a group of supportive adults was able to find multiple ways of maximizing the possibility that the individuals would be able to sustain their involvement in the process of learning.

The group of people supporting the development of a single new talent did considerably more than merely applaud and reward. In fact, perhaps the most difficult task they faced over the years was to support the individual's efforts when interest flagged or skills stalled. There were many examples of such moments in the educational histories of the individuals we studied. There were moments of frustration and disappointment, and attempts at flight from the field. In these moments of failure and discouragement the commitment of parents and teachers was as strong as or stronger than when things were going well. The ability of parents and teachers to provide support after failure as well as after success, and to see less than exceptional performance as a challenge rather than a sign of failure, seem important in the development of talent, although we don't yet understand this well.

The development of talent depended greatly on the efforts of a wide variety of people on behalf of the accomplishment of one. It depended also on the less personal but no less social support provided by larger communities organized around the various fields. The talented individuals in our study were introduced to these communities initially by parents and teachers; over time these communities assumed an increasingly central role in helping to maintain the student's interest and support his or her development.

The larger communities included agemates and slightly older youngsters from other parts of town and the country. They included adults who came to watch the youngsters in public performances and, sometimes, to report on these activities for local newspapers. They included adults who engaged in activity that on the surface was very similar, and who garnered fame (and sometimes fortune) for their work. Exposure to these communities thus placed the child's activity in the context of a valued activity in society, and this context provided substantial support for the student's interest and involvement.

Introduction to the larger communities organized around the different fields seemed to serve various functions. Most obviously, young students were provided with role models of various ages. The oldest and most expert of these models were typically admired from a distance and treated as heroes. They legitimized the activities that the younger students were engaged in, generally without providing much direction for the students' work.

Role models who were closer in age and expertise tended to have more influence on the specific activities our students were engaged with. The slightly older students of the field were used to set an agenda of skills to be mastered and goals to be achieved. They provided a challenge and offered support and guidance. They served as a regular reminder that the individual was not really alone, despite the hours spent in solo pursuit of one sort of mastery or another.

The communities organized around the different fields provided not only role models but also specific and varied opportunities to acquire the knowledge and skills associated with the development of talent. Typically, each community had its own publications which broadened students' opportunities for instruction and inspiration. These talent-specific publications provided information about people, events, and ways of thinking and working; they helped the individuals identify additional resources for learning, and connect to work they were engaged in with teachers. In many cases, each community organized public events of various sorts which provided the individuals in our study both with an audience and with opportunities to see others engaged in similar activity.

Perhaps the most important function of the communities that supported the learning of the individuals we studied was the fact that they provided repeated demonstrations that the students were engaged in learning which was relevant to their lives, rather than merely school learning or learning appropriate only for children. Learning in the process of the development of talent resembled more closely learning out of school, as Resnick (1987) describes it, than learning in school. It often involved a shared experience, and almost always involved direct engagement with the objects and situations that define the field, contextualized reasoning, and the development of situation-specific competencies. Learning connected so directly with our experiences in the world, Dewey (1944) reminds us, has the potential for staying with us longer and making a deeper impression. 'The more human the purpose, or the more it approximates the ends which appeal in daily experience, the more real the knowledge' (p.198).

Learning, for the talented individuals we interviewed, was much more than a matter of acquiring knowledge and skill in the abstract. Most importantly, it was a vital and valued part of their lives, growing from and into their worlds of experience. In this context, distractions were minimized. Even as the individuals grew older, and their lives became more complex, few other activities could compete with the attraction of the field they knew richly and within which they had already developed some skill.

If the hare in *The Hare and the Tortoise* had had the support of its community for the length of the race, if it had been encouraged to defer the immediate satisfaction of food or rest for the sake of an activity all agreed was worthwhile, if the hare had been in the company of others who were leading by a length or nipping at its heels, surely the tortoise never would have turned out to be so outstanding in the long-run. But the race was long and the hare was expected to sustain the activity alone. The talented individuals we interviewed ran a long race too; in this instance, however, they ran with the help of parents, teachers, and the larger community which apparently prevented them from getting so distracted that they lost the chance to excel.

CHALLENGING TRADITIONAL IDEAS ABOUT TALENT DEVELOPMENT

Gruber (1986) has raised serious questions about the necessity and sufficiency of 'the stereotyped idea of a "normal" sequence for a creative life: precocity in childhood, early commitment and achievement, single-minded pursuit of creative goals, a lifetime of elaboration of these beginnings, eventual decline' (p.255). The findings from our study of the development of talent strongly support his argument. The educational histories we collected from clearly talented young adults were remarkably lacking in evidence not only of precocity in early childhood and early achievement, but also of early commitment and single-minded pursuit of field specific goals.

The individuals we studied did not spring to life demonstrating the skills, understandings and dispositions which mark extraordinary talent in the various fields. Instead, they grew into their aptitudes and attitudes, in the context of supportive adults, peers and societies of persons who valued and engaged in activity of a similar sort. Experiences and expectations related to the development of talent were integrated gradually into the individuals' lives and the lives of their families. Thanks to the absence of large goals at the start, there was never so much still to be learned that the task would seem overwhelming.

Aptitudes and attitudes developed in concert, or almost so. The individuals were willing to invest human and material resources in increasingly difficult tasks as the field became an ever more vital and valued part of their lives. They learned to work toward more distant goals as they learned to care about achieving those goals. The students built a reservoir of good feeling about their talent fields, and their abilities, which helped them learn the patience and persistence that apparently are prerequisites of unusually successful achievement.

The process of growing into a person of extraordinary talent involved considerable exposure to and experience with field specific content. As Duckworth (1987) reminds us:

> Intelligence cannot develop without matter to think about. Making new connections depends on knowing enough about something in the first place to provide a basis for thinking of other things to do – of other questions to ask – that demand more complex connections in order to make sense. The more ideas about something people already have at their disposal, the more new ideas occur and the more they can coordinate to build up still more complicated schemes (p.14).

The development of talent involved a clear focus on particular subject matter, with multiple opportunities of various sorts over a long period of time to come to know and appreciate that subject matter.

Cognitive scientists recently have begun making the case that considerable exposure to domain-specific content is an essential early component of the development of human competence. 'The obvious reason for the excellence of experts is that they have a good deal of domain knowledge' (Glaser and Chi, 1988, p.xvii). Rich exposure to domain-specific knowledge is said to have important consequences for the development of automaticity, which in turn is believed to help explain the impressive coding and chunking abilities of experts. The study of expertise is leading increasingly to the assertion that 'the problem of producing an expert may be, to a large extent, that of creating and maintaining the motivation for the long training that is necessary' (Glaser and Chi, p.xxii).

Findings from the study of the development of talent suggest that their conclusion is at least partially correct. Creating and maintaining the conditions which would support the potential for the development of high levels of competence, over the long-term, does seem to be our greatest challenge. To meet this challenge we must become sensitive to the variety of motivations that contribute in different ways at different times to a long-term investment of effort. Our study suggests further that we must recognize the variety of dimensions of teaching and learning which contribute in different ways at different times to the development of people with considerable expertise. Motivating individuals to work at inappropriate tasks in inappropriate ways will hardly do.

To meet the challenge of creating conditions which support long-term involvement with a field of activity, we will have to confront quickly the roles of society in the work of educational institutions. The development of talent apparently requires that students come to know their subject matter in socially meaningful ways. The work of educators apparently cannot be seen in isolation from the values of parents and the influences of larger communities. Educational institutions must learn to make learning a vital and valued part of our students' lives, growing from and into their worlds of experience. In many contexts, this may also require that we work to promote particular values and interests in the larger community.

The development of talent apparently is possible for far greater numbers of people than we ever imagined. Our challenge is to learn to provide appropriate opportunities for its development and to create conditions which support the long-term commitment to learning that is required.

Notes

1. The lack of early and conscious commitment to the field is obvious in multiple ways. The mathematicians provide one example: typically, they made decisions about which colleges to attend as undergraduates without any attention to the quality of the education they might receive in mathematics. Fewer than half were entertaining idea of mathematics as a career at the end of high school (Gustin, 1985). By the time these individuals applied to graduate school, however, the primary and often sole criterion for the selection of a university was the quality of the mathematical experience they believed would be possible.

2. This brief outline of phases in the development of talent necessarily ignores negative evidence. Our data do include examples of instances where learning did *not* proceed smoothly in the manner identified. In fact, these made the pattern all the more obvious because of the 'corrections' that inevitably took place in the individuals' experiences. Some youngsters, for example, were asked to do the work of the phase of precision before they had

developed an intense interest in their talent field. They and their parents remember a point at which they were ready to abandon their work in the field entirely, an option never taken apparently because of the sensitivity of a parent who arranged for a change of teacher who found a more engaging way of working with the student. Other youngsters moved too slowly or too quickly to the third phase, and found themselves floundering until changes were made in teachers or teaching strategies.

REFERENCES

BLOOM, B.S. (Ed.) (1985) *Developing Talent in Young People*. New York: Ballantine Books.

DEWEY, J. (1944) *Democracy and education*. New York: The Free Press.

DUCKWORTH, E. (1987) *The Having of Wonderful Ideas*. New York: Teachers College Press.

GLASER, B. (1965) The constant comparative method of qualitative analysis. *Social Problems*, 12, 436–445.

GLASER, R. and CHI, M.T.H. (1988) Overview. In M.T.H. Chi, R. Glaser and M.J. Farr (Eds), *The Nature of Expertise*. Hillsdale, New Jersey: Lawrence Erlbaum Associates.

GRUBER, H.E. (1986) The self-construction of the extraordinary. In R.J. Sternberg and J.E. Davidson (Eds), *Conceptions of Giftedness*, pp.247–263. Cambridge: Cambridge University Press.

GUSTIN, W.C. (1985) The development of exceptional research mathematicians. In B.S. Bloom, *Developing Talent*, pp.270–331.

RESNICK, L.B. (1987) Learning in school and out. *Educational Researcher*, 16(9), 13–20.

SLOANE, K.D. (1985) Home influences on talent development. In B.S. Bloom, *Developing Talent*, pp.439–476.

SOSNIAK, L.A. (1985a) A long-term commitment to learning. In B.S. Bloom, *Developing Talent*, pp.477–506.

SOSNIAK, L.A. (1985b) Phases of learning. In B.S. Bloom, *Developing Talent*, pp.409–438.

SOSNIAK, L.A. (1987) The nature of change in successful learning. *Teachers College Record*, Vol.88, No.1, 519–535.

SOSNIAK, L.A. (1988) Changing relationships between student and teacher in the development of talent. *Education and Society*, Vol.6, No.s 1 & 2, 79–86.

WHITEHEAD, A.N. (1929) *The Aims of Education*. New York: Macmillan.

MUSICAL EXCELLENCE – HOW DOES IT DEVELOP?

John Sloboda

The language of excellence abounds with pitfalls and hidden assumptions. One such pitfall is to believe that excellence is an absolute quality which can be discerned in some behaviour or product by direct examination. It seems more likely that excellence is normally determined by comparison. To be excellent is to be better than most others. What constitutes excellence in one cultural or historical context may be commonplace or even elementary in another. Furthermore, the criteria employed for judging which of two products is 'better' are subject to immense variation according to social and cultural context, nowhere more so than in the arts. To take a specific example, one aspect of musical excellence has often been taken to be a highly accurate reproduction of the sequence of instructions that constitutes a musical score. It is expected of contemporary classical concert pianists that they play exactly the notes prescribed by a composer. In other cultural contexts (for example, jazz), exact reproduction is given no particular value, and may even be ascribed a negative value. The excellent musician is one who departs from exact reproduction in interesting and appropriate ways.

Another related trap is the tendency to perceive excellence as a stable characteristic of the individual, rather than a characteristic arising from the interaction of a person with specific events and situations. If, as is often the case, the manifestations of excellence are sporadic then this tendency forces us to choose between two alternative accounts of such 'patchiness'. *Either* the individual possesses excellence which is periodically inhibited by certain factors, *or* the individual does not possess excellence and excellent performance is explained as a 'fluke' or an unusual combination of circumstances. The choice between these alternative accounts is highly susceptible to attitudinal bias. For instance, one may be more likely to ascribe excellence to someone who has won a prestigious competition than to someone who has not, even though 'objectively' their attainments may be equivalent.

If we reject the notion of excellence as a stable characteristic, then we do not have to 'account' for patchiness at all. There is no reason to believe that an individual 'develops' excellence in the same way as he or she acquires full physical stature. In physical growth, there is a period of rapid change until late adolescence, followed by a long period of stability, leading to gradual decline. This is not necessarily the best analogy for excellence. That an individual might be an 'excellent' performer at an early age, and average in adulthood, is not inconsistent with the concept of excellence.

The most pessimistic conclusion one can draw from these observations about the concept of excellence is that it is not possible to say anything of general validity about the psychology of excellence, its nature or its development, because excellence is not something which is to be found inside an individual or which can be defined in terms of individual cognitive processes and capacities. It is, rather, a socio-cultural construct whose ascription to individual acts or people is a matter for constant renegotiation in the light of changing social norms and values. One could go even further and suggest that those who wish to study excellence and exceptionality because they believe that this may help increase the incidence of excellence are naïve and deluded. The whole social purpose of the ascription of excellence may be to uphold social class divisions and ensure that the majority of people hold low opinions of themselves and their powers. As the general level of achievement in a population increases, the criteria for excellence are simply shifted upwards so as to ensure that most people are never awarded the accolade of excellence.

However, pessimism about the usefulness of the term 'excellence' need not deter psychologists from examining the development of competence, in this case of musical competence. Within each individual there is a potential for musical growth, from the ability to deal with simple short sequences coded on a few basic dimensions through to the ability to handle complex and lengthy sequences on many subtle dimensions. Within each individual, this growth may be faster or slower, or it may be blocked altogether. It can be studied quite independently of the ascription of excellence, although the two aspects may sometimes go hand in hand. An example of this independence is where a musician judged 'excellent' on conventional grounds is in fact being blocked from further development (as demonstrated, for example, in Bamberger's study of exceptional adolescents discussed later in this chapter). An example of co-ordination is when 'success' leads to new challenges and opportunities for growth. Our questions about music, therefore are:

(a) what is musical growth? and
(b) what factors encourage or inhibit that growth?

My strategy for answering these questions will be to articulate, scrutinize and deconstruct four culturally prevalent myths about musical excellence.

Cultural Myths about Musical Excellence

A lifetime of involvement with people interested in music has convinced me that certain assumptions about the nature and cause of musical excellence are deeply embedded in our cultural consciousness. I call them myths, not to prejudge their truth or falsity, but because they are often illustrated by highly simplified stories or beliefs about particular musicians or musical accomplishments. As is often the case, they seem to come in opposing pairs, the first pair being concerned with

What must a musician do?

The myth of precocity *vs* The myth of diligence.

and the second pair being concerned with

What must a musician have?

The myth of intelligence *vs* The myth of education.

People who argue about musical excellence often align themselves with one or other of the opposing myths. I shall hope to show that none of these myths is fully supported by evidence, and will suggest that belief in any of them may well be a primary inhibitor of musical growth in self and others.

The myth of precocity. According to this myth, to become excellent you have to start excellent. Exceptional musicians in adult life are those who showed exceptional early promise. The prime exemplar of this myth is Mozart who, by all reports, was playing keyboard instruments fluently at the age of three, and producing well-formed compositions at the age of six. Belief in this myth has a number of consequences. People who were not musically active in their early years become discouraged from starting later, or from working for excellence. Parents who fail to see supposed signs of early musical promise in their children come to believe that their children are 'not musical'. Anxieties about the importance of early experience have led to the various 'early learning' industries (notably the Suzuki method, where children are encouraged to start musical instrumental exercises as early as possible). However, there is no clear evidence of any superior long-term benefits to be derived from 'early learning' methods as opposed to more orthodox approaches.

Furthermore, a study of top USA concert pianists by Sosniak (1989; see also her chapter in this volume) shows that none of her sample showed any particular signs of exceptional early promise as children. It was not until the pianists reached the age of 10 to 15 that parents and teachers were able to detect signs of achievement and motivation that indicated the possibility of a professional career.

There is even some suggestion (for example, Bamberger, 1987) that the early excellence of the so-called 'child prodigy' may be positively damaging to the prospects of adult excellence. In Bamberger's studies, gifted young musicians seem to have an ability to 'move their attention freely among the complexity of intersecting musical dimensions that together give unique coherence to even a single moment in a composition'. One consequence of this ability is the extraordinary capacity for 'all-at-once imitation' of a performance style modelled by a teacher or professional. The ability seems intuitive and unreflexive. Children neither represent nor name multiple dimensions as separate.

In adolescence, a major change occurs. The musician begins to self-consciously analyse what he or she is doing, and comes to consider the various dimensions of the music separately. The unself-conscious ease of childhood disappears, and a performance has to be constructed through the conscious meshing of disparate dimensions. And so, in the words of one 16 year old, 'It's easy to feel like your playing has got worse because now we're listening and hearing so much more.' Coming to terms with the loss of 'ease' is hard, and can block further progress.

Although there are no systematic studies across large populations of prodigies there are enough documented cases of adolescent decline (for example, Revesz, 1925) for the myth of precocity to be discredited.

The myth of diligence. This myth states that if you work hard enough and long enough at anything you can become excellent at it. Such a myth is at the heart of the protestant work ethic and the entrepreneurial culture. Although it appears to be an antidote to the myth of precocity, there is a strong element of moral censure in it. You have only yourself, your laziness or your lack of application to blame if you are not excellent (a philosophy turned into a set of pedagogic principles for a whole generation of musicians by Buck, 1944). The myth is expressed through numerous stories of musicians exerting prodigious effort (for example, practising 10 hours a day) and, as Johnson (1980) observes, it underlies commentaries on Beethoven's compositional persistence as shown by his notebooks, where developments of the same material can be traced through as much as 20 years of working and reworking.

With this myth, any advantages conferred by precocity are simply explained by the fact that those who start early have more time to practise, if they avail themselves of the opportunity. Its cultural consequences are an emphasis on extensive practice, repetition and drill, and it forms the backdrop of many a domestic battle between exasperated parent and reluctant child. Practice is presented as a sort of medicine, unpleasant but necessary, and adults often ascribe their lack of musical achievement to the fact that they 'never practised' as children.

The myth of diligence has a great deal more plausibility than the myth of precocity. It is given partial support by the extensive literature on skill and expertise which clearly shows that positive effects can be gained from increased numbers of hours spent on both simple tasks (Siebel, 1963) and complex tasks (Chase and Simon, 1973). In addition, there are well developed theoretical accounts of how practice enhances skill (See Fitts, 1964; Newell and Rosenbloom, 1981; Anderson, 1982; Ericsson, Tesch-Römer and Krampe, this volume). These focus on the acquisition of large amounts of pattern-knowledge which become proceduralized and automatized.

Where the myth fails is in what it leaves out. One important aspect of learning is motivation. Without motivation it is very hard to spend the necessary hours practising a task. There are two broad classes of motivators, *internal* and *external*. Internal motivation comes about through interest in and liking of the activity under question for its own sake. External motivation arises through rewards (such as approval) or punishments (such as humiliation or criticism) contingent on performing the task. There is extensive evidence that material of interest to a particular person is learned quickly (Morris, Tweedy, and Gruneberg, 1985) whereas considerable repetition of uninteresting material does not necessarily lead to improved retention (Craik and Watkins, 1973) and that creative activity only flourishes under conditions of internal motivation (see Amabile, 1983).

For musical growth, then, it would seem necessary that the person concerned likes music, is interested in it, and wants to be engaged in it for its own sake. Only then will 'practice make perfect'. A recent study of mine (Sloboda, 1989) has confirmed the crucial importance of internal motivation in sustaining musical involvement and development. In this study, adults were asked to recall events from the first ten years of life that were in any way connected with music. For each remembered event they were asked to supply answers to a range of questions. These included who they were with; where they were; what event the music formed part of; and what effect or significance the event had for them. They were also asked about subsequent involvement with music and current attainment level.

Recalled significance of events was of two kinds. *Internal* significance came from the music itself, and the effect it had on the subject (for example, 'the music made me feel really happy', 'I loved the tone of the clarinet'). Notably, in 114 usable memories, only one had negative internal significance, when someone remembered disliking the tone of an organ note. In contrast, an event's *external* significance was derived from the context in which the music took place. This could be positive ('it was fun to be with all the family') or negative ('I felt extremely nervous about playing in front of everybody'). Both positive and negative memories were common among the 114 memories.

Two features of the results are of major significance. First, there were no memories in the sample where positive *internal* significance and negative *external* significance occurred together. This suggests that people are incapable of obtaining pleasure from music when they are in situations of discomfort or threat. Second, there was a very strong relationship between the ability to recall an event with positive internal significance, and present level of involvement with music. Those who recalled such events were much more likely to be currently musically active at a high level, suggesting that such events were strong motivators.

What were these events like? Interestingly, they changed according to the age at which the event was experienced. Early memories (before the age of 6) tended to be characterized by feelings of excitement, liking, and fun, stimulated by the general activity level of the music (for example, fast, loud, simple). Later memories (from 7 upwards) were characterized more often by feelings of wonder (for example, enthralled, incredulous, awe-struck, astounded) aroused by emotional or sensual qualities of the music (for example, beautiful, romantic, liquid, funny). Even sadness seemed to be a desired and sought after feeling in some music. Several of these memories seemed to have the quality of 'peak' experiences. People saw them as life changing, and sometimes explicitly told how that had been the spur to seeking music lessons or other intensive engagement with music. One of the questions asked of subjects was the age at which they began formal music lessons, if at all. A majority of these positive experiences occurred prior to formal tuition, and certainly did not arise *through* such tuition.

Indeed, one of the most disturbing findings of the study was that these positive experiences rarely occurred when the subject was in a formal educational setting or was performing. More often, such settings were the occasion for anxiety, humiliation, and even physical punishment. The positive experiences occurred more often when subjects were alone or with family and friends, away from school, and listening to rather than performing music. Although formal education is not necessarily a source of negative reinforcement, this random British sample suggests that schools and teachers are as likely to inhibit the development of musical excellence as they are to help it.

Although these findings are probably not unique to music, they have a particular significance for the growth of musical skill. One of the fundamental aspects of musical skill is the ability to apprehend and communicate emotion through music. Anything which disrupts the ability of children to make appropriate emotional responses to music is likely to endanger the growth of skill in a way that no amount of subsequent practice can overcome.

The myth of intelligence. The two previous myths occupied opposite positions on the question of what someone must do to become excellent. The myth of intelligence is concerned with what someone must have to become excellent. This myth has a broad and a narrow version. The broad version asserts that you have to have high intelligence (as measured by IQ) to be excellent at anything. The narrow version asserts that, regardless of IQ, to be good at music you need to have something called musical talent. In both cases the myth implies that these necessary qualities are innate and unevenly distributed in the population. The broad myth is sustained through stories of musicians and composers who have been highly accomplished in other fields (for example, Schweitzer, Mendelssohn, Wagner). The narrow myth is sustained by examples of musical gifts that run in families (for example, Bach) and by general examples of precocity.

In my experience, this myth seems to have a particularly strong hold on some educators, who observe children (aged 5 or 6) coming into their classes with different levels of musical accomplishment, and cannot conceive that, in the absence of formal instruction, these differences can be due to anything but innate talent. This is because they are also victims of the myth of education (see next section of this chapter). The main damage done by the myth of intelligence is, as in all other fields, to reify performance differences between individuals into permanent capacity differences. Attributing musical excellence to a child or, equally, withholding it, can consequently become a self-fulfilling prophecy (Rosenthal and Jacobsen, 1968; Dweck, 1986).

The broad version of the myth of intelligence is most spectacularly challenged by the existence of the *mono-savant*. This is a term coined by Charness, Clifton and MacDonald (1988) to replace the more common but pejorative *idiot savant*. A mono-savant is a person of generally low accomplishments (usually with an IQ in the range of 40–80) who has one small area of outstanding achievement. Although rare, there have now been several hundred documented cases, among whom musical savants are a significant minority. It is not the intention of this paper to go into specific cases (for recent reviews, see Treffert, 1988; Hermelin, O'Connor and Lee, 1987). I shall simply summarize some features which seem most prevalent in such savants. Common to almost all reported cases is a prodigious memory for music. Several savants have demonstrated the ability to play piano pieces of the length of a sonata movement after one or two hearings under controlled conditions of observation (Charness *et al.*, 1988; Miller, 1987a, 1987b; Sloboda, Hermelin and O'Connor, 1985).

Musical savants seem to display 'intelligence' in their behaviour. They do not simply reproduce music as an unanalysed sound sequence. They show sensitivity to musical structure, in that their errors make musical sense, and their ability is greater for music which conforms to tonal structure than that which does not (Miller, 1987b; Sloboda *et al.*, 1985). They also show the ability to improvise on material in musically appropriate ways (Charness *et al.* 1988; Hermelin *et al.* 1987; Miller, 1987b; Sloboda *et al.*, 1985).

The limitations of musical savants are also very clear. None of them has the capacity to describe or reflect upon their ability, indeed severe verbal retardation is a common feature of many savants. Most cannot read music. Most do not improve or enhance their skills beyond adolescence, and most are incapable of retaining or generating the expressive components of music. This could be a loophole for those wishing to defend the broad version of the myth. One could assert that only the ability to apprehend and convey the expressive aspects of music constitutes real musical skill, and that only those with high IQ can do that. Alternatively one could argue (as Howe, 1989, does) that only by excluding meaning and concentrating exclusively on form are mono-savants able to achieve their extraordinary results. In other words, the affectless nature of their representations is a consequence of the way they carry out their task rather than their low IQ, which in itself might be an outcome of the predilection to concentrate attention on a narrow range of stimuli.

Turning now to the narrow version of the myth, the existence of the mono-savant appears to leave the myth unscathed, since one could simply suppose that the savants in question were endowed with innate musical talent (as distinct from high IQ). In response one could point to the lack of affect mentioned above. What *kind* of innate talent is it that fails to respond to such a central aspect of music? More substantively, there is a very good case to be made for explaining the achievements of mono-savants in terms of a high (even obsessional) level of internal motivation coupled with a lack of social awareness or expectation that makes negative external reinforcement almost impossible. This motivation leads to extraordinarily high levels of mental investment over a long timespan. Anyone who put this amount of effort into a task would achieve comparable results. This obsessiveness is amply documented in almost all known cases of savants, so that what really needs explaining is why some savants choose music as their obsession, while others choose calendars or drawing. It is not inconceivable that savants are 'seeking' an obsession, and latch onto the first activity that fulfils certain criteria. The choice of activity may well be a matter of complete chance.

The most convincing evidence against innate talent is a study by Renninger and Wozniak (1985) which shows how small differences in preferences for objects in very young children can 'snowball' into skill differences. Children spend more time observing objects that they prefer. This leads to better memory and performance in tasks using those objects. Success reinforces the tendency to treat these objects differently, so that skill is skewed further in favour of objects which were initially only slightly preferred. By the age of two or three these events can result in quite substantial individual differences. It is not difficult to imagine how musical stimuli might be the objects of such a selective process, neither is it hard to imagine how small initial preferences could be established essentially by chance.

The myth of education. This myth asserts that musical excellence depends upon individuals receiving formal training or tuition from more experienced musicians. It is almost axiomatic in our culture that the first thing you do if you want to grow as a musician is to enrol for lessons. This myth appears to contradict the myth of intelligence, but in reality lives quite happily alongside it in the minds of many, who have a picture of talent as a potential which will easily go to seed or atrophy unless brought under the discipline of rigorous and challenging training.

The main consequence of this myth is to convince people that if they fail to gain access to limited educational resources (by not having enough money, by living in the wrong place, or by failing some entrance hurdle) they will have no chance of musical growth. Even within the education system itself it is assumed that the 'better' (i.e. the more prestigious, expensive) school or teacher will result in faster growth. People therefore place expectations on themselves or their children relative to their position within the educational hierarchy rather than to their own interest, commitment and motivation.

This myth is, in some ways, the easiest of all four to contradict. Examples abound of musicians who have grown and developed in the absence of anything resembling formal tuition. The mono-savants discussed above constitute one clear example of this. Their low ability to communicate and interact effectively precluded any normal teacher-pupil relationship. Their skills were self-generated. It is only a general cultural incredulity that people can learn without teaching that makes such accomplishments seem inexplicable, and pushes those who witness them into adopting the explanation of innate talent.

Savants can, however, be dismissed by the sceptical as a special case. It is less easy to dismiss the accomplishments of jazz musicians, such as Bix Beiderbecke, Roy Eldridge, and Louis Armstrong, to name but three who were essentially self-taught. Armstrong achieved professional status with little more than a few tips and hints from King Oliver in the later years of his teens. He didn't even own a cornet until he was 16, and the only practice he could do was by begging established players to let him borrow an instrument and 'sit in' for a number. He didn't learn to read music until his early 20s by which time he was already an established professional. (A full account of Armstrong's life is given in Collier, 1983, summarized in Sloboda, 1991).

The factors that seem most important in accounting for untutored development of jazz skill are:

(a) a rich pervasive live musical culture (the street bands and tonk bands of New Orleans);

(b) extensive opportunity to explore actively and autonomously the medium of music (as a boy, Armstrong formed and sang in a street-corner choir for several years to earn money);

(c) opportunities to take part in communal jazz activities where 'mistakes' are tolerated and where one can choose the level of risk and difficulty of one's performance (criteria which were admirably fulfilled in the blues bands of the New Orleans bars).

These factors, together with a growing motivation and commitment to music seem to have been peculiarly available in the New Orleans of the 1900s. They are probably replicated in other non-literate musical cultures about which less is written.

Fortunately, we do not have to look at exceptional Jazz musicians for evidence that musical skills develop without formal training. There is considerable evidence that, at the very least, receptive skills develop in the majority of children irrespective of education. For instance, Zenatti (1969) has shown that children over the age of 7 show a memory advantage for sequences which conform to tonality. This advantage is not shared by younger children, and the implication is that structural knowledge is acquired by normal exposure to music. Other consistent findings are outlined by Sloboda (1985a), including one study in which children's judgements of musical well-formedness were obtained at various ages. There was a general increase of conformity with 'adult' convention, but the rate of increase was quite unaffected by whether or not the child was receiving formal musical tuition.

A further source of evidence is provided by a comparative study of pianists' expressive abilities (Sloboda, 1983, 1985b). This study measured the microvariations in timing and loudness that characterize any human performance. The study showed that these variations were, for a given individual, consistent and replicable. They were not random. It also showed that one major purpose of such variations was to enhance the communication of musical structure to a listener. Most variations could be accounted for by a small number of simple rules relating to the metrical structure of the music, in such a way that metrically strong beats were highlighted. A third finding was that these variations did not have to be premeditated, but could be produced under conditions of sight-reading where pianists had to apply instant musical intuitions.

All of the subjects in the study were adults, ranging from university undergraduates to professional performers of many years' standing. There was a direct relationship between the number of years' experience and the consistency and clarity of the performance variations. In other words, expressive performance skills do not cease developing at the end of formal education, but continue to develop and become more refined through the lifespan.

Conclusions

It would be presumptuous to believe that psychology could provide a definite answer to the question posed in the title of this chapter. I hope to have cast doubt on some rather simplistic, but deeply in-grained, myths about musical development. These myths are, of course, not confined to music. They are, in slightly differing forms, embedded in everyday thinking about nearly every aspect of excel-lence. Furthermore, the myths concentrate on preconditions for ex-cellence rather than on the developmental process, and so my comments have been focused on the evidence for such preconditions. Nothing I have said would be a direct contribution towards a formal model of the cognitive-developmental processes underlying growth of musical skill. Psychology is not at the stage where it could design, even in principle, a learning machine that would simulate the growth of musical accomplishment in an individual.

Nonetheless, a better understanding of the conditions for 'excel-lence' is useful in two ways. First, we gain some indirect pointers as to the nature of the learning organism. If plants need water to grow, that tells us something about what plants are like. Likewise with human growth. Second, we gain some hints about how to encourage and foster growth, even if we do not fully understand the mechan-isms by which this is brought about. To the extent that psychology hopes to be useful, this is an end in itself.

Let me then summarize some of the main conditions for musical growth which are suggested by the evidence I have reviewed. It is not possible to say whether the following list is complete, nor whether conditions are necessary or sufficient, either singly or in combination.

What one can say with a fair degree of confidence is that the more of these conditions that are fulfilled, the more likely there is to be growth.

1. Casual and frequent exposure to the musical forms of the culture from an early age.

2. The opportunity to freely explore a musical medium over an extended time-span.

3. The early opportunity to experience intense positive emotional or aesthetic states in response to music.

4. The absence of threat or anxiety arising from the context of the music (a prerequisite for 3).

5. Resources for extended engagement with music (including time, economic support, social support, etc.).

6. Intrinsic motivation for musical activity (possibly arising from 3).

It seems at least possible that the uneven distribution of these conditions within any population can account for major variations in individual musical accomplishment without any need for recourse to notions of individual differences in capacity. Neither do these conditions suggest that high levels of early performance achievement are necessary or even helpful for later achievement. In direct contradistinction to the mores of our society, it seems that music provides a clear demonstration that enjoyment is every bit as important as labour. Indeed, the latter without the former might produce some kind of technician, but is likely to kill the very thing that often makes musicians so highly valued. This is their ability to pick up the emotional concomitants of musical structure, so that a musician's interpretation of a piece of music lends new force, or meaning, to its musical structures. Serious psychological study of this aspect of music has barely begun.

REFERENCES

AMABILE, T.M. (1983) *The Social Psychology of Creativity*. New York: Springer Verlag.

ANDERSON, J.R. (1982) Acquisition of cognitive skill. *Psychological Review*, 89, 369–406.

BAMBERGER, J. (1987) Cognitive issues in the development of musically gifted children. In R.J. Sternberg (Ed.) *Conceptions of Giftedness*. New York: Cambridge University Press.

BUCK, P.C. (1944) *Psychology for Musicians*. London: Oxford University Press.

CHARNESS, N., CLIFTON, J. and MACDONALD, L. (1988) A case study of a musical mono-savant: A cognitive psychological focus. In L.K. Obler and D.A. Fein (Eds) *The Exceptional Brain: The Neuropsychology of Talent and Special Abilities*. New York: Guildford Press.

CHASE, W.G. and SIMON, H.A. (1973) The mind's eye in chess. In W.G. Chase (Ed.) *Visual Information Processing*. New York: Academic Press.

COLLIER, J.L. (1983) *Louis Armstrong: an American Genius*. New York: Oxford University Press.

CRAIK, F.I.M. and WATKINS, J.J. (1973) The role of rehearsal in short-term memory. *Journal of Verbal Learning and Verbal Behaviour, 12*, 599–607.

DWECK, C. (1986) Motivational processes affecting learning. *American Psychologist, 41*, 1040–8.

FITTS, P.M. (1964) Perceptual-motor skill learning. In A.W. Melton (Ed.) *Categories of Human Learning*. New York: Academic Press.

HERMELIN, B., O'CONNOR, N. and LEE, S. (1987) Musical inventiveness of five idiots-savants. *Psychological Medicine, 17*, 685–694.

HOWE, M.J.A. (1989) The strange achievements of Idiots savants. In A.M. Colman and J.G. Beaumont (Eds) *Psychology Survey 7*. London: BPS Books and Routledge Kegan Paul.

JOHNSON, D.P. (1980) *Beethoven's early sketches in the "Fischof Miscellany" Berlin Autograph 28. Vols 1 and 2*. Ann Arbor, Michigan: UMI Research Press.

MILLER, L.K. (1987a) Developmentally delayed musical savant's sensitivity to tonal structure. *American Journal of Mental Deficiency, 91*, 467–471.

MILLER, L.K. (1987b) Sensitivity to tonal structure in a developmentally disabled musical savant. *Psychology of Music, 15*, 76–89.

MORRIS, P.E., TWEEDY, M. and GRUNEBERG, M.M. (1985) Interest, knowledge and the memorizing of football scores. *British Journal of Psychology, 76*, 417–425.

NEWELL, A. and ROSENBLOOM, P.S. (1981) Mechanisms of skill acquisition and the law of practice. In J.R. Anderson (Ed.) *Cognitive Skills and their Acquisition*. Hillsdale NJ: Erlbaum.

RENNINGER, K.A. and WOZNIAK, R.N. (1985) Effect of interest on attentional shift, recognition and recall in young children. *Developmental Psychology, 21*, 624–632.

REVESZ, G. (1925) *The Psychology of a Musical Prodigy*. London: Kegan Paul, Trench, and Trubner.

ROSENTHAL, R. and JACOBSEN, L. (1968) *Pygmalion in the Classroom: Teacher Expectation and Pupil's Intellectual Development*. New York: Holt, Rinehart and Winston.

SIEBEL, R. (1963) Discrimination reaction time for a 1023 alternative task. *Journal of Experimental Psychology, 66*, 1005–1023.

SLOBODA, J.A. (1983) The communication of musical metre in piano performance. *Quarterly Journal of Experimental Psychology, 30*, 228–236.

SLOBODA, J.A. (1985a) *The Musical Mind: The Cognitive Psychology of Music*. London: Oxford University Press.

SLOBODA, J.A. (1985b) Expressive skill in two pianists: style and effectiveness in music performance. *Canadian Journal of Psychology, 39*, 273–293.

SLOBODA, J.A. (1989) Music as a language. In F. Wilson and F. Roehmann (Eds) *Music and Child Development: Proceedings of the 1987 Biology of Music Making Conference*. St Louis: MMB Music Inc.

SLOBODA, J.A. (1991) Musical expertise. In K.A. Ericsson and J. Smith (Eds) *The Study of Expertise: Prospects and Limits*. London: Cambridge University Press.

SLOBODA, J.A., HERMELIN, B., and O'CONNOR, N. (1985) An exceptional musical memory. *Music Perception*, 3.2, 155–170.

SOSNIAK, L. (1989) From tyro to virtuoso: A long-term commitment to learning. In F. Wilson and F. Roehmann (Eds) *Music and Child Development: Proceedings of the 1987 Biology of Music Making Conference*. St Louis: MMB Music Inc.

SOSNIAK, L. (1990) This volume.

TREFFERT, D.A. (1988) The idiot savant: A review of the syndrome. *American Journal of Psychiatry*, 145.5, 563–572.

ZENATTI, A. (1969) Le développement génétique de la perception musicale. *Monographes Francais Psychologiques*, No 17.

EARLY STIMULATION AND THE DEVELOPMENT OF VERBAL TALENTS

William Fowler

Everyone knows that babies won't learn to talk in a wordless environment (Curtiss, 1977; Davis, 1940; 1947). But can their verbal competence be greatly enhanced through exposure to a highly enriched environment? And if it can, will exceptional verbal mastery early in life promote later excellence? If so, in what way? Just how important is early experience in the development of verbal talents?

Like other skills, competence in language is subject to the developmental interplay of heredity and environment. Verbal talents are not just gifts from on high; they must be developed through experience, beginning early in life and nurtured throughout development. Where language appears to differ from other skills is in the predominant role it serves in underpinning many other competencies – from scholarly learning to literary excellence, and possibly even mathematical abilities. I leave aside the question of specialization of neurological functions, assuming that, however specialized neurologically, all areas of competence are governed by the same interplay of nature and nurture (Kobler and Fein, 1988).

The aim of this chapter is to suggest how norms for language development can be advanced through improving the quality of early language stimulation, indicating possibilities for enhancing environmental control over talent development. We can do little at this stage of science to alter human heredity, even if we choose to, but the possibilities for enriching human development through multiplying opportunities for enhanced experience remain largely untapped. Perhaps most widely overlooked in the nature-nurture equation is how few life histories reflect even a moderate range of opportunities to acquire the skills, motivation and interest needed for excellence in any field. Present norms for development are in fact heavily constrained by cultural practices, which vary considerably. For example, in one study, English-speaking infants were found to utter their first word well in advance of Polish and Bulgarian infants (Bateman,

1917). Development of the average individual can apparently be greatly advanced over present norms.

The evidence to be reviewed is drawn from a variety of sources that indicate how dependent verbal excellence is on experience, in both early and later development. Data are drawn from the literature and the collected language research and case studies of myself and my students, supplemented by case studies of high IQ children and prodigies and biographies of eminent achievers. I shall also touch briefly on a model of the ecological dynamics and other issues in development.

EARLY STIMULATION

Considering the volumes of past research devoted to studying the influence on intellectual development of nature versus nurture, it is surprising how little this issue has influenced study of the development of competence in language. This neglect is probably largely because general intelligence has long been regarded as the primary determinant of human competence (Hunt, 1961). The many studies of the 1920s and 1930s on the effects of schooling, adoption, parent education and social class, twin status and other factors on mental development were centred on general intelligence assessed by IQ tests (Jones, 1954). The same is also true of the research on exceptional ability, and of the numerous investigations of giftedness, beginning with the monumental, life-span investigation of Terman and his associates (for example, Burks *et al.*, 1930; Terman, 1925; Terman and Oden, 1947). Although language development has been extensively studied, the predominant framework was long one of describing the process and charting norms for development (McCarthy, 1954). In the view of Gesell (1954) (perhaps the dominant figure in the field of child development from the 1920s through the 1940s), the development of virtually all abilities including language was a process of maturation, unfolding in response to the basic biology and general intelligence of the organism. Gesell's theories were more age-linked descriptions of behavioural development in several skill areas (language, motor, social and the loosely defined 'adaptive' category) than worked out conceptions of how development progressed (Gesell *et al.*, 1940). Such a climate discouraged both theoretical and empirical study of how language is acquired, even within the limited nature-nurture framework employed in studies of intelligence (IQ) (Jenkins and Paterson, 1961; Jones, 1954).

The arrival of Chomsky's theory of transformational grammar in the 1950s (1957; 1965) generated a tremendous burst of theoretically driven studies on how language is acquired (Gleitman and Wanner,

1984), in part because the strong cognitive basis of his theory linked with the newly emerging emphasis, stimulated by Piaget, on the dominance of cognitive processes in developmental theory. Yet, along with earlier hereditarian viewpoints, Chomsky's view that language follows a developmental timetable governed by a genetically regulated language acquisition device (LAD) has left a legacy that continues to obstruct consideration of how much and in what ways nurture contributes to the development of language, and of the degree to which talent or excellence in language can be induced in the general population.

Research on the influence of early experience on language development has taken three main forms:

- large scale studies on the effects of special schooling on mental development;

- correlational research (mostly on older children);

- short-term experimental studies designed to explore the effects of increased mental stimulation on various components of language learning and development.

Each of these three research approaches will be looked at in turn, before considering a few experimental studies, including those of the author, which have been designed to foster the long-term development of language competence as a total system.

Early Schooling and Intervention with Special Populations

Studies of early schooling reflect the different approaches of their two respective historical periods: from the 1920s to the 1940s the effects of nursery schooling on mental development were studied; the 1960s saw the introduction of the early intervention programmes designed to give children from impoverished environments a cognitive 'Head Start' before entering school.

As noted earlier (and elsewhere, for example, Fowler, 1983), studies in both periods were concerned with the development of general intelligence as measured by IQ tests, reflecting the widespread conception of intelligence and intellectual development as a unitary process. While language stimulation was sometimes emphasized, particularly in the later intervention research, it was characteristically embedded in a global programme of intellectual stimulation aimed at raising IQ scores. As a result, determining which factors influence the development of language competence even when separate measures of language were included in the tests, is a complex problem.

Nursery schooling had no more than modest effects on middle class children: rich home experiences largely paralleled the informal play practices of the nursery school curriculum, which did not really centre on the kind of verbal and academically oriented concepts that IQ tests measure (Anastasi, 1958; Fowler, 1962; 1983; Wellman, 1945).

Children from poor environments however, whose IQs generally ranged from 70 to 90, typically made modest to substantial IQ gains of 5 to 20 points in the research of both periods. Controls were often significantly exceeded by 5 to 10 points and IQ levels of between 90 and 100 attained; IQ levels of 110 or more were occasionally reached in certain intensive programmes with strong verbal-conceptual emphases (Hunt, 1975).

Aside from the problem of the global curriculum and the limited use of language measures, the overriding problem with all research on low IQ children in both eras was that it was essentially remedial. Even when started in early infancy (3 months) intensive cognitive remedial efforts for a brief one or two year period could hardly be expected to countervail the social ecology of poverty and thus to alter significantly the momentum of these children's lives (Gordon *et al.*, 1977). In all studies, without exception, children generally declined in all IQ, language and other cognitive measures in subsequent years, though marginal advantages in school performance over controls (for example, grade placement, avoidance of special placement, and reading and mathematical achievements) were often maintained through their school years (Lazar and Darlington, 1982; The Consortium for Longitudinal Studies, 1983).

In sum, all these studies showed the malleability of these special populations. They responded strongly to early cognitive and language stimulation, though probably without achieving their true verbal-cognitive potential, before gradually declining towards the normative levels of their milieux, in the face of their dominant socialization experiences. Selective early remedial experience, though making some long-term impact, was not a permanent fix.

Correlational Research

Numerous correlational studies suggest how important language experience is to language and mental development. Language stimulation has most often been studied as one of a cluster of variables to determine environmental influences on mental development with little regard to age (for example, Walberg, 1979), though some early investigators studied early development (Van Alstyne, 1929).

Even in recent research the focus on language has often remained blurred. In the many studies using the well known HOME Inventory (Home Observation for Measurement of the Environment) of Bradley and Caldwell (Gottfried, 1984), for example, the component scale that measures language stimulation combines in the same scale five items assessing maternal emotional attitudes with six verbal items (for example, mother's object naming, spontaneous vocalization) as the title of the scale, 'Emotional and Verbal Responsivity of Mother', indicates. In one study the significant correlations between 0.2 and 0.42 with scores on the Bayley at 24 months and the Binet at 48 months (Barnard *et al.*, 1984), typical of those found in other studies using this scale (Gottfried, 1984), may in fact seriously underestimate the influence of language stimulation alone on mental development (as the Clarke-Stewart, 1973, and Carew, 1980, studies summarized on the following pages would suggest).

Certain recent early stimulation studies have brought language into clearer focus, however. McCartney (1984) studied 166 children enrolled for at least 6 months in 9 day care centres for both advantaged and disadvantaged children. She found the overall quality of the centre, and specifically the quality of adult language stimulation, to be highly predictive of children's scores on three measures of language development at the ages of 36 to 68 months. The effects of language stimulation were only examined with regards to later infancy, however, as children did not enter day care until (on average) 19.2 months.

Two longitudinal studies further point up the importance of early language stimulation. In a study of 36 poor, first-born infants between 9 and 18 months, Clarke-Stewart (1973) found that mother's verbal stimulation was by far the most important variable relating to infant competence. It correlated 0.84 (0.70 of the variance) with infant competence, of which the most important loadings were the infant's language development (0.81), Bayley Mental Test scores (0.77) and the complexity of the child's schema (0.69).

Carew (1980) conducted two studies of white infants between 18 and 34 months, one in homes of varied socioeconomic status (N = 23), the other in six upper middle class day care centres. She found that much of the variance in the children's IQ scores at age 3 could be predicted from 'intellectual experiences unilaterally provided' by adults during the second year (55 per cent in the home and 48 per cent in day care), compared to what could be predicted from the child's solitary play (15 per cent in the home and 4 per cent in day care). Moreover, the majority of these intellectually valuable experiences consisted of adult-directed, language mastery types of experience, which significantly predicted 'receptive language' and 'spatial abilities' as well as IQ at age 3. Especially interesting was that in the home (but not day care) the child's ability to generate his or her own experiences in solitary play at 30 to 34 months also correlated with adult-directed, language mastery experiences prior to age 2½. Correlations with later self-directed activity were 0.62, 0.53 and 0.48 with adult verbally-guided stimulation at 12–15, 18–21 and 24–27 months, respectively. By age 3, however, the child's own activity in solitary play also begins to correlate significantly with IQ (0.51).

These investigations underscore the importance of early cognitive stimulation centring on language for the development of verbal and cognitive skills. Perhaps not surprisingly the child's own early explorations of the environment in spatial manipulative play appear to do little to advance the verbal-academic forms of mental development measured by IQ tests. In contrast, adult language-mediated cognitive activity appears to function as the chief agent of verbal-abstract mental development during infancy. But once the child's foundation of language and cognitive competence has begun to take shape, towards age 3, the child is able to make increasing use of these acquired verbal competencies to shape his or her own further mental development, as Carew's study suggests.

Short-term Experimental Studies

Just about all dimensions of language have proved highly responsive to stimulation during the early years. Following Rheingold *et al.*'s (1959) control over vocalization rates through social reinforcement (smiles, caresses and sounds), Hamilton (1977) succeeded in increasing significantly through modelling the vocalization of vowels, consonants and single words over their base rates in 9 to 15 month old infants compared with controls. Irwin (1960) increased phonemic frequencies in infants by having mothers read and discuss picture books and label things from the age of 13 months to the age of 30 months. Shvarchkin (cited in Ervin and Miller, 1963, p.111) over a period of 11 months taught infants to discriminate all of the Russian phonemes by 22 months through presenting a selected series of words, varying one phoneme at a time. Using a word labelling play strategy with picture blocks, Mallitskaya (1960) stimulated infants between 9 and 17 months to acquire a vocabulary of 9 words as early as 11 months, learning new words with no more than two or three trials. Following Cazden (summarized in Fowler, 1983, p.249), Nelson (1977) taught two groups of 2½ year olds different forms of syntactical construction they had never used before. She recast their sentences into either complex verb forms (conditional or future tense) or complex question forms (tag or negative questions). With only five single hour sessions over two months, each group became significantly advantaged over the other in the particular form they were taught.

In many ways Strayer's (1930) classic study on Gesell's identical twins, T and C (for trained and control), epitomizes both the strengths and weaknesses of the short-term experimental approach. She stimulated vocabulary development through labelling in twin T for 5 weeks from 84 to 88 weeks, while twin C remained in a largely speechless environment (ethically questionable today). She then stimulated C for four weeks. As in other studies, the infants proved highly responsive to selective stimulation, *both* twins learning around 30 words. But each twin gained in different ways, contradicting the maturational theories of Gesell which Strayer followed. The brevity, close spacing and narrowness of the training, however, as discussed before (Fowler, 1962; 1983), made a poor test of the cumulative effects of early language stimulation on development.

Taken together these studies focus on brief, not always well-timed stimulation of selected components of language with little regard to the development of competence in language as a total system. Yet with all their shortcomings, they contain a powerful message. They indicate the ease with which the beginning stages of different aspects of language can be manipulated and shaped through stimulation. Language is apparently a highly flexible system whose components can be selectively advanced through manipulating experience during the early stages of first language acquisition.

Total Language Stimulation in Infancy

Effective study of the influence of experience on language development would seem to require as a minimum:

1. stimulating language systematically as a total cognitive system;

2. beginning in early infancy before the language skills normatively expected for a population are acquired through cultural practice;

3. maintaining the special stimulation at least to the stage of mastering the basics of language (for example, syntax, narrative theme skills) to determine the mastery levels and earliness obtainable;

4. ultimately following up experimental results to determine long-term effects. In short, can language talents be experimentally induced in a reliable fashion, and once induced what is needed to maintain them?

Intensive studies in disadvantaged ecologies. Recognizing the severe limitations of the 'hit and run' early interventions, certain investigators attempted massive interventions with the total ecology of disadvantaged children. Hunt (1986; Hunt *et al.*, 1976) conducted a series of interventions with successive randomly selected waves (groups) of foundlings in a Tehran orphanage prior to the Islamic revolution, beginning at four weeks or less. In addition to improved general care and caregiver–infant care ratios (from 1:10 to 1:3 or 1:2) and special attention to toy play, Wave 5 received special language stimulation from caregivers specially trained in Hunt's vocalization interaction dialogue and word labelling techniques. By the average mean age of 88 weeks (20 months) these infants had attained the top levels on all seven of Uzgiris and Hunt's (1975) Piagetian cognitive scales; by 93 weeks (22 months) they had attained the top levels of the language scale, just ahead of the ages (94 weeks) attained by a sample of US infants from professional families. All infants had vocabularies of at least 50 words between 17 and 24 months (Hunt, 1986; Hunt et al., 1976), close to or slightly ahead of US norms of 21 months on the CLAMS Scale (Capute et al., 1987). Wave 4 infants attained top levels on the language scale by 115 weeks (27 months), a remarkable finding considering that their chief form of cognitive and language stimulation consisted only of audiovisual enrichment with tape recorded music, 'mother talk', and special mobiles, contingent on infant activation, and that caregiving followed the low-level institutional routines with ratios remaining at 1:10. At 93 weeks wave 5 was eight months advanced over institutional norms (126 weeks for Wave 1 controls), which virtually guaranteed their eligibility for adoption by affluent, educated families who would ensure the adequacy of their later cognitive and personal development. These outcomes are similar to but generally better than the results of other remedial-adoption results (for example, Dennis, 1973; Skeels, 1966; Flint, 1978), apparently because of the earliness of intervention and the systematic language focus of the stimulation. It cannot be said, however, that the overall results matched the full language or cognitive potentials of the infants.

An even more comprehensive effort by Heber et al. (1972) with severely disadvantaged black children achieved even more impressive results from long-term intensive early stimulation and maternal child care and vocational guidance, though the children followed a regressive course in later cognitive development. Beginning at three to six months and continuing until age six, 20 infants attended a highly structured, individually sequenced, verbal academic programme in a day care centre five days per week for 12 months each year.

From the age of 15 months experimental infants consistently surpassed controls on all IQ, language and other concept measures (Garber and Heber, 1981). Between 18 months and 6 years experimental infants averaged above 120 IQ on the Gesell-Catell-Binet test series used, given at three to four month intervals, control infants gradually falling to about 95 IQ and below from the age of two, with almost no overlap between distributions. The same divergent pattern was evident in language development from the age of 18 months. Experimental infants were four months in advance of Gesell norms and six months in advance of controls by 22 months. On various measures of spontaneous speech activity, experimentals were generally consistently ahead of controls on cumulative vocabulary and syntactic development thereafter, their mean length of utterances (MLU) being comparable to Miller and Chapman's (1981) middle class samples. Both experimental and control groups developed in their traditional black dialect. Experimental infants' language scores on the Illinois Test of Psycholinguistics Abilities at age 6 were 108 against 86 for the respective experimental controls, a difference of 22 IQ equivalent points, comparable to their general IQ differences.

In follow-up assessments, however, experimentals slowly declined toward controls. By age 10 the respective mean scores on the WISC were 105 to 85 (Garber and Heber, 1981). Almost no experimental children fell below 85 IQ, while 60 per cent of the controls were below 85 and 80 per cent of these were below 80 IQ. By age 14 mean IQ score differences had narrowed to 100 versus 94, though experimentals maintained advantages in grade placement and avoidance of special classes, and later in graduation rates (62 per cent to 52 per cent) (Garber, 1988, personal communication), as in other studies. No separate data on later language competence are available.

These findings are encouraging with respect to how far the cognitive and language potentials of children from impoverished environments can be actualized through comprehensive early and long-term programmes. But the findings also underscore the magnitude of the efforts required and the limitations on the results. Though gains were remarkable, children probably fell short of realizing their full potential, and once the research based intensive stimulation was terminated at age 6, the debilitating ecology of their milieux gradually eroded their above-average cognitive foundation, pulling them downwards towards community norms to converge with controls, except for marginal achievement advantages similar to those found in all early intervention studies. Disadvantaged populations would seem to require total transformation of community support and opportunities throughout development to gain any hope of permanently realizing their cognitive and linguistic potentials.

Selected studies in advantaged middle class milieux. Two limited studies suggest greater possibilities for early stimulation in a healthy ecology. Metzl (1980) guided two groups of parents (both parents versus mother only) of 20 first-born infants in vocalization play and various word labelling activities for only $1\frac{1}{2}$ hours at each of three infant ages (6, 12 and 18 weeks). Mean Bayley Mental Scale IQ levels at post-testing (6 months) for the two parent and single mother groups were 112 and 109 respectively, both significantly higher than the 104 for controls (no pretests). At follow up (ages 5 to 6), mean Binet IQs for the respective groups were 125.6, 121.2 and 114.1, while mean scores on the Zimmerman Language Scales were 131, 124 and 116 (cited in Storfer, 1990, chapter 10).

Drash and Stolberg (1977; 1979) modelled and discussed behavioural modification techniques in cognitive, linguistic and social skills with parents for three hours a week over a period of seven months in the case of three 6 month old infants and over 5 months for one three month old infant. Mean Cattell IQs were 136 at post-testing (12 months) and 145 at first follow up (23 months). Mean Binet IQ was 157 (N = 3) at second follow up (43 months). Mean language quotients on the Peabody Picture Vocabulary Test were 149 and 133 at the respective follow ups and Vineland Social Maturity quotients were 169 and 207.

Though only modestly exceeding middle class norms, given the extraordinary brevity of the training, Metzl's results are promising. The high level gains Drash and Stolberg produced, on the other hand, making due account for lack of controls and the miniscule sample, give a hint of what extended early stimulation can offer in the way of exceeding norms and realizing competence potentials in an enriched ecology, as our studies will further indicate.

THE INVESTIGATOR'S RESEARCH: EARLY TOTAL LANGUAGE STIMULATION

This investigator and his students (Fowler, 1983, vol.2; Fowler and Swenson, 1979; Ogston, 1983; Swenson, 1983) have conducted a series of studies on early language stimulation. Parents are guided through stimulation techniques of parent-infant interaction in play, common child care routines and other activities. The methods are conceptualized in terms of a cognitively oriented inquiry strategy designed to facilitate the development of complex verbal concepts and verbally mediated cognitive development.

The heart of the method is guiding parents in word-phrase labelling activities, in the course of interacting with their infants from the first months of development. They are guided in both labelling objects, actions and relationships among components in the child's play initiatives and themselves initiating play and caregiving initiatives that provide items suitable for labelling. The strategy involves sequencing the language labelling, beginning with concrete nouns and simple actions, moving through prepositional relations to more abstract modifiers (adjectives, adverbs), pronouns and various other parts of speech, then phrase–sentence constructions and theme narration, with increasing complexity. Developmental pacing, flexibility, interactiveness, and an informal play orientation have been central to the process. The emphasis is also on language as both a communication and a referential tool to facilitate social and complex, generalized cognitive development.

Individual developmental profiles of common indices of the beginning stages of vocabulary and sentence development are presented in Table 1 for all research and case study infants from all prior studies in middle class families.

The advantage of pooling data from several studies in this instance is to present the results of a series of replications that demonstrate the regularity with which early competence in language can be experimentally produced. As may be seen, all infants without exception were advanced over common scale norms on all word and sentence acquisition indices for available data. (Data are complete for all 30 subjects on most early indices and extensive for 50 word vocabulary and longer sentence constructions.) The advancement is evident even at the beginning stages, when the mean ages for first using two to five words or more are advanced over the REEL Scale norms by between 2.8 and 3.8 months. Later stages of acquiring 10 to 20, then 50 word vocabularies and combining words into two, three and four word phrases are increasingly in advance of norms, by as much as a mean of 18 months by the time infants begin to master sentences of four words or more. The effects of stimulating infants systematically over extended periods of early infancy, compared to following cultural practices are thus cumulative, at least through the periods of development assessed. Rates of development generally accelerated over the course of the infants' second year. The apparent exception is the mean age of acquiring a 50 word vocabulary (6 months advanced versus 8 months advanced for reaching a 10–20 word level). This irregularity can probably be explained by two factors: this item is from a different language scale (The CLAMS); family problems slowed some children down, as is discussed later. The later sentence indices were also often minimum estimates, in many cases children had probably produced sentences of the length given some weeks or months before the lengths recorded in the formal tests.

Every infant was advanced over norms on *all* indices and the overwhelming majority substantially so: 27 (90 per cent) of the 30 infants said their first two words at least 1.5 months ahead of norms (≤ 9 months versus 10.5 months), and *all* were at least two months advanced in saying at least five words (≤ 11 months versus 13 months); 25 (83 per cent) were three to seven months advanced in the ages of saying five words or more. The extent and consistency of acceleration is also indicated by the fact that 16 infants (53 per cent) were from four to seven months ahead of the five plus word norm and 21 of 27 infants (78 per cent) were from 7 to 12 months ahead of the 21 months norm in beginning to use two word phrases.

Looking at these developmental patterns in terms of IQ equivalent Language Quotient (LQ) scores, as Hunt *et al.* (1976) did (MA/CA, using the normative age for item attainment as the MA), it is evident

Table 1.   Profiles of language development and short-term follow-up[a] (middle-class samples)

Study/child	Sex	Starting age (in months)	total vocabulary (no. of words)					sentence length (no. of words)			MEAN LENGTH OF UTTERANCES (MLUs)[b]		SHORT-TERM FOLLOW-UP — mental test quotients					
													30 months		42 months		60 months	
			2	5+	10–20	50	250	2	3	4+	24 months	42 months	LQ	IQ	LQ	IQ	LQ	IQ
Norms			10.5m	13m	19m	21m	36m	21m	23m	36m	1.9	3.7	100LQ	100IQ	100LQ	100IQ	100LQ	100IQ
Study I																		
S1	F	4	8	9	10	14		12	15	16	4.7				181	140		146[dg]
S2	M	4	7	8	9	18		12	18	18	3.9				182	138		144[dg]
53	M	5	8	9	10	13		12	16	17	3.7				171	128		134[dh]
Study IV																		
SA	M	6	7	9	9	11	19	12	12	19								
SK	F	8	9	9	10	12	18	12	17	17			187	140				124[f]
SM	M	5	7	7	10	18	23	10	21	21								140
ST	M	6	9	11	11	14[e]		13[e]	19	27					148	132		160
Ogston																		
L1	F	3	7	9	10	16[e]		12	15				185	157				130
L2	F	4	10	10	11			10					158	133				
L3	M	5	10	10	11				16				121	111				
L4	F	3	8	10	13	17[e]		15							169	130		
L5	F	4	8	9	12	16[e]		11	14				144	142				
L6	M	2	9	9	10	16[e]		11					119	111				

Subject	Sex	Entry	C1	C2	C3	C4	C5	C6	C7	MLU₂₇	MLU₄₈	IQ
Swenson A												
A1	F	4	6	8	10	15	10	11	15		5.3	164[d]
A2	F	3	8	11	14	19[e]	14	13	16		6.1	
A3	F	2	6	10	10	14	10	12		3.0	5.3	
A4	M	2	8	9	12	17[e]	12	13[e]	17		5.1	
A5	F	3	8	10	10	12	10	16[e]		2.5	5.0	120[d]
A6	M	3	8	11	13	19[e]	13	12			5.5	
Swenson B												
B1	F	8	8	10	11	18	11	15	15		5.7	
B2	F	8	9	11	11	17[e]	11	15	15		5.5	
B3	F	6	8	11	11	18	11	15				
B4	M	6	8	9	10	16	15	17	22		5.1	
B5	F	7	9	10	11	16	17	26		4.3	6.1	
B6	M	7	10	10	11	17	17			3.2	5.3	
Case studies												
V	F	3	8	9[e]	10[e]	13[e]	11[e]	12[e]	13[e]	5.0		154[d]
M	F	3	8	10	12	14	11	14				
H	F	2	6	7	9	13	14	16				139[d]
Z	F	0	4	6	10	13	9	9	16	5.1		
A	M	0	3	6	11	15	9	15	19			
Ns		30	30	30	30	26	4	27	20	16	16	
Means		7.7	9.2	10.7	15.4	18.5	15.4	12.2	14.8	18.4		
LQ[a]		136	141	178	136	195	136	172	155	197		

[a] Collected research from subject and case study records. Data are drawn from Fowler, 1983, vol. 2, chapters 3–5; Fowler and Swenson, 1979 and research files of Fowler, Ogston (personal communication) and Swenson (personal communication).

[b] Several cases in which ages varied slightly from ages indicated nevertheless still greatly exceeded norms (e.g. MLUs at 27 and 48 months = 2.4 and 4.3).

[c] Reel Scale (Bzoch and League, 1970), except: 50 and 250 word vocabulary = CLAMS Scale (Capute *et al.*, 1987); 4 + word sentences and all quotient scores = Griffiths Scales (1970) or Binet Scale, where indicated (d); MLUs = Miller and Chapman (1981)

[d] Stanford Binet

[e] Highly probable, by inference

[f] Stanford Binet 128 at 72 months

[g] Stanford Binet at 96 months: S1 = 134, S2 = 145

[h] Stanford Binet at 15 months: 106

that high levels of language competence were attained, generally exceeding those historically defined as gifted at 130 IQ or more, and often by wide margins. Even in the early word learning stages mean LQs ranged between 136 and 141. In later stages mean LQs ranged from 155 to 197 for both vocabulary and sentence length, except for the (still substantial) mean LQ of 136 for 50 word vocabulary.

The importance of the quality of home life (and the child's health) to parental language stimulation emerges in selected cases from our research, in which language failed to progress optimally during certain periods. For example, child L1's rates of development fell off when the parents separated and her mother started to work (apparently delaying his use of three word sentences). L5's development was similarly slowed over later stages (50 word vocabulary and using longer sentences) by the irregularity of his care (both parents working) and a shift to a bilingual environment (French speaking babysitter). L3's development was disrupted and slowed by a family move and continuing remodelling of the new home. L6 was placed on phenobarbital for several weeks, following seizures at 13 months, which seriously distorted pronunciation and parent-child communication, slowing his exceptional progress. Parent responsiveness was also an important factor: for example, good interaction avoids over-directiveness (Ogston, 1983). There were no consistent gender differences in language development, however.

Other ecological circumstances exercised important influences. In two other language stimulation studies, infants from less educated foreign language speaking families (four each from functionally illiterate Italian immigrants and high school educated Chinese immigrants) made substantial language gains over norms, though rates ranged from one to three months behind those of the college educated, English speaking families of Table 1, similar to the Hunt *et al.* (1976) and Heber and Garber (1972) studies. Our research has suggested that shifting family ecologies also apparently erased the initial significant advantage of early starting over later starting programme infants (Swenson's A versus B groups). Language stimulation and development lagged in three of the A group (half the sample) as a result of family problems (A2 = house burning down, financial difficulties and separation; A4 = uninvolved father, separation and bilingual day care; A6 = mother's excessively rapid speech style). While two of the B group experienced home difficulties (B2 = initially uninvolved parents; B3 = generational conflict with grandmother), only one child's difficulties (B3) persisted. Later ecological problems among certain other early starters also interfered with the apparent advantage very early starting conferred. S2's development at nine months levelled off for about three months when his parents left him at home for a week's vacation. The progress of case study child A (first word at three months) was impeded at 11 months by flu, the mother's broken nose, and the father's knee surgery, though parental preoccupation with the first child also contributed to later slowing the early beginnings. First-born status is helpful in motivating and freeing parents to focus stimulation, but not essential however, as the faster pace of case study child H over her elder sibling S2 indicates. Substantially larger samples will be necessary to determine at just what ages and ecological conditions optimal progress can be realized.

Fortunately, in most cases, improved home circumstances renewed children's development during the course of the programme. L1's language development slowed down when the family moved (age 7 months), but when the family moved again (13 months), special attention and unpacking the child's toys immediately, appeared to prevent deceleration. Renewed attention to S2, on the parents' return from vacation, and to case study child A, on the family's recovery from illness and injuries, gradually regenerated their former accelerated rates in a similar way.

Later Development

What of follow-up? How well do these early established foundations of high verbal competence hold up in later development, once professional intervention is terminated? At short-term follow-ups, the mean length of utterances (MLU) at various later ages are greatly advanced over even middle class norms (Table 1). MLUs are widely considered one of the best single measures of development because sentence length increases with growth in the complexity of language (Brown, 1973). All infants for whom data are available (N = 16) produced sentences one to four morpheme units longer than the norms of Miller and Chapman's (1981) parallel middle class sample between ages two to four years. Further evidence of the generally temporary quality of ecological setbacks in the home also show up in the later MLUs of A2, A4 and A6, and of B2, all of whom attained the same high levels of the other children. Only B3 may have lagged (no follow up), as no phrases were evident at programme termination (17–18 months).

Similarly, both the LQ and IQ scores of the children assessed between 30 and 60 months (N = 14) indicated that very high levels of competence, often beyond the gifted level were generally maintained (Table 1). The LQs of all except two children were at least 140, and most were well above 150 on the Griffiths Hearing and Speech Scale. Of the two who fell below 130, L3's (LQ = 121) development may have been further impeded because of continued parent preoccupation with remodelling, and L6 (LQ = 119) may have experienced longer-term effects from his seizures and medicine. The Griffiths

General Quotient (GQ) and Binet IQ scores of all except these two and of one other child, SK (whose LQ was still 140), were similarly around 130 or more. Language scores were almost always considerably higher than IQ scores, reflecting the concentrated development of language skills, but advancing competence in language also mediated concept development in other areas where verbal concepts play important roles (for example, social, mathematical and problem-solving skills). Thus over the short term, in the period immediately following termination of professional guidance, it appeared that most parents assimilated the programme's language interaction concepts well enough to be able to maintain the quality of language based cognitive stimulation and home care at the levels needed to sustain development at the accelerated rates. In this they were aided by the rational orientation, verbal conceptual competencies, and cognitive autonomy infants typically developed over the course of the programme, which frequently led children to initiate projects and explore on their own (extensive question asking was common).

Long-term follow-up assessments of later development are in progress, and will continue into adolescence. Variable amounts of evidence to date on some 11 cases indicate generally advanced reading and other verbal competencies; initiative in pursuing intellectual project activities (especially extensive reading, and some creative writing); generally high IQs (where available) from 130 to 150+, but with declining IQs in two cases, one of which is associated with intense family conflict and behavioural problems; high mathematical and foreign language learning skills in some cases; some grade acceleration or gifted programme participation; and consistently high academic achievement, interest and extracurricular participation in school. Ten out of 13 cases to date developed prereading skills (for example, letter and word identification and printing) before age four, and 6 of 11 children were early readers (between two and five).

These collected studies furnish substantial evidence that serious attention to the quality of cognitively oriented language stimulation during infancy will enable virtually all children enjoying adequate home environments to surpass cultural norms for language development, often reaching levels historically associated with 'giftedness'. It also suggests that, given around twelve months of professional early intervention, most families will assimilate techniques adequately to maintain these levels of mastery for at least a number of years, and (preliminary evidence indicates) in some cases much longer, into adolescence and beyond. These studies also suggest that cognitively oriented language stimulation during infancy may be an important basis for facilitating the development of general processing, academic type competencies reflected in IQ test scores.

THE EARLY LIVES OF THOSE WITH LATER EXCELLENCE

What do early stimulation histories of individuals with proven high abilities in later development and adulthood tell us? Intensive language stimulation during infancy has regularly developed high verbal mastery and indications of promising later development in our research. But if verbal stimulation is essential to later excellence in language-related domains, the early histories of great intellects in verbal fields, those with high IQs, prodigies and renowned historical figures, should also be replete with evidence of exceptional verbal stimulation histories.

Early Verbal Stimulation of High IQ Children

Among the historically 'gifted', exceptional abilities do not appear to develop without exceptional nurture. I recently reviewed numerous case history studies of 140+ IQ children (Fowler, 1981), collected early in the century largely to document accelerated development believed to result from inherited general intelligence measured by IQ tests (for example, Gesell, 1922; Hollingworth, 1926; Terman, 1919, 1925; Witty, 1930; Yates, 1922). Despite the generally biased case history recording, which downplayed the influence of experience, indications of exceptional early verbal nurture frequently crept into the records. For example, highly intensive early home stimulation was evident in 87 per cent of each of the groups of 23 children in two different studies (percentages and numbers of children are coincidentally the same for both studies) with Binet IQs of around 140 or more (Root, 1921; Terman, 1919). (No data were available on the other children.)

I have also located 21 cases of 180+ IQ children with even better infant records (Burks *et al.*, 1930; Bush, 1914; Dvorak, 1923; Gesell, 1922; Goldberg, 1935; Hollingworth, 1942; Jones, 1923; Langenbeck, 1915; Root, 1921; Stedman, 1924; Witty and Jenkins, 1935). What stands out is the enormous amount of attention parents typically devoted to early verbal stimulation that combined both oral language and written symbol stimulation. Among the common activities are extensive word labelling; endless talking with the infant; avoiding 'baby talk'; constant attention to word meaning and vocabulary development; explaining everything; encouraging and answering all questions; and generally employing a highly open-ended but rational, verbal-logical and problem-solving orientation toward guiding their infant's development. Beginning ages are not always specified, but the pattern in all 21 cases appeared to extend from earliest infancy on.

The case of Elizabeth (Langenbeck, 1915), whose IQ at age 5 was 220, contained considerable detail. Reared as an only child by parents and a nurse, everything that engaged the infant's attention was labelled 'precisely' and in all its parts. She 'never heard' baby talk, but instead was read to and taught word meanings constantly. Elizabeth was gradually also taught the alphabet, and, well before the age of four, had learned to read, to spell and to write. In common with such cases, the parents maintained high expectations, kept extensive records from birth, and the child associated mainly with adults. There is even a fascinating case of identical twins (Gesell, 1922), *both* attaining IQs above 180. Their mother was their 'constant companion' from infancy. She stimulated their development 'with the aid of plays and games' (p.312), teaching them, for example, the parts of speech, a wide general knowledge, and at the age of three, to read in English, French and Esperanto.

Attention to written symbols and reading often began in the first or second year of infancy, leading in all except two cases to fluent reading before five, and usually between two and four. (One of the others almost certainly read before school also, as he was reading H.G. Wells by age seven.) Letters and words were typically learned through play with alphabet blocks, typewriter keys (in case D of Hollingworth, 1942, sitting in his mother's lap almost from birth), or signs, as well as with books. One child (case C, Hollingworth, 1942) 'learned to read and talk almost simultaneously' (p.256).

Intensive early verbal stimulation would thus appear to be an important agent in developing excellence in the verbal-logical abilities that IQ tests reflect. Case studies do not of course prove that these relations are invariable or causally connected, but the high frequency of occurrence is certainly provocative. Nor is special, language-focused early stimulation alone sufficient to generate intellectual excellence of this type. Besides the contributions of later developmental stimulation (to be discussed shortly), early stimulation in these cases is typically broadly-based, embedded in teaching problem solving, reasoning and general knowledge, which are also frequently mentioned in the case reports. Learning to use language, to learn letters and to read were not viewed by parents as ends in themselves but as doors opening opportunities to gain knowledge, academic competence or literary excellence, all of which were variously stressed from the beginning. Verbal and reading competencies were the foci and mediators (the codes) for advancing knowledge and logical reasoning, however, underscoring the role early language stimulation plays in the development of high IQs and academic competence.

Early Verbal Stimulation of Child Prodigies and Eminent Intellectuals

Intensive stimulation of language and reading from infancy on is also the hallmark of the child prodigy (defined by precocious intellectual achievements versus IQ; Dolbear, 1912). Historical examples like that of Christian Heinrich Heinekin in the 1820s are sometimes enshrouded in legend: he was said to have mastered the Old and New Testaments by 14 months. Still, through all cases of prodigies runs the same thread of very early intensive language labelling, reasoning, and attention to written symbols and reading found in children with exalted IQs. Emilie Basedow, for example, a renowned eighteenth century prodigy (whose educator-father was inspired by Rousseau), was, at an early age, 'taught [through play] the names and properties of objects by hearing them clearly stated' (p.471), and she learned to read in English before three and in French shortly after (Dolbear, 1912). The education of Karl Witte, an early nineteenth century Dante scholar was planned by his father from birth: his father began by constantly labelling everything as he carried the baby around the house, and gradually encouraged question asking, logical reasoning and wide acquisition of knowledge (Witte, 1914; Dolbear, 1912). Karl was taught to read and spell accurately by four. Later examples include Norbert Wiener, the founder of cybernetics, an important basis for the development of computer science (Newman, 1963). His nurse taught him the alphabet at 18 months by drawing letters in the sand and his father taught him to read by three (Dolbear, 1912; Wiener, 1953). He read Darwin at six. The parents of William James Sidis, perhaps the greatest recent prodigy, educated him systematically through play, starting with alphabet blocks in his first few months (Dolbear, 1912; Wallace, 1986). His first words appeared at six months, he could read and spell by three, type by four, learned several languages in a few years, and completed all school grades in half a year at school. A more recent example is the Susedik family of four Japanese-American children, whose intensive life-long stimulation began at birth with object and alphabet labelling (Bell, 1982). All have 150+ IQs and are well advanced in grade; the eldest is a premedical, second year college student at age 12 (Woodley, 1982).

The early stimulation histories of eminent scholars, writers and scientists are equally rich verbally (Cox, 1926; Dolbear, 1912; Galton, 1925; McCurdy, 1957; Fowler, 1983; 1986). Because so many were taught to read advanced material between three and five, their cognitive foundation almost certainly had to be built with a scaffolding of high quality language experiences prerequisite to mastering fluent reading so young. For example, in the studies of three of my students who each selected randomly five eminent historical figures from three pools of playwrights (Durbach, 1979), Victorian novelists (Este, 1979), and scientists (Tetroe, 1979), at least 11 (and probably 13) out of the total of 15 had been taught to read during the preschool period. Note that, while competence in language is the very fabric out of which plays and novels are woven, science (at least natural science) is generally thought to be more dependent on logical-mathematical skills and specialized knowledge. Yet four of the five scientists (and probably the fifth) were early readers, suggesting the value early excellence in language may contribute to competence in science. These three student studies are summarized in more detail in Fowler (1983, pp.366–367).

Surprisingly, competence in mathematics may also be strongly linked to early verbal stimulation. Note that both Wiener and Sidis began their intensive education in infancy with language and reading. In a biographical study of 25 historically great mathematicians (18 men and 7 women) I found that 16 of them (64 per cent) had been taught to read between three and five (Fowler, 1986). (In the other cases the relevant data is not available.) Moreover, the intensive education of at least 21 of the mathematicians began at least by the age of three with reading the classics and writing, including instruction in foreign languages in 10 cases. Thus verbal stimulation was apparently the common denominator of their early experiences, while special early mathematics stimulation was mentioned in only 16 cases. Bloom (1985) reports a similar trend in his extensive study of the developmental histories of contemporary mathematicians. Intensive early verbal and general cognitive stimulation composed their main fare, with early parental attention to mathematical concepts and reasoning much less frequent.

What of infancy? While records of infancy are sparse, intensive language stimulation was evident or inferrable in at least nine cases (Fowler, 1986). As a result of poor health, Descartes was showered with exceptional attention by his grandmother and nurse from birth, then educated first informally then systematically by his father (a judge devoted to education) beginning at 14 months at his mother's death. Gauss was exposed to letters, reading, numbers and calculation from infancy – informally through such devices as the calendar, in family interaction with a highly devoted mother, a skilled accountant father, and a philosopher uncle. Francis Galton, the psychological statistician, was engaged from birth all day long in play with his 11 year old sister, Adele. She 'taught him his letters in play, and he could point to all before he could speak' (Pearson, 1914, p.630). He could read before three and write by four.

Exceptional mathematical skills also emerged in a number of children in our research on early language stimulation: all three children in Study I, two of the four in Study IV, and one of the four Chinese children (Fowler and Swenson, 1979). Between the ages of three and four, quotients on the Griffiths mathematical scale (counting and measurement skills) ranged from 140 to 180+, four scoring above 160. (Other children were not assessed, because they had not reached the mathematics scale starting age of two.) This trend can be interpreted as the result of close parallels in abstract symbol manipulation demands inherent in both verbal and mathematical language codes. Early intensive stimulation in verbal competence may perhaps easily transfer to interest and competence in mathematical skills, assuming at least some milieu support, as was in fact observed among some of our subjects, and was clearly typical among great mathematicians.

EARLY EXPERIENCE AND LATER DEVELOPMENT

Early experience was of course never the sole cause of the later high IQs and the exceptional competencies and achievements of the intellectually great. If language-based cognitive stimulation started the process toward high competence, many other factors were essential to keep it going. Continued support was never lacking, usually from parents, but commonly also from other relatives, teachers, older peers or benefactors. These supports often also served as models and mentors who directly guided, discussed, furnished resources, or otherwise interacted in intellectually stimulating ways.

The five playwrights (Durbach, 1979) and five novelists (Este, 1979) all enjoyed tutors and association with models and mentors of literary excellence. From babyhood Eugene O'Neill grew up in the theatre, surrounded by actors, attending plays, evaluating their quality, often with his father, an actor. Yeats associated with literary figures throughout childhood. From his earliest days Hardy heard endless stories around the family hearth from his grandfather and others; he was also guided in advanced literature by his mother. The great mathematicians, men and women alike, probably all had special tutors, schooling and mentors in various combinations throughout development (Fowler, 1986). Descartes' highly educated father educated his son intensively until eight, when he enjoyed fine mathematics and philosophy teachers and the company of a stimulating older mathematics student in Jesuit school. Gauss enjoyed various mentors and had numerous intellectual discussions with his philosopher uncle. The woman mathematician, Noether, grew up participating in the seminars of her mathematics professor father, held in the home (because her father was lame). Galton's sister educated him intensively until he was sent to a special school at eight (Pearson, 1914).

High IQ children and child prodigies followed the same course of intensive verbally stimulating activities throughout development (or as far as reported). Intensive parental effort continued but the forms of guidance gradually altered. Parents (and other mentors) interacted in projects and intellectual discussions, increasingly as equals. Parents encouraged and supported independent project activity, actively intervened with schools for grade acceleration, taught or arranged for special instruction (in, for example, mathematics, history and foreign languages), and above all provided an intellectual climate of ideas, skills and strong interest in and expectations for learning. In some cases, teachers or principals took a special interest, recommending or supplying advanced books and generally providing encouragement and an intellectual dialogue.

Among prodigies, the brilliant fathers of both Wiener and Sidis tutored their sons in a broad array of subjects (mathematics, history and foreign languages) over many years, both entering college in the early teens (Wallace, 1986; Wiener, 1953). Here too the form of interaction gradually changed to become relations between equals, especially with Sidis whose mathematical competencies exceeded those of his father by the time he entered and lectured at Harvard at the age of 11. Feldman (1986) reports similar strategies among his verbal prodigies, with parents also engaging other fine minds to support their child's exceptional talent development. The Susedik family's high scholarship educational programme for their children continued at least until they entered college (Bell, 1982).

Not all high IQ children and child prodigies followed smooth courses of development, of course. All children experienced vicissitudes of one sort or another, such as teachers unreceptive to brilliant, independent-thinking children who could not fit in easily and could not profit from rigid, lock step school curricula and rituals, or social ostracism from peers (Horowitz and O'Brien, 1985). Some children fell by the wayside to one degree or another, their IQs and skills declining as a result of shifting ecological circumstances (McCall *et al.*, 1973) similar to those described above in our research, underscoring the importance of maintaining a healthy intellectual ecology and stimulating cognitive activity throughout all phases of development. For the most part, the cases reviewed here were developmental successes by selection, especially the eminent intellectuals. Yet even among these selected cases, signs of the impact of adverse experiences upon development appeared. The most renowned example is William James Sidis, whose later career seemed to fall short of his early prodigious promise. Contrary to popular opinion, however, it was not his early intensive intellectual education that later 'burned him out' (Wallace, 1986). Rather, his father made him a public showpiece of his theories in a way which galvanized media hostility, particularly because of young Sidis' naïvety and later radical political activities. He continued to produce brilliant works throughout his life, but not in the mould of an institutionally supported career. (Two notable examples of erudite books are his *The Animate and Inanimate,* a complex treatise on the theory of black holes, years ahead of any other work on the subject, and a 1,200 page (unpublished) revisionist history of the United States, also antedating later works on the life of native Americans prior to the European conquest.) Norbert Wiener followed a more conventional path to great achievements (except for his early college entry), but his psychosocial problems originated less in adverse publicity than in the overly dominating style of his father, which required years to overcome and for Norbert to establish his personal identity.

Several high IQ cases also reveal signs of ecological conflicts emerging during later development. Most of them centre on peer or curriculum conflicts over their discrepantly high abilities that eventually become resolved in high school where academic pursuits become more interesting and acceptable (for example, the case of Madeline; see Burks *et al.*, 1930, p.268), though not always. Certain cases of girls appear to demonstrate closed career choices for women in earlier eras. For example, Elizabeth (Hirt, 1922), at age 22 remained at home writing poetry; yet as with the case of Emily Dickenson (or William James Sidis), formal career success is not the only criterion of high verbal intellectual achievement in adulthood. In any case, nearly all the cases reviewed here are of more conventional high-level careers which were ecologically well supported through the periods reported.

THE CONTRIBUTIONS OF EARLINESS

If earliness followed by continued emphasis on exceptional verbal stimulation are apparently both indispensable to the development of later excellence in verbal fields, can the special contributions of early stimulation be identified? The question is in some ways easy to answer. Earliness establishes a complex foundation that makes it possible for the child to respond to increasingly complex stimulation at successive ages. If any consistent strand can be traced through all cases of exceptional verbal-cognitive skills from all sources, it is that the education of preschoolers who emerge from infancy with advanced verbal skills and concepts requires a far more complex curriculum than that of the average preschooler. Later excellence builds on early mastery. Later stimulation must be tailored to the skills acquired: the more complex the early skills the more complex the later curriculum. Early mastery thus above all establishes the *potential* for later excellence.

Early mastery is not merely complex, however: it involves other special characteristics, such as intense curiosity and motivation to inquire and learn, along with the tools to solve problems, learn, produce and create with comparative cognitive autonomy, as I have documented in detail in earlier studies (Fowler, 1981). One of the most important tools for harnessing the curiosity and the drive to learn stems from the early establishment of reading skills found in the vast majority of cases. Once able to decipher written text fluently, typically between three and five years, children are assured of a vehicle for exploring broader horizons on their own, as the advanced material children commonly read (at least by school age) testifies. The readiness of many of the language-stimulated children who participate in our research to respond readily to written symbols and explore the reading process, even in the absence of special focus, illustrates one way self-propelled interest systems begin, (a pattern similar to that reported by many parents of high IQ children seeking help on learning to read).

Early mastery is however also a question of initiating enquiries and complex projects that appeared very early in development, initiatives that frequently never develop at all in many children. Among 180+ IQ children Elizabeth (Langenbeck, 1915) was writing and illustrating her own stories by four; case D (Hollingworth, 1926) constructed an imaginary community with extensive rules, designs and history between the ages of four and seven (which occurred in one of our cases – excluded because of limited early records – between 10 and 11), and wrote and circulated a neighbourhood newspaper by seven; case 3 (Stedman; 1924) wrote stories by five, composing every day and enjoyed solving arithmetic problems by nine. Among Terman's (1919) 140+ IQ cases, case 6 wrote poetry at seven, case 36, very complex poetry by nine; case 12 ran his own circulating library of 50 books for neighbourhood children before nine; and case 19 enthusiastically taught several neighbourhood children before 11.

Among prodigies, Sidis invented a perpetual calendar by five (later patented and marketed at 20; Wallace, 1986). Among biographical figures, eight of the ten novelists (Este, 1979) and playwrights (Durbach, 1979) were writing literature by age 12 (one of the others was severely handicapped by eye disease, the other began in his teens), seven by age nine, and one between six and nine. Early reading was typical (eight out of ten), as it was in all categories, including mathematicians, whose other early independent activities tended more toward mathematics and science (Fowler, 1986). For example, Newton experimented constantly from early childhood and the women mathematicians Somerville and Germain pursued mathematics from middle childhood almost alone (with only one or two mentors) in the face of intensive family and other social opposition to careers for women.

THE DEVELOPMENTAL LEARNING ECOLOGY AND
DYNAMICS OF VERBAL TALENTS

Developmental learning patterns for the course of exceptional abilities have been discussed several times elsewhere (Fowler, 1967; 1971a; 1971b; 1981; 1983; 1986). In a detailed model, based on case studies of high IQ children, the chief experiential factors and stages of development for verbal-logical competencies were represented as following two separate strands (Fowler, 1981). One was based on deliberately parent-planned stimulation from infancy. The other was based on incidental stimulation by parents in apparent response to their infant's early emerging skills and curiosity. Differences in belief concerning the role of heredity and experience appeared to be the only important distinction dividing the two groups, however, since the developmental consequences of exceptional IQ, high curiosity and independence in learning, and the methods of verbal stimulation in interactive play employed were hardly distinguishable. The outline presented here thus combines both models into a single course, which appears to be equally valid for the additional sources of data reviewed in this chapter.

The following is a summary of the factors around which developmental experiences are organized to determine exceptional verbally mediated cognitive competencies.

Early stimulation: Intensive verbal symbol manipulation (oral and often written) and rational cognitive learning of means and ends and knowledge seeking, starting at birth or within the first year.

Agents: Family members (and sometimes nurses' or parents' network of intellectual associations) during early years. Later, models, mentors and resource persons, who stimulate or otherwise facilitate development.

Methods: Labelling, explanations, an emphasis on rational problem solving and enquiry and, above all, interaction, often informally in play; an evolving spiral of *developmental interaction* in which mutual adult-infant responsiveness revolves around verbal-cognitive interchange; this evolves through successive stages of widening and longer range project activities that are often increasingly initiated by the child from infancy as a result of precocious, complex symbol manipulation and cognitive processing skills (language and reading), intensive motivation, curiosity, and autonomy in cognitive processing.

Intellectual climate and values: Home ecology peopled with models (parents and association network) whose values and interests reflect

Table 2.   Stages in the development of verbal talents

1. *Infancy* (0–3 years)	2. *Early Childhood* (3–6 years)	3. *Middle Childhood* (6–12 years)	4. *Later Childhood* (from 12 years)
Establishing a self-propelled verbal-cognitive system	Consolidating language and reading skills Initiating project activities	Extending skill mastery Organizing extended projects Beginning field specialization	Beginning original contributions to fields

highly verbal-cognitive activities, concentrated in various fields (for example, literature, science, theatre), rational analysis, and high expectations toward constant learning, understanding, individual responsibility, and a work and achievement ethic in chosen cultural or scientific fields.

Continued support: High familial involvement in child's development maintained indefinitely, throughout development, often even as child gradually extends activities into the community (for example, school, outside mentors).

Later influences: Child's verbal-cognitive precocity defines social role of creative intellectual which, along with special achievements, fortuitously attracts attention from resource persons and special mentors, who reinforce efforts, provide opportunities (for example, special courses, gifted programmes), and high level stimulation and collaboration if competent themselves.

The stages are outlined in Table 2. Note that ages and stages overlap and the course and sequence of adult-child developmental interaction vary considerably. For example, children read, initiate and pursue projects, specialize and make original contributions at different ages.

Conclusions

Several conclusions seem warranted, though many questions remain. First, uncommon cognitive experiences play an enormous role in stimulating children to develop their mental competencies to their full potentials, whether originating in exceptional cultural-familial intellectual ambiances in the home or induced through professionally planned guidance of parents in ecologically healthy homes. Second, while a multiplicity of factors must work in concert to bring about such favourable courses of development (for example, interactive, enquiry-oriented strategies that develop cognitive autonomy, an ambience where the intellect is valued, models and mentors), the exceptionally stimulating experiences must apparently embrace both early and later development. All cases of later excellence (with adequate data) combined both exceptional early and later verbal stimulation. In our research, early language stimulation consistently accelerated development to realize exceptional verbal competencies in infancy, but if ecological difficulties arose and stimulation later lagged development also lagged. Indeed, the appearance of interruptions at any age or from any sources to the optimal forms of adult–child cognitive interactions and other highly favourable circumstances that marked these children's development – family trauma, moving, divorce, shift of caregivers, or sudden thrust into a bilingual environment – at least temporarily impeded the favourable course of development. Given these patterns, the later development of children in our research would be predicted to depend on how well later developmental conditions build on the high language competencies developed in infancy, as the limited data on differential outcomes emerging during preschool and later development suggest. Finally, language and written symbols appear to function critically as mediating agents for the development of superior cognitive competencies in many fields – literary, scientific and perhaps even mathematics.

Among key questions still to be answered are, how does experience dovetail or interact with biology to determine high skill levels. Given exceptional early (and continuing) stimulation, how important is heredity in determining outcome levels, indexed for example by IQ scores of 140+ versus 180+ or by the differing literary or scientific levels of the individual's work? Just how plastic is development, particularly early development? There is at least some evidence, both from our research and from the cases of later excellence, that parents varied considerably in the zeal, efficacy and persistence with which they undertook their infant's education, and that these efforts were correlated with the quality of verbal-intellectual development realized. Presumably, as Feldman (1986) observes, optimal circumstances and optimal heredity must coincide to produce the highest levels of excellence.

Yet my reading of the equation would also indicate that there is plenty of room in the cognitive potentials of at least the advantaged strata of the general population for generating competence levels much beyond current norms, without removing wide individual differences. Given adequate ecologies and well planned early guidance to parents, nearly all children can attain high levels of competence, and often attain what are now considered 'superior' or gifted levels, at least in verbally mediated competencies. Even in disadvantaged ecologies, the evidence strongly indicates that many children can be aided to reach or approach superior levels during the early years, though the evidence indicates with equal strength that without large-scale efforts to upgrade the ecology of family life in disadvantaged communities the early attainments will fade with the debilitating circumstances associated with poverty.

In other words, it may well be possible to raise the level of verbally based competencies for the general population through adopting improved practices of early stimulation throughout society – including upgrading the social ecology as needed, bringing along with the general rise an increase in talents at the highest levels. Individual differences would not be eliminated (though they might be narrowed in broad strata of the population), because inherent differences in potential would continue to place different limits on attainment, and because even with greatly enriched practices of verbal and cognitive stimulation, differences with which they were implemented would also remain – albeit in an enriched developmental framework.

REFERENCES

ANASTASI, A. (1958) *Differential Psychology*, 3rd ed. New York: Macmillan.

BARNARD, K.E., BEE, H.L. and HAMMOND, M.A. (1984) Home environment and cognitive development in a healthy low-risk sample: The Seattle study. In A.W. Gottfried (Ed.) *Home Environment and Early Cognitive Development*. New York: Academic Press.

BATEMAN, W.G. (1917) Papers on language development: I. The first word. *Pedagogical Seminary*, 24, 391–398.

BELL, S. (1982) The super Susedik kids. *Families, June 1982*, 95–100.

BLOOM, B.S. (1985) *Developing Talent in Young People*. New York: Ballantine.

BROWN, R. (1973) *A First Language*. Cambridge, MA: Harvard University Press.

BURKS, B.S., JENSEN, D.W. and TERMAN, L.M. (1930) *The Promise of Youth. Genetic Studies of Genius, Vol.3*. Stanford, CA: Stanford University Press.

BUSH, A.D. (1914) Binet-Simon Tests of a thirty-nine months old child. *Psychological Clinic*, 7, 250–257.

BZOCH, K.R. (1970) *The Bzoch-League Receptive-Expressive Emergent Language Scale*. Austin, Texas: Pro-Ed.

CAPUTE, A.J., SHAPIRO, B.K. and PALMER, F.B. (1987) *Clinical Linguistic and Auditory Milestone Scale*. Baltimore: Kennedy Institute for Handicapped Children.

CAREW, J. (1980) Experience and the development of intelligence in young children at home and in day care. *Monographs of the Society for Research in Child Development*, 45, Serial no.187.

CHOMSKY, N. (1957) *Syntactic Structures*. The Hague: Mouton.

CHOMSKY, N. (1965) *Aspects of a Theory of Syntax*. Cambridge, MA: MIT Press.

CLARKE-STEWART, K.A. (1973) Interactions between mothers and their young children: Characteristics and consequences. *Monographs of the Society for Research in Child Development, 38, Serial no.153.*

COX, C.M. (1926) *The Early Mental Traits of Three Hundred Geniuses. Genetic Studies of Genius, Vol.2.* Stanford, CA: Stanford University Press.

CURTISS, S. (1977) *Genie.* New York: Academic Press.

DAVIS, K. (1940) Extreme social isolation of a child. *American Journal of Sociology, 45,* 554–565.

DAVIS, K. (1947) Final note on a case of extreme social isolation. *American Journal of Sociology, 52,* 432–437.

DENNIS, W. (1973) *Children of the Creche.* New York: Appleton-Century-Crofts.

DOLBEAR, K.E. (1912) Precocious Children. *Pedagogical Seminary, 19,* 461–491.

DRASH, P.W. and STOLBERG, A.L. (1977) *Acceleration of cognitive, linguistic and social development in the normal infant.* Tallahassee, FL: Florida State Department of Health and Rehabilitation Services. (ERIC Document Reproduction Service No. ED 145 938).

DRASH, P.W. and STOLBERG, A.L. (1979) *Intellectual acceleration in normal and Down's Syndrome Children through Infant Stimulation and Language Training.* (ERIC Document Reproduction Service No. ED-176482). Southeastern Proceedings: Psychological Association, New Orleans, LA.

DVORAK, H.D. (1921) The mental tests of a superior child. *Mental Hygiene, 7,* 250–257.

ERVIN, S.M. and MILLER, W.R. (1963) Language development. In H.W. Stevenson (Ed.), *Child Psychology: Yearbook of the National Society for the Study of Education: Part 2.*

FELDMAN, D. (1986) *Nature's Gambit.* New York: Basic Books.

FLINT, B.M. (1978) *New Hope for Deprived Children.* Toronto: University of Toronto Press.

FOWLER, W. (1962) Cognitive learning in infancy and early childhood. *Psychological Bulletin, 59,* 116–152.

FOWLER, W. (1967) The dimensions for environmental control over developmental learning. *Psychologia Wychowawcza, 10, No.3,* 265–281.

FOWLER, W. (1971a) Cognitive baselines in early childhood: Developmental learning and differentiation of competence rule systems. In J. Hellmuth (Ed.), *Cognitive Studies. Vol.2. Cognitive Deficits.* New York: Brunner/Mazel.

FOWLER, W. (1971b) Mental prodigies. In *Encyclopedia of Education.* New York: Macmillan.

FOWLER, W. (1981) Case studies of cognitive precocity: The role of exogenous and endogenous stimulation in early mental development. *Journal of Applied Developmental Psychology, 2,* 319–367.

FOWLER, W. (1983) *Potentials of Childhood. Vol.1: A Historical View of Early Experience.* Lexington, MA: Lexington Books.

FOWLER, W. (1986) Early experiences of great men and women mathematicians. In W. Fowler (Ed.), *Early Experience and the Development of Competence. New Directions in Child Development, No.32.* San Francisco: Jossey-Bass.

FOWLER, W. and SWENSON, A. (1979) The influence of early language stimulation on development: Four studies. *Genetic Psychology Monographs, 100,* 73–109.

GALTON, F. (1925) *Hereditary Genius: An Inquiry into its Laws and Consequences,* 2nd ed. London: Macmillan.

GARBER, H.L. and HEBER, R. (1981) The efficacy of early intervention with family rehabilitation. In M.J. Begab, H.C. Haywood and H.L. Garber (Eds) *Strategies for improving competence. Psychosocial Influences in Retarded Performance, Vol.2*, Baltimore: University Park Press.

GESELL, A. (1922) Mental and physical correspondence in twins. *The Scientific Monthly, 14*, 305–331, 415–428.

GESELL, A. (1954) The ontogenesis of infant behavior. In L. Carmichael (Ed.) *Manual of Child Psychology*, 2nd ed. New York: Wiley.

GESELL, A., HALVERSON, H.M., THOMPSON, H., ILG, F.L., CASTNER, B.M., AMES, L.B. and AMATRUDA, C.S. (1940) *The First Five Years of Life: A Guide to the Study of the Preschool Child*. New York: Harper.

GLEITMAN, L.R. and WANNER, E. (1984) Current issues in language learning. In M.H. Bornstein and M.E. Lamb (Eds) *Developmental Psychology*. Hillsdale, NJ: Erlbaum.

GOLDBERG, S.L. (1934) A clinical study of K., IQ 196. *Journal of Applied Psychology, 18*, 550–560.

GORDON, I.J., GUINAGH, B. and JESTER, R.E. (1977) The Florida parent education infant and toddler programs. In M.C. Day and R.K. Parker (Eds) *The Preschool in Action*, 2nd ed. Boston: Allyn & Bacon.

GOTTFRIED, A.W. (1984) *Home Environment and Early Cognitive Development*. New York: Academic Press.

GRIFFITHS, R. (1970) *The Abilities of Young Children*. London: Child Development Research Centre.

HAMILTON, M.L. (1977) Social learning and the transition from babbling to words. *Journal of Genetic Psychology, 130*, 211–270.

HEBER, R., GARBER, H., HARRINGTON, S., HOFFMAN, C. and FALENDER, C. (1972) *Rehabilitation of families at risk for mental retardation: Progress Report*. Madison, Wisc: University of Wisconsin.

HIRT, Z.I. (1922) A gifted child. *Training School Bulletin, 19*, 49–54.

HOLLINGWORTH, L.S. (1929) *Gifted Children*. New York: Macmillan.

HOLLINGWORTH, L.S. (1942) *Children Above 180 IQ, Stanford Binet*. New York: World Book.

HOROWITZ, F.D. and O'BRIEN, M. (Eds) (1985) *The Gifted and Talented: Developmental Perspectives*. Washington, DC: American Psychological Association.

HUNT, J.McV. (1961) *Intelligence and Experience*. New York: Ronald.

HUNT, J.McV. (1975) Reflections on a decade of early education. *Journal of Abnormal Child Psychology, 3*, 275–330.

HUNT, J.McV. (1986) The effect of variations in quality and type of early child care on development. In W. Fowler (Ed.) *Early Experience and the development of competence: Vol.32. New Directions for Child Development*. San Francisco: Jossey-Bass.

HUNT, J.McV., KHOSSROW, M., GHODSSI, M. and AKIYAMA, M. (1976) The psychological development of orphanage-reared infants: Interventions with outcomes (Tehran). *Genetic Psychology Monographs, 94*, 177–226.

IRWIN, O.C. (1960) Infant speech: Effect of systematic reading of stories. *Journal of Speech and Hearing Research, 3*, 187–190.

JENKINS, J.L. and PATERSON, D.G. (1961) *Studies in Individual Differences: The Search for Intelligence*. New York: Appleton-Century-Crofts.

JONES, A.M. (1923) The superior child: A series of case studies. *Psychological Clinic, 15*, 1–8; 116–123; 130–137.

JONES, H.E. (1954) The environment and mental development. In L. Carmichael (Ed.) *Manual of Child Psychology*, 2nd ed. New York: Wiley.

KOBLER, L.K. and FEIN, D. (1988) *The Exceptional Brain*. New York: Guilford Press.

LANGENBECK, M. (1915) A study of a five year old child. *Pedagogical Seminary*, 22, 65–88.

LAZAR, I. and DARLINGTON, R. (1982) Lasting effects of early education: A report from The Consortium for Longitudinal Studies. *Monographs of the Society for Research in Child Development*, 47, Serial no.195.

McCALL, R.B., APPELBAUM, M.I. and HOGARTY, P.S. (1973) Developmental changes in mental performance. *Monographs of the Society for Research in Child Development*, 38, Serial no.150.

McCARTHY, D. (1954) Language development in preschool children. In L. Carmichael (Ed.) *Manual of Child Psychology*, 2nd ed. New York: Wiley.

McCARTNEY, K. (1984) Effect of quality day care environment on children's language development. *Developmental Psychology*, 20, 244–260.

McCURDY, H.G. (1975) The childhood pattern of genius. *Journal of the Elisha Mitchell Society*, 73, 448–462.

MALLITSKAYA, M.K. (1960) K motodike ispol'zovaniya kartionok dlya razvitiya ponimaniya rechi u detei v contse pervogo i na vtorom godu zhizni (A method for using pictures to develop speech comprehension in children at the end of the first and in the second year of life). *Vosprosy Psicholologii (Questions of Psychology)*, 3, 122–126.

METZL, M.N. (1980) Teaching parents a strategy for enhancing infant development. *Child Development*, 51, 583–586.

MILLER, J. and CHAPMAN, R. (1981) The relation between age and mean length of utterance in morphemes. *Journal of Speech and Hearing Research*, 24, 154–161.

NELSON, K. (1977) Facilitating children's syntax acquisition. *Developmental Psychology*, 13, 101–107.

NEWMAN, J.R. (Ed.) (1963) *The Harper Encyclopedia of Science, Vol.4*. New York: Harper and Row.

OGSTON, K. (1983) The effects of gross-motor and language stimulation on infant development. In W. Fowler (Ed.), *Potentials of Childhood, Vol.2*. Lexington, MA: Lexington Books.

PEARSON, K. (1914) *The Life, Letters and Labours of Francis Galton, Vol.1, Birth 1822 to Marriage 1853*. Cambridge, ENG: Cambridge University Press.

RHEINGOLD, H.L., GEWIRTZ, J.L. and ROSS, H.W. (1959) Social conditioning of vocalization in the infant. *Journal of Comparative and Physiological Psychology*, 52, 68–73.

ROOT, W.T. (1921) A socio-psychological study of fifty-three supernormal children. *Psychological Monographs*, 29, no.133.

RUSK, R.R. (1917) A case of precocity. *Child Study*, 10, 27–28.

SKEELS, H.M. (1966) Adult status of children with contrasting early life experiences. *Monographs of the Society for Research in Child Development*, 31, Serial no.105.

STEDMAN, L.M. (1924) *Education of Gifted Children*. Yonkers-on-Hudson, New York: World Book.

STORFER, M. (1990) *Intelligence and Giftedness: The Contributions of Heredity and Early Environment*. San Francisco: Jossey-Bass.

STRAYER, L.C. (1930) Language and growth: The relative efficacy of early and deferred vocabulary training, studied by the method of co-twin control. *Genetic Psychology Monographs, 8,* 209–317.

SWENSON, A. (1983) Toward an ecological approach to theory and research in child language acquisition. In W. Fowler (Ed.), *Potentials of Childhood, Vol.2.* Lexington, MA: Lexington Books.

THE CONSORTIUM FOR LONGITUDINAL STUDIES. (1983) *As the Twig is Bent.* Hillsdale, NJ: Lawrence Erlbaum.

TERMAN, L.M. (1919) *The Intelligence of School Children.* Boston: Houghton Mifflin.

TERMAN, L.M. (1925) *Mental and Physical Traits of a Thousand Gifted Children. Genetic Studies of Genius, Vol.1.* Stanford, CA: Stanford University Press.

TERMAN, L.M. and ODEN, M.H. (1947) *The Gifted Child Grows Up: Twenty-five Years' Follow-up of a Superior Group. Genetic Studies of Genius, Vol. 4.* Stanford, CA: Stanford University Press.

UZGIRIS, I. and HUNT, J.McV. (1975) *Assessment in Infancy: Ordinal Scales of Psychological Development.* Champaign: University of Illinois Press.

VAN ALSTYNE, D. (1929) The environment of three year old children: Factors related to intelligence and vocabulary tests. Columbia University, *Teachers College Contributions to Education. Serial no.366.*

WALBERG, H.J. (Ed.) (1979) *Educational Environments and Effects.* Berkeley, CA: McCutchan.

WALLACE, A. (1986) *The Prodigy.* New York: Dutton.

WELLMAN, B.L. (1945) IQ Changes of preschool and nonpreschool groups during the preschool years: A summary of the literature. *Journal of Psychology, 20,* 347–368.

WIENER, N. (1953) *Ex-prodigy: My Childhood and Youth.* New York: Simon & Schuster.

WITTE, K. (1914) *The Education of Karl Witte.* (H.A. Bruce, Ed. and L. Wiener, trans.). New York: Crowell.

WITTY, P.A. (1930) A Study of one hundred gifted children. *University of Kansas Bulletin of Education, 2, no.7.*

WITTY, P.A. and JENKINS, M.D. (1935) The case of 'B' – A gifted Negro girl. *Journal of Social Psychology, 6,* 117–124.

WOODLEY, R. (1982) Want to raise a genius? The Susediks have a formula that has worked every time. *People, August 30, 1982,* 32–34.

YATES, D.H. (1922) *A Study of High School Seniors of Superior Intelligence.* Bloomington, IL: Public School.

FINDING AND HELPING YOUNG PEOPLE WITH EXCEPTIONAL MATHEMATICAL REASONING ABILITY

Julian C. Stanley

Find young people who *reason* exceptionally well mathematically; make them and their parents and teachers aware of their great potential for learning mathematics and related subjects such as physics, computer science, engineering, and chemistry far faster and better than is typical of their age-mates; and offer them special educational opportunities. This is the model that the Johns Hopkins University Study of Mathematically Precocious Youth (SMPY) pioneered in 1971 and has disseminated across the United States and into other lands, especially the People's Republic of China (Stanley *et al.*, 1986). It is meant to help bridge the transition from about age 12 into college at age 18 or younger for such students, who constitute a precious 'natural resource'. Excellent quantitative reasoning ability underpins achievements in science, technology, and many other scholarly or professional fields. Much, or even most, of that ability is wasted because few students and their parents and teachers are aware of the extent of the individual's mathematical aptitude and the great learning ability it confers.

For example, in the United States, the first year of high school algebra is usually a dreary wasteland for most boys and girls who before age 13 score at least 500 on the mathematical part of the College Board Scholastic Aptitude Test (SAT–M), which is meant mainly for above average 17 and 18 year old students. *Before* taking that course, about half of them know the year's work better than the typical student will after completing it. They are ready for intensified, compressed, more rigorous treatment of the subject matter. Since 1971, under the stimulus of SMPY many special educational opportunities for mathematically talented young people have arisen. Currently, annual university-sponsored talent searches using the Scholastic Aptitude Test are available to young students in all 50 states of the USA. Thus, quantitatively apt boys and girls can be found and helped in many ways.

THE RATIONALE OF SMPY

SMPY began 19 years ago with a purpose that has survived the interval. For 13 years it was aided greatly by substantial grants from the Spencer Foundation of Chicago. From the start SMPY was meant to identify students who reason exceptionally well mathematically and then help them find the special, supplemental educational opportunities every such student needs in order to learn mathematics, physics, computer science, chemistry, and related subjects faster and better than can be done in most public or private junior or senior high schools. By 1980, however, SMPY itself was concentrating not simply on those young students who reason well mathematically, but on those who do so exceptionally well.

From the beginning the emphasis was on individual programming, year by year. One pupil's other abilities, geographical setting, interests, and parental financial situation might differ radically from another's, even though both had earned exactly the same score on a difficult test of mathematical reasoning ability at the same age. There could be no one programme. One size would not fit all, nor should it.

SMPY conducted its first talent search in March of 1972. At its core was the mathematical part of the College Board Scholastic Aptitude Test (SAT–M), which is intended mainly for above-average students in the last two years of high school in the United States (Grades 11–12, ages 16–18). A different form of that college admission test has been used in each of the 16 subsequent annual talent searches conducted by Johns Hopkins University. A total of 396 students, mostly far above average seventh and eighth graders (11–14 years old), took SAT–M (and other tests) in 1972. By January of 1990 the annual number had risen to almost 37,000, chiefly seventh graders less than 13 years old, in the search conducted by the Johns Hopkins University Center for the Advancement of Academically Talented Youth (CTY). Since 1980, CTY has handled the annual talent searches and summer programme that SMPY started in 1972. Though on the same campus, SMPY and CTY have no formal relationship with each other. By helping create CTY in 1979, SMPY freed itself from most of the operational aspect in order to concentrate on the ablest students and do applied research designed to understand their educational needs better.

The talent searching and educational facilitation began in the Greater Baltimore area. Initially, it was reported by Keating and Stanley (1972) in an article in the first volume of the *Educational Researcher*, by Stanley (1973) the next year in the *Educational Psychologist*, and by Stanley *et al.* (1974) in a book. SMPY's rationale is set forth extensively in Stanley (1977) and Stanley and Benbow (1986). Initial longitudinal results were reported in Benbow and Stanley (1983).

By 1980 the concepts had spread to Duke University, whose Talent Identification Program (TIP) still flourishes in the Southeast below Virginia, in the Southwest, and in Iowa and Nebraska. Soon every state of the Union, including Alaska and Hawaii, plus China, were covered by a talent search and associated special academic pro- grammes. These operate in Johns Hopkins and Duke Universities, Northwestern University, the University of Denver, the University of Wisconsin at Eau Claire, Iowa State University, Arizona State Univer- sity, Sacramento State University, the University of Washington, the University of North Texas, the State of Illinois, and Tianjin, People's Republic of China. Whereas virtually no persons less than 13 or 14 years old took the SAT in 1971, by 1988 about 100,000 did each year. Many of their scores are impressive.

Those with Scores of 500–800 on SAT–M before age 13

'Exceptional' mathematical reasoning ability was defined, tentatively for investigative purposes, as being suggested by a score of at least 500 on SAT–M achieved before age 13. About 13 per cent of males and 6 per cent of females scored that well in CTY's 1989 talent search (CTY, 1989). Because persons entering that search average at least in the top 5 per cent of their age group with respect to quantitative aptitude, we estimate that the high-scoring boys are in about the top 1 per cent of males of their age, and the girls are in about the top $\frac{1}{2}$ per cent of females of their age. Clearly, they are exceptional mathemat- ical reasoners, as judged by their SAT–M scores. Also, compared with college-bound twelfth-graders, whose mean SAT–M score is 500 for males and 454 for females (College Board, 1989), they are remarkable. They have one of the most essential abilities needed to learn math- ematics and related academic subjects much faster and better than most of their age-in-grade courses permit.

At this point, to prevent misunderstandings, let me make two points explicitly:

1.) We started SMPY in large part to help determine what conse- quences a high score on SAT–M at an early age has, rather than assuming that it indicates great talent for becoming a mathemat- ician. Even initially, it seemed likely to us that the type of mathe- matical reasoning ability SAT–M measures would, for a given individual, be moderated rather strongly by that person's other abilities, interests, and circumstances.

2.) The founders of SMPY (Stanley, Keating and Fox) were all psy- chologists, not mathematicians or mathematics teachers.[1] They did not plan to produce mathematicians, or even to help every student who scored at least 500M before age 13 learn to think like a mathematician. They viewed mathematics, from first year algebra to calculus, differential equations, linear algebra, probability, and statistics, as an invaluable *tool* for scientists and quantitatively oriented social scientists. Their goal was, and still is, to help young people learn as much of that 'applied' mathematics as fast and as well as is feasible so that at an early age they will have it available to use. The students who go on to courses in analysis, number theory, topology, higher algebra, and/or mathematical logic at excellent colleges and universities or in special summer programmes for high school students can then get a true introduction to 'pure' mathematics. Of them, a few will become seized with the abstract beauty of mathematics and court it for the rest of their lives. Fundamental research in mathematics is not likely to attract many, even of those scoring high on a test of mathematical reasoning ability before age 13, nor probably should it. Modern societies need relatively few really good university mathematicians but many excellent chemists, engineers, computer scientists, and physicists. We must try to ensure that great quantitative aptitude is used well in the context of other individual factors.[2] It must not be squandered because of slow pacing or inept teaching.

Those with Scores of 700–800 on SAT–M before age 13

After helping create other groups such as CTY at Johns Hopkins in 1979 and TIP at Duke a year later, SMPY moved toward working exclusively with the quantitatively most apt youths in the country. Each of these had scored at least 700 on SAT–M, higher than all but 7 per cent of college-bound male high school seniors. Only about one twelve year old in 10,000 would score that high. The females average 4.43 standard deviations above the mean of the girls participating in the annual CTY talent search, and the males average 3.38 above such boys (Stanley, 1988a). Truly, this is a most exceptional group. It seems reasonable to expect that many of the ablest mathematicians and scientists of the next generation will come from youths who reason this well mathematically. Much preliminary evidence supports that expectation.

Those with Scores of 640–690 on SAT–M before age 13

The 700–800M scorers are chiefly male. Among Asian Americans the gender ratio is 4 males to every one female, the same as it is for Chinese in the People's Republic of China (Lupkowski and Stanley, 1988). Among non-Asian Americans it is about 16 to 1, but seems to be lessening a bit as some girls who are unusually competent at mathematics are being introduced to algebra and geometry at a younger age. As noted earlier, the percentile rank of an SAT–M score of 700 is 93 for college-bound male twelfth-graders. The 93rd percentile for such females is a score of 640: in a percentile-equivalent sense, 700 for males equals 640 for females. Therefore, in order to find more females to help educationally, in 1986 SMPY created a special group, restricted to females who scored 640 to 690 on SAT–M before age 13. Though somewhat less accelerated than the 700–800M females, these girls are so able that by age 17 or 18 they can expect to score at or near the ceiling of SAT–M's score scale, in the top 1 per cent of college-bound twelfth-graders.

SMORGASBORD OF SPECIAL EDUCATIONAL OPPORTUNITIES

Once found, the young person who is talented at mathematics needs several things:

1. He or she should be helped to understand clearly what great academic potential the SAT–M score probably reflects.

2. Other test scores should be considered, because often they serve as moderating variables. Perhaps the most important of these is the individual's score on the verbal part of the SAT, which measures reading comprehension, analogical ability, antonym ability, and ability to fill in blanks in sentences so as to make them logically and grammatically correct. Overall, SAT–V scores of those who score 700 or more on SAT–M before age 13 vary from 250, which is only 20 points above chance, to 780, which is 20 points below the highest possible score. They average 521, which is the 78th percentile of college-bound high-school seniors – 20 percentile points below their SAT–M mean. It is obvious that, despite this great variability, the average verbal reasoning ability of SMPY's top SAT–M group is high (Stanley, 1988a). The discrepancy between the percentile rank of the mean SAT–M score and that of the mean SAT–V score is about 1 and $\frac{3}{10}$ ths of the norm group's standard deviation. Galtonian regression toward the mean works here, as it does elsewhere. A group of persons chosen specifically for scoring quite high on one variable will average less high on any other variable that is not perfectly correlated with the selection variable.

Working with the SAT–M scale vs the SAT–V scale is confusing. Though set up in 1941 to be comparable, the two scales long since wandered away from each other. For example, in percentile rank terms a score of 700 earned on SAT–M by a male college-bound twelfth-grader is equivalent to an SAT–V score of 610. For girls, 700M is equivalent to 660V (College Board, 1989). This gender discrepancy does not complicate our argument, however, because we work via percentile ranks or standard scores. The main point to be gleaned from this technical aside is that some members of the 700–800M group reason verbally much better than others. We have found this source of variability to be related to interest in learning advanced mathematics fast and the ability to do so. If the percentile rank of a student's SAT–V score is higher than the percentile rank of his or her SAT–M score, there seems to be less readiness to benefit from intensive mathematics courses than if the percentile rank of the SAT–M score appreciably exceeds that of the SAT–V score. One of the fastest learners of precalculus and calculus we ever knew scored 760M and 310V at age 12, but seemed somewhat deficient in abstract ability. A relatively slow 12 year old mathematics learner scored 750V and 720M, equivalent to being about 120 points more able verbally than mathematically. In college, he majored in music. *Perhaps* the optimum SAT–V score for a 700–800M scorer before age 13 is about 600, if he or she aspires to earning a top-flight PhD degree in mathematics, science, or engineering. This needs to be studied further.

3. All ingenuity available should be used to find for every student the special, supplemental educational opportunities needed at each stage of development. SMPY emphasizes acceleration in academic subjects in the students' areas of greatest ability and interest. Benbow (1979) listed 13 of the many ways mathematically talented young people can be provided a comprehensive 'smorgasbord of accelerative options'. These range from entering kindergarten early to earning a master's degree concurrently with the bachelor's.

4. SMPY stresses academic summer programmes and college level Advanced Placement (AP) programme courses in high school, followed by AP examinations, to provide both depth and breadth. Residential academic summer programmes can contribute much to the young person's scholastic, social and emotional development. There, the gifted student is free to interact naturally with his or her true intellectual peers with far less fear of being stigmatized as a 'brain', 'nerd', 'wimp', or 'greasy grind' than in regular school. A more realistic self-assessment of academic and personal potentialities is likely to ensue. Usually, the young person goes home after three or six weeks more confident but less arrogant or defensive.

5. Especially for helping keen mathematical reasoners learn precalculus mathematics fast and well, SMPY developed its DT-PI model: diagnostic testing followed by prescribed instruction (Stanley, 1978; 1986). A skilled tester-mentor determines system-

atically what the brilliant student does not know and helps him or her learn just those points quickly but thoroughly. This saves much of the time usually devoted in class and at home to working through the textbook from page one to the end, thereby going so slowly that the exceptional student often becomes bored and inattentive.

For example, in Dr Camilla Benbow's special three week residential summer programme at Iowa State University, where the DT-PI model is used, the typical mathematics student covers the equivalent of two years of school mathematics (at least 270 classroom hours) readily. Some accomplish more than that; virtually no one finishes less than a school year's work. They return to school with heightened skills and confidence, ready for the next level.

This is instruction guided by pre- and post-testing, but not coaching toward the test itself. All aspects of the material, such as algebra or geometry, must be learned extremely well. No '70 per cent is passing' philosophy underlies this DT-PI model. No student fails, but instead a pupil does not move on to the next level (as from Algebra I to Algebra II) until completely ready. Mastery learning, but without wasting time, is the goal.

6. Mentors and role models figure prominently in SMPY's facilitation efforts.

7. Wide dissemination of the results of studies it conducts has been a major activity of SMPY since its founding. Some ten books and more than a hundred articles make this feasible. The latter are sent out, without charge, in tailored-to-order packets by SMPY at Johns Hopkins University to those who request them from all over the world – at least 500 per year.

8. Currently, SMPY's chief contact with most of the members of its '700–800 on SAT–M before age 13' and '640–690 on SAT–M before age 13' groups born in 1972 or later is via a quarterly pre-college newsletter.[3] Single-spaced, this usually runs to 20 pages or so per issue. It serves to inform, stimulate, motivate, and inter-relate members of the group. There is also a twice yearly alumni newsletter for members of the group who are beyond high school. Knowing, when young, what special educational opportunities are available from the beginning of junior high school (or even earlier) through senior high school, and what other members of the group have done with those opportunities, gives each member a motivational head start.

9. SMPY's DT-PI approach has been extended to the basic high school sciences (Stanley and Stanley, 1986).

ACCOMPLISHMENTS

Many of the students have performed spectacularly in educational events. For example, although the oldest members of SMPY's formally facilitated 700–800M group were only 21 years old in 1989, quite a few had already earned a bachelor's or even a master's degree from an outstanding university. The number one graduate of the huge baccalaureate class at the University of California at Berkeley in the spring of 1988 was a 19 year old female member, majoring in philosophy and becoming a Marshall scholar at Oxford University. The top mathematics graduate there was a male 19 year old member of SMPY. A 17 year old female has completed six semesters at a major state university with all A grades, and a 19 year old female at MIT graduated with an all A grade record.

About a dozen SMPYers achieve honours in the annual Westinghouse Science Talent Search. In 1987, three of them ranked in the top six in that prestigious national competition and won large scholarships (Stanley, 1987b).

Of the 78 youths who studied pure mathematics in Professor Arnold Ross's famed programme at The Ohio State University during the summer of 1988, 30 were SMPYers. Of 56 Americans chosen to attend the 1989 national Research Science Institute, 18 were from the group. A number have been designated Presidential Scholars. About half of the United States team in the high school International Mathematical Olympiad (IMO) each year is from the group (Stanley, 1987a), including the youngest ever from this country (Jeremy A. Kahn), who became the only four time contender. Also, the day before his 13th birthday an Australian member of the group (Terence C.-S. Tao) won a gold medal in the 1988 IMO, probably the youngest person in the world ever to do so in the 30 year history of that competition. He had won a silver medal at age 11 and a bronze medal at age 10. SMPY helped nurture him educationally from the time he was eight years old.

The other honours, awards, and achievements of the group are extremely impressive. Most of the members of SMPY's groups are far better students than one would expect on the basis of their mathematical reasoning ability alone.

ASPECTS OF THE MODEL

SMPY's model is simple. Find students who have a certain special ability at an extremely high level, understand as much as is feasible about each one, and help each pupil to tailor an individualized educational programme that maximizes the use of the special talent

(Wallach, 1978). As much of that programme as possible should be within the pupil's own school, but almost inevitably a great deal is likely to be outside the school. Stimulation via newsletters, access to special academic summer or school year programmes, college courses taken as a part-time student while still enrolled in high school, peer support via networks of true intellectual peers, and excellent role models are components of SMPY's efforts to provide the needed supplemental educational opportunities.

We of SMPY prefer that able students be helped in school by '*coordinators* of special educational opportunities for intellectually highly talented youths', rather than by 'teachers of the highly gifted'. This is more than a play on words. To expect any one teacher, however well prepared, to be able to meet all the educational needs of a diverse group of intellectually highly talented boys and girls usually stretches one human being's abilities and education too far.

We advocate enrichment *and* acceleration, rather than enrichment *versus* acceleration (George *et al.*, 1979). In order to be effective, accelerated subject matter must be enriched, that is, presented at a higher level of rigour, generality, abstractness, or applicability. Similarly, enrichment without acceleration of some sort will eventually leave the enriched student more bored than ever in those school areas in which he or she excels (Stanley, 1976; 1980).

Like most simple-seeming models, the model of the Study of Mathematically Precocious Youth requires great skill in order to be implemented effectively. It is rather robust, however, because of the enormous educational potentialities of the young people for whom it is intended. Often, a small amount of relevant input produces a multiplier effect that greatly boosts the output. From SMPY's efforts with a tiny percentage of intellectually talented students will come many top-level scientists, mathematicians, engineers, and physicians. Other fields will also be represented. As mentioned earlier, Berkeley's top graduate majored in philosophy and won a Marshall Scholarship to study at Oxford University. One of SMPY's older protégés was the number one graduate of a top law school at age 21. He also won a Marshall Scholarship to Oxford to study philosophy. The two met there and continued the type of interaction that augments the other effects of SMPY's model.

Professor Camilla P. Benbow plans to conduct longitudinal studies of this group, among others, for many years to come. It should be interesting to determine what contributions to their country's intellectual welfare they make, and how self-fulfilled they become. In both areas we predict a high level for many of them.[4]

Acknowledgement: I thank Susan G. Assouline, Linda E. Brody, Ann E. Lupowski and Barbara S.K. Stanley for their assistance.

Notes

1. Stanley has, however, been a Fellow of the American Statistical Association since 1967.

2. A related, also much-neglected, ability is mechanical aptitude.

3. Students in these two groups were born in 1968 or more recently. Earlier, however, SMPY had found other youths who scored 700–800M before age 13, two of them as far back as 1972. Those two received PhD degrees at age 24, one in computer science from Cornell University and the other in mathematics from MIT.

4. She is the Director of SMPY at ISU, Department of Psychology, Iowa State University, Ames, Iowa 50011. There is also an SMPY at Teachers Advanced Study College, Hong Quao District, Tianjin 300123, People's Republic of China, and an SMPY at the University of North Texas, Denton 76203. The former is headed by Professor Feng Cheng De, and the latter by Professor Ann E. Lupkowski. Each of the four SMPYs has a somewhat different mission from the other three. Each operates independently of the others. SMPY at Tianjin coordinates talent searching and educational facilitation in the People's Republic of China. Thus far, 225 members of the 700M group have been found there. One of them became an undergraduate at Yale University in 1989 and made an all-A record in the first semester. Some others are preparing to do their graduate work in the United States or elsewhere outside China.

REFERENCES

BENBOW, C.P. (1979) The components of SMPY's smorgasbord of accelerative options. *Intellectually Talented Youth Bulletin*, 5, 21–23.

BENBOW, C.P. and STANLEY, J.C. (Eds) (1983) *Academic Precocity: Aspects of its Development*. Baltimore: Johns Hopkins University Press.

COLLEGE BOARD (1989) *National Percentiles, College-bound Seniors*. New York: College Entrance Examination Board.

CTY (1989) *The 1989 Talent Search Report*. Baltimore: Center for the Advancement of Academically Talented Youth, Johns Hopkins University.

GEORGE, W.C., COHN, S.J. and STANLEY, J.C. (Eds) (1979) *Educating the Gifted: Acceleration and Enrichment*. Baltimore: Johns Hopkins University Press.

KEATING, D.P. and STANLEY, J.C. (1972) Extreme measures for the exceptionally gifted in mathematics and science. *Educational Researcher*, 1, 3–7.

LUPKOWSKI, A.E. and STANLEY, J.C. (1988) Comparing Asians and non-Asians who reason *extremely* well mathematically. Paper presented at the Cornell Symposium on Asian Americans: Asian Americans and Higher Education, Cornell University, May 5–6. Available from Professor Julian C. Stanley, SMPY, 430 Gilman Hall, Johns Hopkins University, Baltimore, MD 21218, USA.

STANLEY, J.C. (1973) Accelerating the educational progress of intellectually gifted youths. *Educational Psychologist, 10*, 1973, 133–146. Reprinted in W. Dennis and M.W. Dennis (Eds) *The Intellectually Gifted: An Overview* (pp.179–196). New York: Grune & Stratton, 1976.

STANLEY, J.C. (1976) Identifying and nurturing the intellectually gifted. *Phi Delta Kappan, 58,* 234–237.

STANLEY, J.C. (1977) Rationale of the Study of Mathematically Precocious Youth (SMPY) during its first five years of promoting educational acceleration. In J.C. Stanley, W.C. George and C.H. Solano (Eds), *The Gifted and the Creative: A Fifty-year Perspective* (pp.75–112). London: Johns Hopkins University Press.

STANLEY, J.C. (1978) SMPY's DT-PI model: Diagnostic testing followed by prescriptive instruction. *Intellectually Talented Youth Bulletin, 4,* 7–8.

STANLEY, J.C. (1980) On educating the gifted. *Educational Researcher, 9,* 8–12.

STANLEY, J.C. (1986) Fostering use of mathematical talent in the USA: SMPY's rationale. In A.J. Cropley, K.K. Urban, H. Wagner and W. Wieczerkowski (Eds) *Giftedness: A Continuing Worldwide Challenge.* New York: Trillium (pp.227–243). Also published in *Journal of the Illinois Council for the Gifted, 1986, Vol.5,* pp.18–24.

STANLEY, J.C. (1987a) Making the IMO team: The power of early identification and encouragement. *Gifted Child Today, 10,* 22–23.

STANLEY, J.C. (1987b) Johns Hopkins group tops Science Talent Search. *Gifted Child Today, 10,* 57.

STANLEY, J.C. (1988) Some characteristics of SMPY's '700–800 on SAT–M Before Age 13 Group': Youths who reason *extremely* well mathematically. *Gifted Child Quarterly, 32,* 205–209.

STANLEY, J.C. and BENBOW, C.P. (1986) Youths who reason exceptionally well mathematically. In R.J. Sternberg and J.E. Davidson (Eds) *Conceptions of Giftedness.* New York: Cambridge University Press (pp.361–387).

STANLEY, J.C., HUANG, J. and ZHU, X. (1986) SAT scores of highly selected students in Shanghai tested when less than 13 years old. *College Board Review, No.140, Summer,* 10–13 & 28.

STANLEY, J.C., KEATING, D.P. and FOX, L.H. (Eds) (1974) *Mathematical Talent: Discovery, Description, and Development.* Baltimore: Johns Hopkins University Press.

STANLEY, J.C. and STANLEY, B.S.K. (1986) High-school biology, chemistry or physics learned well in three weeks. *Journal of Research in Science Teaching, 23,* 237–250.

WALLACH, M.A. (1978) Care and feeding of the gifted. *Contemporary Psychology, 23,* 616–617.

THE EMERGENCE AND NURTURANCE OF MULTIPLE INTELLIGENCES: THE PROJECT SPECTRUM APPROACH

Mara Krechevsky and Howard Gardner

Standardized tests were invented, in part, as one way to identify unusual talents, and they are certainly capable of revealing scholastic prodigies. But consider the individuals who do not perform well on such assessments. How can we assess their strengths, and what would it mean to do so?

Jacob is a four year old boy who was asked to participate in two forms of assessment during the 1987–1988 school year: the Stanford-Binet Intelligence Scale (4th ed.) and a new approach to assessment called Project Spectrum. Jacob refused to be tested on the Stanford-Binet. Three subtests were attempted and partially completed, after which Jacob ran out of the testing room, left the building, and climbed a tree. On the Spectrum battery, which includes 15 different tasks spanning a wide range of domains, Jacob participated in most of the activities, and demonstrated outstanding strength in the areas of visual arts and numbers. He revealed a consuming love of different materials, and worked with every possible medium in the art area. On other activities, even when he resisted engaging in the task at hand, he always expressed interest in the materials out of which the games were made, for example, the small figures on a storytelling board, the metal of the bells for the music activity, etc. This passion for the physicality of materials extended to almost every area: his exploration of the discovery or natural science area focused at one point on an examination of bones and how they fit together, and led to a remarkably accurate sculpture of a bone fashioned from clay.

Of all the activities in the Spectrum battery, Jacob was least interested in movement and music. At first, he also resisted participating in a numbers task embedded in a bus game. However, when he at last became engaged, he seemed to take special delight in figuring out the correct number of people boarding and leaving the bus. Tapping Jacob's understanding of numbers in a context which was meaningful and familiar to him seemed to help elicit abilities which might otherwise have remained hidden.

The above comparison suggests that while the Spectrum and Stanford-Binet assessments can reveal similar qualities, there are distinct advantages to an assessment conducted over time with rich materials in the child's own environment. The example of Jacob indicates four ways in which the Spectrum assessment system might benefit children. First, Spectrum engages children through games which are meaningful and contextualized. Second, Spectrum blurs the line between curriculum and assessment, thereby integrating assessment more effectively into the regular educational programme. Third, the Spectrum approach to assessment makes the measures 'intelligence-fair' by using instruments which look directly at the intelligence in operation, instead of through a linguistic or logical-mathematical lens. Fourth, Spectrum suggests how a child's strength may provide access to more forbidding areas (areas in which the child shows less promise).

In this chapter, we consider the possibility that children's exceptional talents can be identified at an early age and that the profile of abilities exhibited by preschoolers can be clearly distinguished from one another. We also consider some of the educational implications of an approach which focuses on the early identification of areas of strength and weakness. After a brief introduction to the theoretical background and framework of the Spectrum approach to assessment, we will discuss some of the research findings and offer some preliminary conclusions.

THE THEORETICAL BACKGROUND

Traditionally, intelligence has been conceptualized as a singular faculty which can be brought to bear on any problem-solving situation, no matter what the domain. Intelligence is commonly considered to be a general ability that is found in varying degrees in all individuals, and is especially central to one's performance in school. One's intelligence can also be reliably measured by standardized tests which predict successful performance in school (although such tests have been shown to have only modest predictive value for success in life when other variables, like social class, have been controlled; Jencks, 1972). This unitary view of the mind as a comprehensive and coherent entity is deeply entrenched in Western thought, starting with Plato and continuing through Descartes to Kant.

Although the first intelligence tests developed by Alfred Binet at the turn of the century were originally intended to diagnose different degrees of mental retardation, Lewis Terman at Stanford University modified and standardized the scales to yield the 'intelligence quotient' or 'IQ' in the Stanford-Binet Scale in 1916 (Sattler, 1988). As Jenkins and Paterson noted, 'probably no psychological innovation has had more impact on the societies of the Western world than the development of the Binet-Simon scales ' (1961, p.81).Testing is now a common practice in schools, clinics, industry, and the military. In education, test scores determine admission to academic settings from preschool to graduate school, and IQ scores are the most frequent (and often the only) criterion used for admission to programmes for the gifted, no matter whether the area of talent is language, art, or dance (Sternberg and Davidson, 1985).

Recently, a number of researchers working in the cognitive and neural sciences have offered new support for a pluralistic view of cognition, suggesting that the mind is organized into relatively discrete realms of functioning (Ceci, 1990; Feldman, 1980; Fodor, 1983; Gardner, 1983; Keil, 1984, 1986). Gardner, for example, defines intelligence as the ability to solve problems or fashion products that are valued in one or more cultural settings. In his theory of multiple intelligences (hereinafter referred to as MI theory), Gardner proposes that all normal individuals are capable of at least seven relatively autonomous forms of intellectual accomplishment: linguistic, musical, logical-mathematical, spatial, bodily-kinaesthetic, interpersonal and intrapersonal (see Gardner, 1983, for a detailed discussion).

To identify an 'intelligence', Gardner uses information from a variety of sources. These include knowledge about normal development and development in gifted individuals; information about the breakdown of cognitive capacities under conditions of brain-damage; studies of exceptional populations, including *idiots savants*, prodigies, and autistic children; a plausible evolutionary history; support from tasks in experimental psychology and psychometric findings; and cross-cultural accounts of cognition. Moreover, each intelligence must have an identifiable core operation or set of operations (which may be modelled as information processing mechanisms) which can make sense of specific kinds of input. For example, sensitivity to pitch relations is a core operation of musical intelligence, whilst the capacity to conjure up mental (usually visual) images and perform mental operations upon them is a core operation of spatial intelligence. An intelligence must also be susceptible to encoding in a symbol system – a culturally contrived system of meaning which captures and conveys important information. Language, picturing, and mathematics are three important symbol systems which have become critical for survival and productivity.

Each intelligence is based, at least initially, on a biological potential, which then gets expressed as a result of the interplay of genetic and environmental factors. Although one may view an intelligence in isolation in exceptional individuals such as *idiots savants*, in general, individuals exhibit a blend of several intelligences. Indeed, after early infancy, intelligences are never encountered in pure form. Rather, they are embedded in various symbol systems, such as spoken language and picturing systems; notational systems, like maps and musical or mathematical notation; and fields of knowledge, such as journalism and mechanical engineering. Thus, education at any point in time represents the cultivation of intelligences as they have come to be represented over time in a variety of culturally fashioned systems.

These intelligences are best thought of as biopsychological constructs: they constitute cognitive resources by virtue of which an individual may effect a meaningful connection to a content area. However, to round out this perspective of intelligences as they are espoused in any culture, we need to consider two additional components as well: the epistemological perspective of the 'domain' and the social perspective of the 'field'.[1] The structure of a domain of knowledge represents the organization of a particular area of study or competence at a given historical moment. These 'domains' undergo reorganization at different points in time, as for example the advent of jazz or the twelve tone system in music. A 'field', on the other hand, includes the range of roles (composers, performers, critics) and institutions (conservatories, orchestras, professional competitions) that make up the culturally defined realms in which learning and performance necessarily take place.

Nearly all cultural roles and tasks in any domain or field require a combination or blend of intelligences. For example, becoming a successful concert violinist requires not only a high degree of musical intelligence, but both bodily-kinaesthetic dexterity and the interpersonal skills of relating to an audience and, in a different way, of choosing a manager. To become an architect requires skills in spatial, logical-mathematical, bodily-kinaesthetic, and interpersonal intelligences in varying degrees. If Jacob goes on to become a sculptor, he will probably need to draw on spatial, bodily-kinaesthetic and interpersonal intelligences.

THE SPECTRUM APPROACH TO ASSESSMENT

Once these intelligences have been identified, the question arises of how to assess them in an ecologically valid way. In the following pages, we describe Project Spectrum, an innovative attempt to measure the profile of 'intelligences' and working styles of young children. Spectrum is a long-term, collaborative research project undertaken by several researchers at Harvard Project Zero with our colleague, David Feldman at Tufts University (see Feldman and

Gardner, 1989; Malkus *et al.*, 1988; and Ramos-Ford *et al.*, 1988). Spectrum begins with the assumption that every child has the potential to develop strength in one or several areas. The Project's focus on preschool children has both a scientific and a practical thrust. On the scientific side, we address the question of how early individual differences can be reliably detected, and the predictive value of such early identification (see also, Lewis, 1976). On the practical side, parents and teachers are likely to benefit most from information about their children's cognitive competences during this time when the young child's brain is especially 'plastic', when schools are likely to be more flexible and where a free choice component is typically built into most curricula.

Although Spectrum started out with a search for the early indices of the seven intelligences, it soon became apparent that many more competences warranted examination. To be sure, we identified a number of core capacities in each intelligence; but rather than attempting to look at intelligences in 'pure' form, we looked at the domains of accomplishment of the culture through those forms taken up by children (Feldman, 1986). For example, we address both production and perception in music; both invented and descriptive narrative in language; and expressive and athletic movement in the bodily-kinaesthetic realm. We also used the notion of adult end states to help us focus on those skills and abilities which are relevant to achieving significant and rewarding adult roles in our society, rather than just focusing on skills which are useful in the school context. Thus, instead of looking at logical-mathematical skills in the abstract, we examine competences which may culminate in mechanical inventiveness; instead of examining competence at repeating a series of sentences, we look at the child's ability to tell a story or provide a descriptive account of an experience.

In order to capture fully a child's approach to a task, we found it important to look at cognitive or working styles as well as 'sheer' intellectual capacities. Working styles describe the way a child interacts with the materials of a content area, such as ability to plan an activity and to reflect on a task, and level of persistence. While some individuals exhibit working styles which determine their approach to any task, no matter what the content area, others have styles which are much more domain-specific. Such information may be particularly important for fashioning an effective educational intervention for a child. At the present time, we address 15 areas of cognitive ability and 18 stylistic features (see Tables 1 and 2).

IMPLEMENTATION OF THE SPECTRUM APPROACH

How does Spectrum work in practice? First, we became convinced that one cannot assess children in a vacuum – one is always assessing earlier experiences in some domain. In order to assess a child in a given domain, we had to provide the child with some experience interacting with materials before a particular competence could be developed; otherwise, there was nothing to assess. Thus, the Spectrum approach ensures that children are exposed to rich and engaging materials both informally, in their classroom environment, and in more structured task situations. In the classroom, most children gravitate naturally to the different materials and show through their play activities their particular combination of strengths and interests. Supplementing this enriched environment are the more structured tasks which provide rough-and-ready measures of level of skill in the different areas. All of the Spectrum materials invite children to become involved in the content area, regardless of their initial level of skill. In our view, this quite deliberate blurring of the line between assessment and curriculum leads to a more ecologically valid assessment, which ideally takes place over time and in the child's environment.

In order not to confound competences, we tried as much as possible not to rely exclusively on logical and linguistic measures; instead we used measures which were 'intelligence-fair' (Gardner, 1990). We also tried to avoid hypothetical situations and abstract formulations. Instead, we provided children with something concrete to manipulate no matter which domain was being assessed. For example, Spectrum's social analysis measure, the classroom model, provides children with small figures of their peers and teachers, offering a tangible structure within which to consider children's knowledge of friends, social roles, and classroom dynamics. The music perception task provides children with Montessori bells with which they can play a pitch matching game.

As Table 1 indicates, Spectrum measures range from relatively structured and targetted tasks (for example, in the number and music domains) to relatively unstructured measures and natural observations (in the science and social domains). These measures are implemented throughout the course of a year – one part of a classroom is equipped with engaging materials, games, puzzles, and learning areas. Documentation takes a variety of forms, from score sheets and observation checklists to portfolios and tape-recordings. Although most teachers will not find it practical to administer formally all 15 measures to each child, we have used such a procedure for research purposes.

Table 1. Areas of cognitive ability examined in Project Spectrum

NUMBERS

Dinosaur Game: designed as a measure of a child's understanding of number concepts, counting skills, ability to adhere to rules, and use of strategy.

Bus Game: assesses a child's ability to create a useful notation system, perform mental calculations, and organize number information for one or more variables.

SCIENCE

Assembly Activity: designed to measure a child's mechanical ability. Successful completion of the activity depends on fine motor skills and visual-spatial, observational and problem-solving abilities.

Treasure Hunt Game: assesses a child's ability to make logical inferences. The child is asked to organize information to discover the rule governing the placement of various treasures.

Water Activity: used to assess a child's ability to generate hypotheses based on observations and to conduct simple experiments.

Discovery Area: includes year-round activities which elicit a child's observations, appreciation, and understanding of natural phenomena.

MUSIC

Music Production Activity: designed to assess a child's ability to maintain accurate pitch and rhythm while singing, and to recall a song's musical properties.

Music Perception Activity: assesses a child's ability to discriminate pitch. The activity consists of song recognition, error recognition, and pitch discrimination.

LANGUAGE

Storyboard Activity: measures a range of language skills including complexity of vocabulary and sentence structure, use of connectors, use of descriptive language and dialogue, and ability to pursue a storyline.

Reporting Activity: assesses a child's ability to describe an event with regard to the following criteria: ability to report content accurately, level of detail, sentence structure and vocabulary.

VISUAL ARTS

Art Portfolios: reviewed twice a year, and assessed on criteria that include use of lines and shapes, colour, space, detail, and representation and design. Children also participate in three structured drawing activities. The drawings are assessed on criteria similar to those used in the portfolio assessment.

MOVEMENT

Creative Movement: the ongoing movement curriculum focuses on children's abilities in five areas of dance and creative movement: sensitivity to rhythm, expressiveness, body control, generation of movement ideas, and responsiveness to music.

Athletic Movement: an obstacle course focuses on the types of skills found in many different sports such as co-ordination, timing, balance, and power.

SOCIAL

Classroom Model: the purpose of the Classroom Model activity is to assess a child's ability to observe and analyse social events and experiences in the classroom.

Peer Interaction Checklist: a behavioural checklist is used to assess the behaviours in which children engage when interacting with peers. Different patterns of behaviour yield distinctive social roles such as facilitator and leader.

Table 2. Stylistic features examined in Project Spectrum

The child is:

    easily engaged / reluctant to engage in activity
    confident / tentative
    playful / serious
    focused / distractible
    persistent / frustrated by task
    reflects on own work / impulsive
    apt to work slowly / apt to work quickly

The child:

    responds to visual / auditory / kinaesthetic cues
    demonstrates methodical approach
    brings personal agenda / strength to task
    finds humour in content area
    uses materials in unexpected ways
    shows pride in accomplishment
    shows attention to detail / is observant
    is curious about materials
    shows concern over 'correct' answer
    focuses on interaction with adult
    transforms task / material

At the end of the year, all of the information gathered on each child becomes the basis for a 'Spectrum Profile' – a description in straight-forward language of a child's intellectual strengths and weaknesses. The report delineates each child's strengths relative to that individual's personal profile of strengths and weaknesses, and occasionally, in relation to peers. However, of equal importance to the trajectory of strengths outlined in the report is the list of recommendations which are offered. As a general rule, we believe psychologists should spend more time trying to help students and less time trying to rank them. Accordingly, we include in the Profile concrete suggestions for home, school, and wider community activities. A Parent Activities Manual accompanies each profile with suggestions for activities in the different domains addressed by Spectrum. Most of the activities use readily accessible and affordable materials; however, a cautionary note to parents is added regarding premature streaming or fast-tracking of a child: the idea is not to make each child a prodigy in the area of greatest strength. Rather, Project Spectrum stresses the notion that every child is unique: parents and teachers deserve to have a description faithful to the child, as well as suggestions for the kinds of experiences appropriate to the child's particular configuration of strengths and weaknesses.

PRELIMINARY RESULTS

Having provided a general overview of the Spectrum assessment model, we now turn to a discussion of the results of our research to date. Because Project Spectrum is a pilot study, the following comparisons should be regarded as preliminary and suggestive, rather than definitive. Given the limited scope of our sample population, we are not prepared to draw general conclusions about four year old children. The major part of the analysis centres on the 1987–1988 sample on whom more complete data were gathered. However, we do report on the 1986–1987 sample where it seems instructive to do so.

The analyses presented in this section are based on data collected during the 1986–1987 and 1987–1988 school years. We were primarily interested in the following questions:

(1) Do young children have domain specific as well as more general strengths?

(2) Was there any correlation between performances in different activities?

(3) Does a child's strength in one domain facilitate or hinder performance in other domains?

We now report on each question in turn.

1. The Spectrum battery was administered in two preschool classrooms at the Eliot-Pearson Children's School at Tufts University in Medford, Massachusetts. The 1986–1987 class consisted of 19 children between the ages of three and four, drawn chiefly from a relatively homogeneous, white, middle and upper income population. Except where otherwise noted, we restrict the present discussion to our population of four year olds. (Although three year old children yielded distinctive intellectual profiles as well, we decided to limit the 1986–1987 sample to the 13 four year olds in the class, given that it was the age for which most of our activities were developed.) Ages of the subjects in the 1986–1987 class ranged from 48 to 59 months at the start of the school year; the mean age was 52 months. Eight of the 15 Spectrum activities were included in the analysis (the remaining activities did not yet have complete scoring systems).

   The 1987–1988 class was comprised of 20 children, also drawn primarily from a white, middle and upper income population. The children ranged in age from 42 to 58 months at the beginning of the school year; the mean age was 53 months. Ten of the 15 Spectrum activities were included in this part of the analysis.

   In each of the two samples, we looked at a child's strengths and weaknesses, both in relation to the group and to the self. Children who scored one standard deviation or more above the mean on the Spectrum measures were considered to have a 'strength' in a domain, while children who scored one standard deviation or more below the mean were considered to demonstrate a 'weakness'. The majority of the children in the 1986–1987 class revealed a strength in at least one domain (10 out of 13 children), and a weakness in at least one domain (9 out of 13). Four children exhibited one or more strengths across Spectrum activities and no weaknesses, and three children exhibited no strengths and one or more weaknesses. Finally, every child exhibited at least one strength and one weakness relative to him or herself.

   In the 1987–1988 sample, 15 of the 20 children demonstrated a strength in at least one domain, and 12 children demonstrated a weakness in one or more domains. Seven children in the sample revealed strengths in one or more areas and no weaknesses, and 4 children demonstrated a weakness in one or more areas and no strengths. One child was also identified as having no strengths or weaknesses. (Her scores ranged from -0.985 to $+0.87$ standard deviations from the mean, with an average of -0.03.)

   The results from the two samples are strikingly similar. For the majority of children, strengths and/or weaknesses were identified in relation to the group, and in all cases, areas of relative strength and weakness were identified for each child.

2. In order to determine the degree of correlation between performances on the different activities, we created a matrix of correlations between pairs of the ten activities used with the 1987–1988 sample. The results indicated that there was very little correlation between the activities, reinforcing the notion that the Spectrum measures identify a range of non-overlapping capabilities in different content areas. Only one pair was significant at the $p<0.01$ level: the two number activities, the Dinosaur Game and the Bus Game ($r = 0.78$). In contrast, the two music and the two science activities included in the sample were not significantly correlated ($r = -0.07$ and $r = 0.08$, respectively).

3. There was also some evidence that a child's strength in one area might facilitate performance in another. For example, one child exhibited a keen sensitivity to colour, and demonstrated both interest and ability in the area of visual arts. While playing the treasure hunt game, which focuses on logical inference skills, this child's attentiveness to colours seemed to help her identify the rule governing the placement of treasures under colour-coded flags. Another child, who was identified as having a strength in music production (singing), found it easier in the creative movement sessions to synchronize his movements to the underlying rhythm of a piece of music if he sang while he moved. His musical talents also characterized his performance on the invented narrative task: he created both a theme song and a death march for the characters in his story.

A third child, who exhibited outstanding ability in story-telling, yet remained motionless in the creative movement sessions, moved with uncharacteristic expressiveness when storyboard props were used as a catalyst in one of the exercises. She also transformed tasks in visual arts, social analysis, and mathematics into occasions for further story-telling (cf. Renninger, 1988, on the effect of children's interests on their attention and memory for tasks and types of play). Her drawings in art often served to illustrate accompanying narratives. Her mother reported that she often made puppets and dolls at home, modelling them on characters from the books she was 'reading'. She also used the classroom model as a reality based storyboard, creating vignettes with the figures of her classmates. On the bus game, however, she became so involved in the motivations for the different figures boarding and leaving the bus, that she was distracted from recording the correct numerical information.

It seems that strength in an area can also interfere with one's performance. One child exhibited outstanding strength in visual arts, demonstrating an unusual sensitivity to line, colour and composition. However his sensitivity to visual cues led him to misinterpret directional signs when using dice which had a '+' and '−' on their sides. He interpreted the crossing lines (+) to mean that the player could move in two directions, while the single horizontal line (−) meant that the player could proceed in only one direction.

WORKING STYLES

As noted earlier, in addition to recording a child's performance, we also recorded 'working style' or the way in which each activity was approached (see Table 2). We were primarily interested in two issues:

(1) Do children utilize distinctive working styles when solving problems from different domains? (And if so, what is the nature of the differences in a child's areas of strength and weakness?)

(2) Are some working styles more effective than others in particular domains?

1. *Consistency across tasks.* With regard to the first issue, it seemed that for the majority of children, while one or two working styles usually obtained across domains, other working styles depended more on the content of the area being explored. Approximately three-quarters of the children in the sample exhibited general working styles which, in specific instances, combined with one or two others to yield domain specific configurations. For example, one girl displayed attention to detail only on the classroom model activity, her one area of strength, and was impulsive only in the music perception activity, her area of weakness. Another child was easily engaged and confident, even in areas of weakness, as long as the task involved a performance aspect.

Not surprisingly, performances in an area of strength were typically characterized by 'easy to engage', 'confident', and 'focused' working styles. In contrast, weak performances were characterized by 'distractible', 'impulsive', and 'reluctant to engage' working styles. 'Playfulness' characterized both strengths and weaknesses. Also, a number of children showed reflectiveness and attention to detail in their area of strength. Three of the five children who exhibited no strengths relative to their peers never reflected on their own work, and eight children only reflected on their work in areas of strength.

Five of the children demonstrated working styles which were highly domain specific. One child found it very difficult to remain focused on most of the Spectrum and classroom activities. However, when she was presented with the materials for the assembly activity, she worked in a focused and persistent manner until she had completely taken apart and reassembled the objects. This result gave the teacher valuable information about how she might use this child's strength to engage her in focused work in the classroom. Also Jacob, the boy described in the introduction, exhibited confidence, attention to detail, seriousness, planning skills, and reflectiveness *only* in the visual arts and numbers domains – his areas of strength.

2. *Styles which help and hamper: from the confident to the over-confident.* Some of the children who exhibited a consistent working style were clearly helped by their content-neutral style, whereas others were probably hindered by it. One child worked in a serious and focused manner across domains, which helped him to complete activities in which he experienced difficulty as well as those where he exhibited competence. Every child exhibited confidence in at least one activity, and one girl, who revealed no strengths relative to her peers, nonetheless demonstrated 'pride in accomplishment' on more tasks than any other child, perhaps indicating a resilience which augurs well for her scholastic prospects. Ironically, it may be that too general a confidence inhibits successful performance across tasks. The child who was identified as having the most weaknesses of any child (five) and no strengths relative to her peers, never showed any tentativeness, whereas all but three of the rest were 'tentative' in their approach at least once.

One child brought his own programme of ideas to every Spectrum activity. Although his ideas were often compelling, his unwillingness to attend to the task caused him to perform poorly on many of the activities. On the music perception activity, for example, he was most interested in how the metal bells, which looked exactly the same, could produce different sounds. To explore this phenomenon, he examined the differences in their vibrations after hitting them with his mallet. He also invented new rules for the dinosaur game, and tried to fashion tools out of the parts of the two food grinders in the assembly activity. Because he was so interested in exploring his own ideas, he often resisted exploring the ideas of others. When he experienced difficulty with an activity, he would become frustrated and turn to his sense of humour to distract the adult from the task at hand.

It also appeared that the structure of the tasks (or sometimes their lack of it) served to inhibit the performances of some children. In the less structured environment of the classroom, the boy just described demonstrated great experimental ability, and constantly formulated and tested hypotheses to find out more about the world around him. Jacob was another child who required very little structure, so immersed in the materials did he become. Unfortunately, his intense focus on materials to the exclusion of other people – whether child or adult – is likely to present problems for his future scholastic performance.

A COMPARISON OF VIEWS: PARENTS, TEACHERS AND SPECTRUM

While it seems clear that the Spectrum measures identified domain specific strengths in the children, it also seemed important to determine whether we were uncovering abilities hitherto unrecognized by teachers and parents. To address this question, we asked parents and teachers of the 1987–1988 class to fill out a questionnaire indicating the level of ability shown by each child in a number of different areas. We also sent response forms to parents to solicit their reactions to the Spectrum profiles.

Seventeen of the 20 sets of parents returned a completed questionnaire. In general, parents were quite generous in identifying their child as demonstrating outstanding ability in an area. The average number of areas checked by parents for their child was 8 out of 30. On the other hand, the teachers rarely scored a child as exhibiting outstanding ability in any area, averaging one out of 30. This discrepancy between parent and teacher ratings may reflect the broader frame of reference available to teachers who see each child in the context of his or her peer group. While parents may understandably be biased, they also have fewer opportunities to view the strengths of a large number of children. These factors should be kept in mind in the following comparison. A child was considered to have an outstanding strength by Spectrum only if the score in a given domain of activity was at least one standard deviation above the mean.

The comparison revealed that Spectrum identified outstanding strengths that had not otherwise been identified in 8 of the 17 children. In all, Spectrum identified 12 strengths that had not been identified by *either* parent *or* teacher. The domains of strength included science, visual arts, music, and social understanding. Also, seven children were identified as exhibiting outstanding strengths by parents and teachers, but not by Spectrum. In most of these cases, although Spectrum identified relative strengths, they were not considered outstanding in relation to the group. For a number of other children, strengths scoring close to, but less than, one standard deviation above the mean were identified by Spectrum, but not by parents or teachers. Finally, parents, teachers, and Spectrum identified the same areas of outstanding ability in 9 of the 17 children in the comparison.

It appears that some areas, like language and numbers, can be relatively easily identified regardless of whether the child is at home or at school, but other areas are not so easily noticed, like music perception, mechanical skills, or social analysis. In fact, Spectrum never identified language or numbers as outstanding strengths, where they were not already identified by parent or teacher. However, even in a commonly recognized area of ability like language, Spectrum provides a breakdown of the area into component skills (vocabulary, sentence structure, use of descriptive language, etc.) employed in the service of a meaningful endeavour (story-telling).

Of course, many competent preschool teachers simply cannot provide experiences in all areas, especially those with which they may be relatively unfamiliar, like music perception and logical inference tasks. The assembly activity, in particular, helps to break down gender preconceptions by providing girls with the same opportunity as boys to reveal a strength and become engaged in an area traditionally considered masculine. The profile response forms also revealed that the areas where parents were most surprised to learn of strengths included music perception, mechanical ability and creative movement. Because the information in the profiles is generated from contextualized tasks, it may be easier for parents to translate it into meaningful follow-up activities.

A COMPARISON OF SPECTRUM RESULTS WITH STANFORD-BINET INTELLIGENCE SCALE

A professional psychometrician administered the Stanford-Binet Intelligence Scale (4th ed.) to 19 of the 20 children in the 1987–1988 Spectrum class. Two of the 19 children did not complete the measure, and are therefore not included in the analysis. The results from this sample, while useful for providing a very general sense of how the two measures compare, should be read with the following caveats in mind.

First, Spectrum addresses seven domains of ability through fifteen activities, ten of which are included in the analysis, whereas the Stanford-Binet focuses on four areas or factors (verbal reasoning, abstract/visual reasoning, quantitative reasoning, and short-term memory) through eight subtests. Second, the battery of Spectrum activities is administered seriatim over the course of a year, whereas the Stanford-Binet is administered in a one to two hour session. Finally, the Stanford-Binet is a standardized measure and Spectrum is not. Thus, the findings presented in the following comparison should be considered tentative.

The 17 children in the sample who completed the Stanford-Binet assessment scored in the low-average to very superior range, with composite scores ranging from 86 to 133. The average score was 113. As with the preceding analysis, a child was considered to demonstrate a strength and/or weakness on a Spectrum activity only if he or she scored one or more standard deviations above or below the mean of the group.

To determine whether Stanford-Binet composite scores were predictive of performance on some or all Spectrum activities, we ranked the composite scores of the children to see how the top five children (with composite scores from 125 to 133) and the bottom five children (with scores from 86 to 105 – the 'low average' to 'average' range) performed on the Spectrum battery. Of the five children earning the highest Stanford-Binet composite scores, one child demonstrated a strength on three of the ten Spectrum activities in the analysis, three displayed strengths in two of the activities, and one child exhibited one strength. The areas Spectrum identified as strengths for these children are as follows: two in narrative language; four in music perception and production; two in the visual arts; one in social understanding; and one in science (logical inference).

The movement, numbers, and mechanical component of the science domains were not identified as strengths for any of the children and, in fact, movement and numbers were identified as areas of weakness for two of them. Moreover, only one of the three children who displayed three or more strengths on the Spectrum measures was among the top five scorers of the Stanford-Binet. One of the top three Spectrum scorers was also the top scorer on the combined Spectrum mathematics activities.

It seems that the Stanford-Binet Intelligence Scale did not predict successful performance either across or on a consistent subset of Spectrum activities. The one qualification is the possibility of a connection between the Stanford-Binet composite scores and performance on the Spectrum music tasks. Four of the five strengths in music identified by the Spectrum measures were displayed by the children receiving the highest Stanford-Binet composite scores. However, in general, no correlation was found between Stanford-Binet subscores and the individual Spectrum activities. Of course, without a much larger sample, no firm conclusions can be drawn.

The Stanford-Binet also did not seem to predict lack of success across Spectrum tasks, although it did identify three of the lowest scoring children (children with no strengths and zero to five weaknesses). Of the five children with the lowest Stanford-Binet composite scores, one child exhibited one strength (social understanding) and one weakness (music perception), and another exhibited no weaknesses and three strengths (mechanical ability, language, and music perception). The remaining three children displayed no strengths on the Spectrum activities, and between zero and five weaknesses.

The child who received the lowest composite score in the group (86) was also identified by the Spectrum battery as the lowest scoring child across tasks: she exhibited no strengths and five weaknesses on the Spectrum activities (two more weaknesses than any other child). However, Spectrum did identify two relative strengths displayed by this child in the domains of social understanding and creative movement. The Stanford-Binet subtests also revealed some scatter (the verbal reasoning skills and memory for sentences subscores were in the 53rd and 49th percentiles, respectively, while bead memory and pattern analysis scores fell in the 39th and 40th percentiles).

These data suggest that although the Stanford-Binet Intelligence Scale does yield a range of factor scores and subtest variability within factors, the Spectrum measures produced more jagged profiles. Part of this difference can be attributed to the number of domains addressed by each measure: 8 tasks in four content areas for Stanford-Binet vs. 15 tasks (10 in the current analysis) in 7 areas for Spectrum. But Spectrum does more than simply expand the areas addressed by the Stanford-Binet. All of the Stanford-Binet subtests can be considered either good or fair measures of 'g', the general intelligence factor (see Sattler, 1988, for a full discussion). Spectrum, however, does not postulate 'g' as a general intelligence factor which is present in a wide range of mental abilities, and which accounts for children's performances in different content areas. Rather, the Spectrum model suggests that the jagged profiles represent domain specific abilities, which reflect real world problem-solving in the context of meaningful activities: for example, analysis of one's own social environment, assembling a mechanical object, telling a story, etc. The information gained from the Spectrum inventory may therefore be potentially more useful in designing appropriate educational interventions for children.

A PRELIMINARY LOOK AT FOLLOW-UP DATA FROM THE CLASS OF 1986–1987

A preliminary look at longitudinal data collected on 17 of the 19 children in the 1986–1987 class (including five three year olds) suggests that strengths and working styles in the Spectrum cohort remained constant, at least during a one to two year follow-up period. Follow-up information on the children in the 1986–1987 group was gathered from interviews with parents and teachers, and second year participation in a Spectrum classroom. Of the 19 children in the 1986–1987 sample, six remained in a Spectrum related classroom at the Eliot-Pearson Children's School the following year, six were in a non-Spectrum kindergarten class at Eliot-Pearson, and seven attended other kindergarten programmes.

Five of the children participated in an expanded set of the year-long activities for a second time in the 1987–1988 Spectrum class. Four of the five children demonstrated strengths consistent with those identified by Spectrum the previous year, with one child exhibiting an additional strength in the language domain. The fifth child, who had not exhibited any strengths during the first year, was identified as having a relative strength in experimental science (through the newly added water activity).

The working styles for the five children remained relatively consistent over the one to two year follow-up period. One child, who seemed serious and focused on many of the tasks in his first year, only became more so during year 2, continuing to show great concern with task demands. Another girl took the same uncharacteristically forward thinking, focused, and reflective approach to the assembly activity that she had exhibited during the first year, in contrast to her more distractible style on other tasks.

For the remaining twelve children in the sample, information in the Spectrum profile was compared to information obtained through interviews with parents and/or teachers. Eleven of the twelve children were identified by their parents or teachers as having abilities consistent with those identified by Spectrum in the first year. One girl, who had demonstrated a strength in logical inference, continued to be fascinated with things logical: she made up her own rules for backgammon and other games, and reportedly derived great satisfaction from trying to figure out how different relatives were related to her. At a subsequent two year follow-up conducted on seven of the eleven children (through teacher and parent questionnaires and checklists), the majority of strengths remained unchanged. (One girl, who identified 'snack' as the activity she enjoyed the most during Year 1 of Spectrum, reported to her mother that one of the activities she did best two years later was 'eating lunch'.)

Of note for the social domain, two teachers considered their students' social skills to be areas where they exhibited least ability, although both Spectrum and parents had identified the areas as strengths. The definition of social ability provided to teachers was 'knowledge of one's own and others' abilities, interests, likes, dislikes, and feelings'. In the teachers' descriptions of the two girls, it was clear that the girls exhibited such knowledge; however they put it to inappropriate use. One was a quite successful and subtle manipulator of others, as well as an effective leader in her group; while the other, also an effective leader, often attempted to control those around her. Unlike other domains, the social realm seems to be an area where 'ability' does not always take on a neutral cast. One's judgement is influenced by concern for how such ability is used.

The twelve children also exhibited relatively consistent working styles from year to year. The children who were serious, focused, and forward thinking across tasks remained so. Likewise, the more impulsive and stubborn children remained the same. Again, this consistency was also true for the seven children in the two year follow-up. Sometimes, the particular configuration of a child's working style and areas of strength determined whether or not a strength would resurface. For example, one girl who 'liked to shine', according to her teacher, was not the most able in her group at the writing table or book area. Consequently, she frequented the art and construction areas where she would be more likely to stand out. Given the context of her relative standing within the group, there was less of a chance that her previously identified ability in language would re-emerge and develop during the year.

Furthermore, if a child's interests did not match his or her strengths, or if an individual chose to focus on the same set of materials or to explore new skill areas, opportunities to observe ability in other domains would be correspondingly reduced. One girl who had demonstrated both interest and ability in art while in the Spectrum classroom, in kindergarten became much more interested in learning how to read and avoided the art area. On the other hand, a child who had been an outstanding story-teller was very reluctant to start writing, and experienced difficulty both with his fine motor co-ordination and sound–letter connections. At the two year follow-up, he was reported still to love listening to stories and performing in class plays. It should also be noted that written language may well involve a different set of skills from spoken language (Olson, 1977).

Responses from parents in the sample revealed that the area which they seemed to have encouraged most at the one year follow-up was drama. This activity seems to have been considered an effective way to combine ability in the story-telling and social domains with the performance aspect of the movement domain. Music perception and production was another area where many parents were surprised and pleased to discover the enjoyment their child showed in the domain. Music appeared to be an area which enriched a child's life, regardless of level of ability. A number of parents also spoke of the usefulness of having a written document to which they could refer and compare more recent views of their child.

Thus, a number of factors and conditions seem to work in concert to determine whether a strength will ultimately resurface and have a chance to develop in a given year: the range of areas provided and emphasized in the classroom; family knowledge and interest in an area; the child's own fluctuating interests (which depend on the areas to which he or she is exposed as well as the context of the child's peer group); and the nature of the domain at the particular point in the child's development.

Some Limitations and Long-term Implications of Project Spectrum

At this point, it may be worthwhile to raise explicitly several issues which are likely to be on the reader's mind. Clearly, the current study has a number of limitations. Because of the small sample which received the Spectrum battery, the study should be regarded as generating hypotheses rather than as conclusive in any sense. At present the Spectrum activities still lack norms and in some cases are still being refined.[2] In addition, the data presented in the comparison of children's strengths identified by parents, teachers and Spectrum and the longitudinal follow-up may well suffer from parental bias in the identification of strengths.

However, we can identify some of the potential benefits of Spectrum in comparison with other assessment approaches, such as the Stanford-Binet. First, Spectrum provides an opportunity to involve children more actively in the assessment, giving them a chance to reflect on their experience and their own sense of their interests and strengths. Children also become actively involved in helping to collect and document their work in the Spectrum model: saving their work for the art portfolios, taping stories and songs, and bringing in items for the discovery or natural science area. Such involvement conveys to children the sense that their products are being taken seriously, and includes them in the process of monitoring their own growth.

For children who are unusually sensitive about performance issues, Spectrum may have information to offer which a one session, decontextualized, heavily verbal measure does not (Gardner, 1990). For example, as part of the intrapersonal component of the social analytic activity, children are shown pictures of the different Spectrum activities and asked which activities they consider their favourite, their best, and the hardest. One boy who had remained unengaged in either Spectrum activities or the Stanford-Binet subtests (the Stanford-Binet testing had to be discontinued because of his great anxiety about his performance), showed a surprising degree of interest in answering questions about his reactions to the different activities. He seemed to have an accurate sense about his areas of relative interest and strength. He identified the storyboard as his best activity and, indeed, it was the only one of the eight tasks he completed where his score was above the group mean. He also selected the water activity as his favourite, and although he was reluctant to try out his ideas for sinking and floating experiments during the task, he became so excited about a discovery he made at one point, that he called his teacher over to the area in an uncharacteristic display of enthusiasm.

Of course, the Stanford-Binet Intelligence Scale has advantages as well. It is a standardized measure, with excellent internal consistency and high reliability. The measure is easily and efficiently administered, and the areas examined map readily on to the standard school curriculum. While we do not yet know whether a Spectrum assessment can predict scholastic success with the reliability of standardized forms of assessment, the Spectrum measures do identify distinctive areas of strength with immediate implications for further avenues to explore, both inside and outside school. The Spectrum battery also allows teachers and parents to perceive individual differences in areas traditionally considered important only with regard to passage through universal stages of development (Feldman, 1980) or as a reflection of general intelligence.

However, the Spectrum approach contains its own risks. The danger of premature streaming of children must be weighed against the benefits of giving every child a chance to do well. There is also the potential for achievement oriented parents to push their children to excel not just in the traditional academic areas, but in all seven domains, increasing an already powerful pressure on children to achieve. Moreover, families outside the mainstream culture may quite properly be less concerned with performance in domains like visual arts and music, and more concerned with those areas which continue to be valued most by those in power – language and logic.

Clearly, family environment determines in part both the use and the usefulness of the information contained in the Spectrum profile. As one parent reported, because the family members were either not interested in music, or were simply non-musical, her child's musical capabilities might never have surfaced without Spectrum, or even if they had, they would not have been recognized as talent. This result can be contrasted with the case of a mother who considered music to be an important part of her son's life and greatly encouraged his interest in it. At the one year follow-up, she reported that he loved watching musical and operatic performances, and would sit through them attentively, without talking or moving. While no one really knows the exact relationship between early talents and later achievements, the identification of strengths early on may become a self-fulfilling prophecy.

Could a Spectrum perspective lead to a reasonable curriculum for the primary years? Our data suggest the potential influence of the structure of the environment on the particular qualities which can be discerned in children. They emphasize the importance of continuing to provide a rich set of stimulating materials across diverse curricular areas. Creative movement and mechanical skills cannot be recognized in a kindergarten which does not offer these areas in the curriculum. Also, starting in first grade, many children are taught subjects like art, music, movement, and science by specialists once or twice a week. Unless these specialists communicate with the classroom teachers, the latter may be unaware of a child's abilities in a particular area. At a minimum, teachers may find it easier to be good teachers in the Spectrum framework, both in terms of documenting their observations and individualizing their curriculum.

The emphasis on end states may also provide a more direct link between identification of a strength and a decision on what to do once it has been identified. An apprenticeship model emerges as a particularly attractive alternative educational approach. Once an end state has been defined, the possibility arises for staking out an educational regimen towards its realization. Apprenticeships embed the learning of skills in a social and functional context, with well-defined stages of mastery. In our view, the apprenticeship model, where students receive frequent and informal feedback on their progress in highly contextualized settings, holds much promise educationally. Thus, in the case of a child like Jacob, we would recommend that if he continues to exhibit interest in his chosen domain, he could well benefit from the guidance of an expert in a variety of rich, hands-on learning situations.

Finally, although Spectrum reflects in part a value system of pluralism associated with the middle class, it may also have something to offer children from a less privileged background. The Spectrum assessment system has the potential for revealing unsuspected areas of strength and bringing about enhanced self-esteem, particularly for those children who do not excel in the standard school curriculum. Towards this end, we are currently engaged in a study to determine whether a modified version of the Spectrum measures can yield fruitful information on the sources of school adjustment problems for less privileged, school age children (Gardner and Hatch, 1989).

The Spectrum model presents one approach to recognizing and supporting a wider range of competences, with the potential for involving the home, school, and community. It encourages the development of a child's abilities and interests by providing greater opportunities for an early and meaningful connection to a content area. The Spectrum approach may even help foster extraordinary performances by identifying an emerging strength at an early point in life, suggesting a pattern of continued growth, and putting forth alternative methods for fostering that growth. The promise of the Spectrum model will be realized when more people are able to find rewarding niches in our increasingly diversified society.

244   *Mara Krechevsky and Howard Gardner*

Acknowledgements: The work described in this chapter was supported in part by grants from the Spencer Foundation, the William T. Grant Foundation, and the Rockefeller Brothers Fund.

Notes

1. In drawing this distinction, we rely heavily on collaborative work with David Feldman of Tufts University (1980, 1986) and Mihaly Csikszentmihalyi of the University of Chicago (Csikszentmihalyi and Robinson, 1986).

2. The Project is currently engaged in refining the scoring systems and preparing a Spectrum Activities Handbook. The Handbook, updated in July 1989, will be made available to the public at cost. For further information, write to the authors at: Project Zero, Harvard Graduate School of Education, Cambridge, MA 02138, USA.

REFERENCES

CECI, S.J. (1990) *On Intelligence . . . More or Less: a Bio-ecological Treatise on Intellectual Development*. Englewood Cliffs, NJ: Prentice-Hall.

CSIKSZENTMIHALYI, M. and ROBINSON, R. (1986) Culture, time and the development of talent. In R. Sternberg and J. Davidson (Eds) *Conceptions of Giftedness*. New York: Cambridge University Press.

FELDMAN, D.H. (1980) *Beyond Universals in Cognitive Development*. Norwood, NJ: Ablex.

FELDMAN, D.H. (1986) *Nature's Gambit*. New York: Basic Books.

FELDMAN, D.H. and GARDNER, H. (1989) *Project Spectrum: July 1987 – June 1989*, (Final Annual Report to the Spencer Foundation).

FODOR, J. (1983) *Modularity of Mind*. Cambridge, MA: MIT Bradford Press.

GARDNER, H. (1983) *Frames of Mind: The Theory of Multiple Intelligences*. New York: Basic Books.

GARDNER, H. (1990) Assessment in context: The alternative to standardized testing. In B. Gifford (Ed.), *Report of the Commission on Testing and Public Policy*. Boston: Kluwer

GARDNER, H. and HATCH, T. (1989) Multiple intelligences go to school: The educational implications of the theory of multiple intelligences. *Educational Researcher, 18*, 4–10.

JENCKS, C. (1972) *Inequality*. New York: Basic Books.

JENKINS, J.J. and PATTERSON, D.G. (Eds) (1961) *Studies in Individual Differences*. New York: Appleton-Century-Crofts.

KEIL, F.C. (1984) Mechanics in cognitive development and the structure of knowledge. In R. Sternberg (Ed.), *Mechanics of Cognitive Development*. San Francisco: W.H. Freeman.

KEIL, F.C. (1986) On the structure-dependent nature of stages in cognitive development. In I. Levin (Ed.), *Stage and Structure*. Norwood, NJ: Ablex.

LEWIS, M. (Ed.) (1976) *Origins of Intelligence*. New York: Plenum Press.

MALKUS, U., FELDMAN, D.H. and GARDNER, H. (1988) Dimensions of mind in early childhood. In A. Pellegrini (Ed.) *The Psychological Bases of Early Education*. Chichester, England: Wiley.

OLSON, D. (1977) From utterance to text: The basis of language in speech and writing. *Harvard Educational Review*, 47, 257–82.

RAMOS-FORD, V., FELDMAN, D.H. and GARDNER, H. (1988) A new look at intelligence through Project Spectrum. *New Horizons for Learning*, 8 (3), 6–7, 15.

RENNINGER, A.K. (1988) Do individual interests make a difference? In *Essays by the Spencer Fellows 1987–1988*. Cambridge: National Academy of Education.

SATTLER, J.M. (1988) *Assessment of Children*, 3rd ed. San Diego: Sattler.

STERNBERG, R.J. and DAVIDSON, J.E. (1985) Cognitive development of the gifted and talented. In F.D. Horowitz and M. O'Brien (Eds), *The Gifted and Talented: Developmental Perspectives*. Washington, D.C.: American Psychological Association.

Author Index

Subject Index